Study Guide to Accompany

CHILD AND ADOLESCENT DEVELOPMENT
Second Edition

Edward P. Sarafino
Trenton State College

James W. Armstrong
Bucks County Community College

West Publishing Company
St. Paul   New York   Los Angeles   San Francisco

COPYRIGHT © 1986 by WEST PUBLISHING CO.
50 West Kellogg Boulevard
P.O. Box 64526
St. Paul, MN 55164-1003
All rights reserved
Printed in the United States of America

ISBN   O-314-93412-X

CONTENTS

Introduction	. . . .	1
Chapter 1.	Overview: The Study of Child Development	5
Chapter 2.	Theories of Development	19
Chapter 3.	Heredity, Prenatal Development, and Birth	35
Chapter 4.	Infant Physical, Cognitive, and Language Development	53
Chapter 5.	Infant Social, Emotional, and Personality Development	71
Chapter 6.	Physical and Motor Development in Childhood	87
Chapter 7.	Child Cognition I: Perception, Learning and Memory	103
Chapter 8.	Child Cognition II: Thinking, Reasoning and Intelligence	119
Chapter 9.	Language Development in Childhood	137
Chapter 10.	Social Relations in the Family . . .	153
Chapter 11.	Socialization and Society: Peers, School, and Television	171

Chapter 12.	The Self: Building a Personal Identity	187
Chapter 13.	Emotions and Psychological Problems in Childhood	205
Chapter 14.	Adolescent Physical, Cognitive, and Sexual Development	221
Chapter 15.	Adolescent Social, Emotional, and Personality Development	237

INTRODUCTION

We have written this <u>Study guide</u> as a teaching tool. It supplements and coordinates with the learning aids in the textbook to help you master the material in <u>Child and Adolescent Development</u> (2nd edition) by Sarafino and Armstrong. Using this guide will enable you to understand the concepts and principles of developmental psychology better and help you earn a higher grade in the course.

At the beginning of the textbook, there is a section called "To the Student" that describes how to use the book's many learning aids, such as the progress checks, key terms, and key questions. Be sure to read and follow the suggestions in To the Student--use the <u>Study Guide</u> when you follow step number 7 of our suggestions.

HOW TO USE THIS STUDY GUIDE

We have organized the <u>Study Guide</u> to match the organization of the text. Fifteen chapters of study materials make up most of the guide. The answer key for each chapter appears at the end of that chapter in the guide.

Which study materials in each chapter of the guide should you use first? Do the exercises in the order in which they appear. They are organized so that they build your knowledge from one exercise to the next. Each chapter contains seven exercises. Let's see what they are.

1. <u>Summary in Outline</u>

The first section of each <u>Study Guide</u> chapter presents an outline of an entire text chapter in detail. Examine it very carefully to create a mental picture of the chapter and refresh your memory of the major points you have read.

2. Guided Review

The guided review summarizes a chapter, using a fill-in-the-blank format. Write the missing word or phrase in the blank space. After completing the entire exercise, check your answers against those in the Answer Section at the end of the <u>Study Guide</u> chapter.

3. Terms and Definitions Quiz

The third exercise has you construct a glossary for the key terms of the chapter, using a matching procedure. All of the terms and definitions are given--you just need to match them up. Select the correct term and write it in the blank space that precedes the definition. Check your selections with those in the Answer Section. You can then use this glossary as another study aid.

4. Matching Quiz

This exercise uses the standard matching format, with two columns of terms and phrases. For each item in the left column, select the matching phrase from the right column and write its designated letter in the space provided in the left column. Check your answers with those in the Answer Section when you have finished the exercise. There, you will also find the textbook page number on which the material in each item is covered.

5. Self Test

The self test gives you lots of useful practice on questions like those you may have on your course examination, if it contains objective items. Our questions include multiple-choice and true/false items. Circle the answer you choose for each question and, after completing the self test, consult the Answer Section. Use the page numbers given with the answers to refer back to the text material for questions you missed.

6. Important Details to Know

Sometimes important details in a chapter are difficult for students to pick out. This exercise has you consult the textbook to answer questions about important details you may have missed. Study the answers later.

7. Test Your Recall

Answer these questions without consulting the text. Jot down ideas or information that you recall from your reading. Then, use the page numbers given with each question to look up the relevant material in the text to get feedback on your answers. If you are studying for an essay examination, expand and organize your answers.

A FEW MORE SUGGESTIONS

    Use the <u>Study Guide</u> to diagnose the weak spots in your learning. Do each exercise as if it is a test in class, and look up answers after you finish it. If you see that many of your errors relate to certain topics in the text, go back and reread that material. This all takes time, of course, but we're confident you'll be pleased by the effect on your performance in your course.
    We hope you enjoy our text and this guide. We know you will learn many important things about child psychology in your course.

CHAPTER 1

Overview: The Study of Child Development

SUMMARY IN OUTLINE

WHY STUDY ABOUT CHILDREN? (p. 4)

   To learn more about normal and abnormal behavior patterns and individual differences
   To make informed decisions

THE FIELD OF DEVELOPMENTAL PSYCHOLOGY (p. 5)

   A DEFINITION OF DEVELOPMENTAL PSYCHOLOGY
      The scientific discipline concerned with the physical, behavior, cognitive, and personality changes that occur throughout the life cycle.

   DEVELOPMENTAL CHANGES: ARE THEY GRADUAL OR ABRUPT?
      Some psychologists divide development into qualitatively different stages.
      Growth rates vary within and between individuals.
      Chronological periods (prenatal, infancy, childhood, adolescence, adulthood and old age)
      Robert Havighurst described developmental tasks.

   GOALS OF DEVELOPMENTAL PSYCHOLOGY--description, explanation, prediction, and control.

   RELATION TO OTHER DISCIPLINES
      Biological sciences (genetics, embryology, physiology, biochemistry, neurology and ethology)
      Sociology studies human social life.
      Anthropology includes the study of human cultures.

DEVELOPMENTAL DETERMINANTS
   Maturation is guided by our genetic masterplan.
   In learning, information is incorporated into memory.
   Canalization describes the combined influence of genetic
      and environmental factors on a trait. Highly canalized
      means heredity has a strong influence.

STUDYING CHILD AND ADOLESCENT DEVELOPMENT

HISTORICAL BACKGROUND (p. 12)

THE MIDDLE AGES
   High infant mortality
   Infanticide and hardening
   Children viewed as "miniture adults"
   Adult activities by 7 years of age

AFTER THE RENAISSANCE
   New concept of childhood with unique treatment given to
      children
   Compulsory education and child labor laws

THE SCIENTIFIC BEGINNINGS
   Baby biographies by Pestalozzi, Tiedeman, Darwin, and
      Preyer
   Hall, Baldwin, and Gesell

RESEARCH METHODS IN DEVELOPMENTAL PSYCHOLOGY (p. 17)

EXPERIMENTAL METHODS--independent and dependent variables
   An Example--fear of strangers experiment with experimental
      and control groups
   Single-Subject Design

NONEXPERIMENTAL METHODS--does not manipulate an independent
   variable or test for cause-effect relationships
   Naturalistic Observation--baby biographies and case
      studies
   Correlational Research
      A correlation is a joint relation between variables.
      Correlation coefficient (+1.0 to 0.0 to -1.0)
   Research Using Preselected Categories does not lead to
      causal conclusions.
   "Age" as a Variable--cannot be manipulated
      Cross-sectional approach
      Longitudinal approach
      Cross-sectional/longitudinal design
      Cohort effects

ISSUES IN ACTION (p. 27)

TRADITIONAL BELIEFS--regarding parental discipline, firstborns and laterborns, and righthanders and lefthanders

EXPLAINING WHY SOME CHILDREN DEVELOP NORMALLY AND OTHERS DO
   NOT

Chapter 1

"Nature-nurture" debate
Maturational and learning factors interact.

GUIDED REVIEW

1. Although developmental psychology is concerned with the entire life span, it has focused on the study of children. Some psychologists view development as a gradual and continuous process, but others see changes as occurring _abruptly_ and divide development into a series of _stages_.

2. The chronological divisions in the human life cycle are the prenatal period, _infancy_, childhood, _adolesense_, adulthood, and old age.

3. Havighurst has outlined specific goals or "developmental _tasks_" for infancy, childhood, and adolescence--such as learning to walk, developing verbal and mathematical skills, and preparing for a career.

4. Developmental psychology has as its primary goals the description, explanation, _prediction_, and control of developmental processes.

5. Sociology and anthropology provide knowledge about social life and customs, and biology adds to an understanding of developmental psychology through the fields of _embryology_ which focuses on prenatal growth; _gerontology_ which deals with the aging process; and _ethology_ which focuses on the behavior of organisms in their natural environment.

6. Human development is influenced by two sets of determinants: _hereditary_ and _environmental_. The process of growth toward the potential of one's genetic masterplan is called _maturation_.

7. One model of the way genetic and environmental factors interact proposes that development tends to follow a path which has a structure and form that is determined by _genetic_ factors. The tendency for development to stick to the path in the face of environmental influences is called _canalization_.

8. During the Middle Ages, life expectancy was short and survival was difficult. The killing of unwanted babies, called _infanticide_, was common. Those that were not killed were often subjected to _hardening_ which was thought to toughen or strengthen the infant.

9. Young children in the Middle Ages were viewed as _miniature_ adults. They wore clothing like that of adults and participated in most adult activities. By

_____7_____ years of age most children were required to perform adult activities. During the _Renaissance_ (after 1500 A.D.) attitudes concerning children began to change radically.

10. The scientific study of chidren's behavior did not begin until the late 1700s when the first _baby-biography_ was published in diary form. However, it wasn't until the turn of the ___20TH___ century that research and theories concerning psychological development began to emerge. Even then, early research was mostly conducted to describe development.

11. Experimental research methods may yield _cause-effect_ conclusions because they demand rigorous control and direct _manipulation_ of variables.

12. The manipulated variable in experimental research is called the _independent_ variable; the level or value of the _dependent_ variable is expected to depend on the level of the manipulated variable.

13. In nonexperimental methods, the researcher does not manipulate variables and usually has less _control_. Consequently, they do not provide a direct test of cause-effect relationships. Baby biographies and case studies are types of _naturalistic_ observation research. Correlational research attempts to determine _relationships_ between variables. A study of attitudes toward teachers, which compared the opinions of high versus low-IQ students, would be an example of research using _preselected_ categories.

14. The age variable is a crucial one for developmental psychology. A study of 2-, 5-, and 8-year-olds that examines different children at each age over a short time period is using the _cross-sectional_ approach. The _longitudinal_ approach, which studies the same individuals over many years, takes more time, but it provides a long-term evaluation of the _stability_ of behavioral characteristics.

15. Research examining traditional beliefs has disconfirmed the notions that the firstborn child is _innately_ superior to siblings and that left-handed children are more likely to develop problems in reading and _language_ skills.

TERMS AND DEFINITIONS QUIZ

SET 1 (Match each term in the set with its definition below.):

ANTHROPOLOGY, BIOLOGY, DEVELOPMENTAL PSYCHOLOGY, DEVELOPMENTAL TASK, DEVELOPMENTAL TREND, LEARNING, MATURATION, NORMS, SOCIOLOGY, STAGE

1. __LEARNING__   The process of acquiring a relatively permanent behavior tendency as a result of experience.

2. __NORMS__   Data describing levels of characteristics (e.g., height, intelligence) that are considered normal or average for a particular group of people.

3. __SOCIOLOGY__   The science of human social life, particularly the behavior of people in groups.

4. __MATURATION__   The process of growth toward the fulfillment of our genetic potential.

5. __DEVELOPMENTAL TASK__   A culturally recognized achievement, such as walking, learning to read, or choosing a career, usually undertaken during a specific phase of the life cycle.

6. __ANTHROPOLOGY__   The study of human beings--their evolution, distribution, and cultures.

7. __STAGE__   A period of time during which a set of processes or behaviors are qualitatively different from those preceding or following it.

8. __BIOLOGY__   The science of living things. It includes such fields as genetics, embryology, and ethology.

9. __DEVELOPMENTAL PSYCHOLOGY__   The scientific study of the behavioral, cognitive, and personality changes that occur throughout the life cycles of organisms.

10. __DEVELOPMENTAL TREND__   A pattern of change that characterizes some aspect of development from one age to another.

SET 2: BABY BIOGRAPHIES, CANALIZATION, CONTROL GROUP, DEPENDENT VARIABLE, EXPERIMENTAL GROUP, EXPERIMENTAL METHODS, INDEPENDENT VARIABLE, INFANTICIDE, VARIABLE

1. __INDEPENDENT VARIABLE__   A characteristic of people, objects, or events that the researcher manipulates directly and independently of other variables to determine its effect on behavior.

2. __EXPERIMENTAL METHODS__   Controlled methods whereby variables are manipulated and observed in order to test hypotheses and to make cause-effect conclusions.

Chapter 1

3. __DEPENDENT VARIABLE__ A characteristic of people, objects, or events that the researcher expects will change as a result of his or her experimental manipulation(s).

4. __BABY BIOGRAPHIES__ Diary descriptions of infant and child development.

5. __CANALIZATION__ The tendency for an individual's development to follow the course dictated by heredity.

6. __VARIABLE__ Any measurable characteristic of people, objects, or events which may change in quantity or quality.

7. __CONTROL__ In an experiment, a group of subjects that does not experience the experimental treatment.

8. __infanticide__ The murder of a baby--a practice used for unwanted babies in some societies.

9. __EXPERIMENTAL GROUP__ A group of subjects in an experiment that receives the experimental treatment.

SET 3: CASE STUDY METHOD, COHORT EFFECT, CORRELATION COEFFICIENT, CORRELATIONAL RESEARCH, CROSS-SECTIONAL APPROACH, LONGITUDINAL APPROACH, NATURALISTIC OBSERVATION, NONEXPERIMENTAL METHODS, PRESELECTED CATEGORIES

1. __NATURALISTIC OBSERVATION__ Nonexperimental methods for data collection in the subjects' natural environment with relatively little intervention by the researcher.

2. __CORRELATIONAL COEFICIENT__ A statistic that reflects the degree and direction of relationship between two variables.

3. __PRESELECTED CATEGORIES__ Levels of a variable selected (not manipulated) by the researcher for a study (e.g., age and sex).

4. __CASE STUDY METHOD__ A nonexperimental method in which a trained researcher constructs a systematic biography from records of a child's history, interviews, and current observation.

5. __CORRELATIONAL RESEARCH__ A nonexperimental method by which the degree and direction of a relationshp between two variables is studied and statistically analyzed.

6. __COHORT EFFECT__ The influence of having been born in different years; it can be assessed in cross-sectional/longitudinal research.

7. __CROSS-SECTIONAL APPROACH__ Method of studying developmental trends by observing different groups of people of different ages within a relatively short time period.

8. __LONGITUDINAL APPROACH__ Method of studying developmental changes

in same individuals by making observations over a long period of time.

9. __NON-EXPERIMENTAL METHODS__ Research methods that include correlational research, naturalistic observation, and research using preselected categories, but do not involve manipulation of variables.

MATCHING QUIZ

1. __i__ stage
2. __j__ Robert Havighurst
3. __f__ embryology
4. __g__ sociology
5. __b__ canalization
6. __h__ Dieterich Tiedeman
7. __c__ G. Stanley Hall
8. __a__ Arnold Gesell
9. __d__ independent variable
10. __e__ correlation coefficient

a. norms for motor development
b. genetic/environmental interaction
c. questionnaire
d. a cause or "treatment"
e. degree of association
f. prenatal structures and processes
g. groups and mass media
h. early baby biography
i. a period that is qualitatively unique
j. developmental task

SELF TEST

1. The scientific study of the physical, behavioral, and mental changes that occur throughout the life cycle is called
   a. ethology.
   b. **developmental psychology.**
   c. gerontology.
   d. physical anthropology.

2. Chronological divisions of the life cycle that are characterized by qualitative changes in physical structures and behaviors are called
   a. abrupt trends
   b. norms
   c. cross-sections
   d. **stages**

3. The period of time called childhood lasts from _____ years of age to about 13 years, when the period called _____ begins.
   a. 1½; adolescence ✓
   b. 1; adulthood
   c. 2; adolescence
   d. none of the above

4. According to Havighurst, getting ready to read and learning sex differences and modesty are developmental tasks of
   a. infancy and early childhood. ✓
   b. middle childhood.
   c. late childhood.
   d. all ages of childhood.

5. Norms enable psychologists to predict how the typical child progresses and to answer questions, such as: When do infants begin to walk?
   a. True ✓
   b. False

6. Embryology is the field of study which focuses on physical development in early infancy.
   a. True
   b. False ✓

7. Environmental determinants in development include physical factors, such as nutrients and sunlight, and social factors, such as
   a. school.
   b. the family.
   c. television.
   d. all of the above. ✓

8. The process of maturation is related most closely to the concept of
   a. nature. ✓
   b. cohort effects.
   c. nurture.
   d. integration.

9. A mildly canalized trait is easily influenced by environmental factors.
   a. True ✓
   b. False

10. If development of a trait follows a path that is narrow and deep, it is described as
    a. very mature
    b. strongly nurtured.
    c. highly canalized. ✓
    d. weakly canalized.

11. During the Middle Ages infanticide was outlawed throughout the world and rarely practiced.
    a. True

(b.) False

12. To make babies healthier, parents in the Middle Ages used hardening techniques, which involved
    a. feeding with high-calcium foods to strengthen the bones.
    b. careful hygiene practices.
    (c.) harsh caretaking practices.
    d. exercising the baby's muscles.

13. Initiation rites were special jobs children performed when they began an apprenticeship in the Middle Ages.
    a. True
    (b.) False

14. Preyer published the first baby biography that examined the psychological development of a child for more than a year.
    a. True
    (b.) False

15. Which of the following is a variable?
    a. the income of a child's family
    b. a child's age
    c. the grades a child gets in school
    (d.) all of the above

16. A scientific experiment involves the systematic _____ of a variable by the researcher to determine its effect on another variable.
    a. correlation
    b. observation
    (c.) manipulation
    d. cross-sectioning

17. In an experiment, manipulation of the independent variable is expected to cause the value of the _____ to change.
    a. controlling factor
    b. correlated categories
    c. cohort effects
    (d.) dependent variable

18. In the fear of strangers experiment described in the text, fear behavior was the dependent variable.
    (a.) True
    b. False

19. In an experiment, a control group
    a. is not always used.
    b. is compared with the group receiving the experimental treatment.
    c. receives no treatment.
    (d.) all of the above.

20. Two research methods that use naturalistic observation are the baby biography and case-study.
    (a.) True

b. False

21. Some of the information acquired for case studies is retrospective and, therefore, subject to errors in recall.
    a. True
    b. False

22. If one variable increases as another variable decreases, the two variables are
    a. causally related.
    b. cohorts.
    c. positively correlated.
    d. negatively correlated.

23. Which correlation coefficient represents the weakest relationship between two variables?
    a. -1.0
    b. +0.8
    c. +0.1
    d. -0.2

24. If researchers find a very strong correlation between two variables, they can conclude that there is a cause-effect relationship between the two.
    a. True
    b. False

25. Research using _____ often look like experiments because they have separate groups of subjects, but no variable is manipulated.
    a. case study methods
    b. dependent variables
    c. preselected categories
    d. longitudinal approaches

26. In doing an experiment, the gender of the subjects could be used as an independent variable.
    a. True
    b. False

27. Research that involves the repeated observation of the same individuals over a long period of time is called a _____ study.
    a. cross-sectional
    b. longitudinal
    c. correlational
    d. cohort

28. Which of the following is a strength of the cross-sectional/longitudinal design?
    a. It allows examination of individual growth across time.
    b. It can show the stability of behavioral characteristics over time.
    c. It permits examination of the influence of having been born in different years.
    d. All of the above are strengths.

29. Which of the following beliefs have been disconfirmed by research?
    a. Children's development is enhanced if parents are very permissive.
    b. Firstborn children are much more socially and intellectually capable than their later-born siblings.
    c. Left-handed children are more likely to develop problems in reading and language skills than right-handers are.
    d. All of the above have been disconfirmed.

30. Many people argue that if reading problems are primarily determined by _____, then remedial education would be of _____ value.
    a. "nurture"; little
    b. genetics; great
    c. "nature"; little
    d. nutrition; great

IMPORTANT DETAILS TO KNOW

1. What are the ages (see Table 1.2) for the prenatal, infancy, and childhood periods of development? (p. 6)

2. At what age did children take on adult work roles in the Middle Ages? (p. 13)

3. Between what years were compulsory education laws being enacted in the United States? (p. 15)

4. Name the date and author of the first baby biography to "trace the psychological development of a normal child for more than a year..." (p. 16)

5. Who was the first to develop and use questionnaires in the study of children? (p. 16)

6. Name the psychologist at the turn of the century who proposed that the child's thinking advances through a series of stages. (p. 16)

7. Name an early researcher who developed norms for childhood characteristics. (p. 16)

8. What is the RANGE of a correlation coefficient? (p. 23)

TEST YOUR RECALL

1. Suggest three practical reasons for studying child development. (pp. 4-5)

2. Define the term developmental psychology? (p. 5)

Chapter 1

3. What is a stage? (p. 6)

4. List the major chronological periods sequentially from conception to death. (p. 6)

5. List and briefly describe the four goals of developmental psychology. (pp. 7-8)

6. Cite one example for each discipline--biology, sociology, and anthropology--to illustrate how each is important to the study of human development. (pp. 8-9)

7. Briefly discuss how physical growth is affected by genetic and environmental influences. (pp. 9-11)

8. Define canalization using the terms maturation and learning. (p. 10)

9. Define the term hardening. (p. 13)

10. During the Middle Ages, how were children below the age of 7 typically treated? (p. 13)

11. What is an initiation rite? (p. 14)

12. Briefly describe how the lives of children changed after the Renaissance. (p. 15)

13. List the contributions of G. Stanley Hall and James Mark Baldwin to the study of child development. (p. 16)

14. What were the two major "approaches" to the study of child psychology that emerged in the early 20th century? (p. 16)

15. What is a variable? (p. 18)

16. List four ethical standards that researchers are required to follow when studying children. See Highlight 1.2. (p. 19)

17. In the example experiment on FEAR OF STRANGERS in the text, what were the independent variable and dependent variable? (pp. 18-19)

18. Cite an important limitation of the experimental method. (p. 21)

19. What are the strengths and weaknesses of naturalistic observation? (pp. 22-23)

20. How does a positive correlation differ from a negative correlation? (p. 23)

21. Why is it NOT POSSIBLE to draw cause-effect conclusions from nonexperimental (i.e., correlational) research designs? (pp. 23-24)

22. Why is "age" a correlational variable? (p. 25)

23. State the essential differences between the cross-sectional and longitudinal research approaches. (p. 25)

24. Define the term cohort effects. (p. 25)

25. Discuss two traditional beliefs that have been partly or fully disconfirmed by scientific research. (pp. 27-28)

ANSWER SECTION

GUIDED REVIEW:

1. abruptly; stages
2. infancy; adolescence
3. tasks
4. prediction
5. embryology; gerontology; ethology
6. hereditary; environmental; maturation
7. genetic; canalization
8. infanticide; hardening
9. "miniature"; 7; Renaissance
10. baby biography; twentieth
11. cause-effect; manipulation
12. independent; dependent
13. control; naturalistic; associations (relationships); preselected
14. cross-sectional; longitudinal; stability
15. innately (born); language

TERMS AND DEFINITIONS QUIZ:

SET 1:
1. learning
2. norms
3. sociology
4. maturation
5. developmental task
6. anthropology
7. stage
8. biology
9. developmental psychology
10. developmental trend

SET 2:
1. independent variable
2. experimental methods
3. dependent variable
4. baby biographies
5. canalization
6. variable
7. control group
8. infanticide
9. experimental group

SET 3: 1. naturalistic observation
        2. correlation coefficient
        3. preselected categories
        4. case study method
        5. correlational research
        6. cohort effect
        7. cross-sectional approach
        8. longitudinal approach
        9. nonexperimental methods

MATCHING QUIZ:

    1. i   (p. 6)   6. h   (p. 16)
    2. j   (p. 6)   7. c   (p. 16)
    3. f   (p. 8)   8. a   (p. 16)
    4. g   (p. 9)   9. d   (p. 18)
    5. b   (p. 10)   10. e   (p. 23)

SELF TEST:

    1. b   (p. 5)   16. c   (p. 18)
    2. d   (p. 6)   17. d   (p. 18)
    3. a   (p. 6)   18. a   (p. 18)
    4. a   (p. 7)   19. d   (p. 20)
    5. a   (p. 8)   20. a   (p. 22)
    6. b   (p. 8)   21. a   (p. 22)
    7. d   (p. 10)   22. d   (p. 23)
    8. a   (p. 10)   23. c   (p. 23)
    9. a   (pp. 10-11) 24. b   (p. 24)
   10. c   (p. 11)   25. c   (p. 24)
   11. b   (p. 13)   26. b   (pp. 24-25)
   12. c   (p. 13)   27. b   (p. 25)
   13. b   (p. 14)   28. d   (pp 25-26)
   14. b   (p. 16)   29. d   (pp. 27-28)
   15. d   (p. 18)   30. c   (p. 29)

CHAPTER 2

Theories of Development

SUMMARY IN OUTLINE

   WHAT ARE THEORIES? (p. 36)

     A scientific theory is a tentative explanation that is clearly stated, organizes and relates known facts, and leads to testable hypotheses.
     Epigenetic theories view development as the product of genetic/environment interactions.

   SKILL AND INTELLECTUAL DEVELOPMENT (p. 37)

     LEARNING THEORY--derives from 17th century philosophy (Locke and Hobbes) and behaviorism.
        <u>Classical or Respondent Conditioning</u>
            History and Definition--Pavlov and Watson
                Classical conditioning is the basic learning process by which a stimulus (the CS) gains the ability to elicit a response through association with a stimulus (the US) that already elicits that response.
        <u>Operant or Instrumental Conditioning</u>
            History and Definition--Skinner
                In operant conditioning behavior is changed because of its consequences.
        <u>Complex Learning</u>--Gagné's learning theory describes a hierarchy of types of learning.

     INFORMATION-PROCESSING THEORY
        Uses computer models to study intellect and describe information flow in the nervous system.
        Types of codes: visual, acoustical, semantic, episodic.

COGNITIVE-STAGE THEORY--epigenetic view that derives from 18th century philosophy (Kant and Rousseau).
  <u>Stages in Cognitive Growth</u>--Piaget
    Sensorimotor (0-2 yrs.)
    Preoperational (2-7 yrs.)
    Concrete operational (7-12 yrs.)
    Formal operational (after 12 yrs.)
  <u>Processes in Cognitive Growth</u>
    A schema is a basic unit of knowledge.
    Organization, adaptation (assimilation, accommodation), equilibration.
    Jerome Bruner's theory stresses the role of language.

AN EVALUATION
  Learning theory
    Contributions: emphasis on environment; successful applications.
    Limitations: emphasis on quantitative differences in learning; failure to fully explain qualitative differences in learning; omission of maturational and innate factors.
  Cognitive-stage theory
    Contributions: emphasis on maturation and qualitative description.
    Limitations: some concepts are vaguely and inconsistently described; underestimates children's cognitive abilities in some areas.
  Information-processing theory--promising new approach that focuses on detailed analysis and examines quantitative and qualitative aspects of cognitive development.

<u>SOCIAL AND PERSONALITY DEVELOPMENT</u>   (p. 50)

  SOCIAL LEARNING THEORY
    Based on behaviorism and observational learning.
    Personality traits are learned behavior patterns.
    Bandura's work has focused on learning without external reinforcement, characteristics of effective models, and conditioning as a predictive function via cognition.

  PSYCHOANALYTIC THEORY--emphasizes an epigentic approach to explain personality development; innate instincts and drives; stages with certain goals of maturity; the mind consists of conscious and unconscious processes.
    <u>Freud's Theory</u>
      Personality consists of id, ego, and superego.
      Psychosexual stages--erogenous zones
        Oral (0-2 yrs.)
        Anal (2-4 yrs.)
        Phallic (4-6 yrs.)
        Latency (6-puberty)
        Genital (after puberty)
      Libido, fixated growth, Oedipus complex, Electra complex.
      Freud's followers made important contributions--Adler (striving for superiority), Horney (insecurity and

anxiety), and Sullivan (zones of interaction, six
stages)
- Erikson's Theory
  - Based on psychoanalytic approach and Freud's ideas.
  - Departures from Freud--psychosocial emphasis; stresses importance of the ego; focus on healthy personality and prevention of problems; covers full life cycle.
  - Eight stages of "crisis" resolution and psychosocial development:
    - Basic trust vs. basic mistrust (0-1 yr.)
    - Autonomy vs. shame or doubt (1-3 yrs.)
    - Initiative vs. guilt (4-5 yrs.)
    - Industry vs. inferiority (6-11 yrs.)
    - Identity vs. role confusion (12-18 yrs.)
    - Intimacy vs. isolation (young adulthood)
    - Generativity vs. self-absorption (middle adulthood)
    - Integrity vs. despair (old age)

THEORIES OF INBORN MECHANISMS
- Temperament Theory--innate temperaments (EASI) and experience shape personality.
- Ethological Theory
  - Focuses on biological sources of behavior.
  - Species-specific behavior, sign stimuli

AN EVALUATION
- Social learning theory
  - Overlooks the importance of maturation.
  - Beginning to include cognitive processes.
- Psychoanalytic theories
  - Contributions: concern with innate, internal, and unconscious processes; emphasis on early childhood experiences; focus on overcoming childhood problems.
  - Limitations:
    - Many aspects of Freud's theory not testable; effects of fixation generally not confirmed; some stages may be culture bound.
    - Concepts in Erikson's theory lack scientific and logical rigor.
- Temperament theory and ethological theory
  - Relatively new; promising explanations about inborn mechanisms are being formed.

ISSUES IN ACTION (p. 62)

THEORIES PARENTS HAVE--parents' beliefs, such as "Spare the rod and spoil the child," affect the parent/child relationship.

GUIDED REVIEW

1. Theories attempt to _____ why events occur. A good theory produces clear hypotheses which are _____. Since theoretical guesses, or hypotheses, are continuously being tested, all theories should be regarded as _____.

2. Theories of skill and intellectual development include learning theories, _____-processing theories, and _____-stage theories. The epigenetic approach, as opposed to the environmental approach, is taken by the _____ theories.

3. Behaviorism was founded by _____, who stressed the importance of learning experiences while denying the existence of _____ ideas. Skinner made major contributions in formulating the principles of _____ conditioning.

4. Learning theories view intellectual development as a cumulative process. For example, Gagné has described a taxonomy of eight types of learning arranged in a _____. The most complex form of learning in Gagné's hierarchy is _____, because it builds upon all other forms of learning.

5. Information processing theory attempts to explain cognitive development on the basis of changes in the way children pay attention to stimuli, convert or _____ this information, and _____ their experiences in memory.

6. According to Piaget, children pass through a sequence of cognitive stages: the sensorimotor, preoperational, _____ operational, and formal operational stages. Thinking during the preoperational stage is _____ rather than logical.

7. Piaget's epigenetic theory of cognitive development proproses three inborn processes: organization, adaptation, and _____. Adaptation involves two processes of taking in information; the one that requires modifications to existing schemas is called _____.

8. In contrast to Piaget's view, Bruner's cognitive-stage theory proposes that older children's big cognitive leap occurs chiefly through the acquisition of _____ skills.

9. The development of social behavior and personality is partially explained by social _____ theories, psychoanalytic theories, and theories of _____ mechanisms.

10. Bandura discovered that observational learning could occur

without the use of external _____ and emphasized that conditioning also serves a _____ function.

11. Psychoanalytic theories use an _____ approach to explain social and personality development, and emphasize that the mind functions on conscious and _____ levels.

12. Freud's concept of _____ feelings and gratification was very broad; it included feelings that result from almost any activity that produces bodily _____.

13. Freud's theory holds that the earliest part of personality is the _____. The id's store of basic drives, or _____, is checked by the maturing ego. Gradually, the child acquires a conscience, or _____, which attempts to guide the ego according to cultural values and rules. These personality components emerge as children pass through five _____ stages: anal, oral, _____, latency, and genital. The phallic stage is highlighted by the onset and resolution of the Oedipus and _____ complexes. If a child is deprived or overstimulated at any stage, the personality is likely to become _____ at that stage.

14. Other psychoanalysts differed with Freud over the importance of the id, and emphasized the role of the child's _____ environment. Adler held that developing personalities were striving for social _____. Horney stressed the influence of social neglect or overprotection on the child's sense of anxiety and insecurity. Sullivan proposed _____ of interaction as the initial avenue for contact with a social world.

15. Erikson's psychoanalytic personality theory encompasses the life span from birth to old age. He deemphasized Freud's psychosexual orientation and stressed a psycho-_____ orientation. In his view, the id is not as central to personality development as the _____, which matures by resolving a major _____ during each of eight successive stages of personality growth. For example, in infancy the baby tries to resolve the conflict between _____ and basic mistrust. The healthy personality resolves each conflict with a favorable _____ of positive-to-negative ego qualities. The positive ego qualities at each stage, in order, are: basic trust, _____, initiative, _____, identity, _____, generativity, and integrity.

16. Theories of inborn mechanisms have provided explanations for relatively specific traits and behavior. T_____ theory proposes that certain personality dispositions are inherited and then modified through the child's experiences. Ethological theory emphasizes the role of instinctive _____-specific behaviors, such as aggressive and courtship activities, that are elicited by _____.

24   Chapter 2

17. Although social learning theory has made valuable contributions toward an explanation of social/personality development, it has been criticized for failing to include a role for _____ factors. Psychoanalytic theory also has made important contributions, particularly in focusing on early childhood _____ and the importance of unconscious processes. However, predictions from Freud's description of _____ stages have not been confirmed.

TERMS AND DEFINITIONS QUIZ

SET 1 (Match each term in the set with its definition below.):

BEHAVIORISM, CLASSICAL CONDITIONING, CONDITIONED RESPONSE, CONDITIONED STIMULUS, ENCODE, INFORMATION PROCESSING, OPERANT CONDITIONING, PUNISHMENT, REINFORCER, THEORY, UNCONDITIONED RESPONSE, UNCONDITIONED STIMULUS,

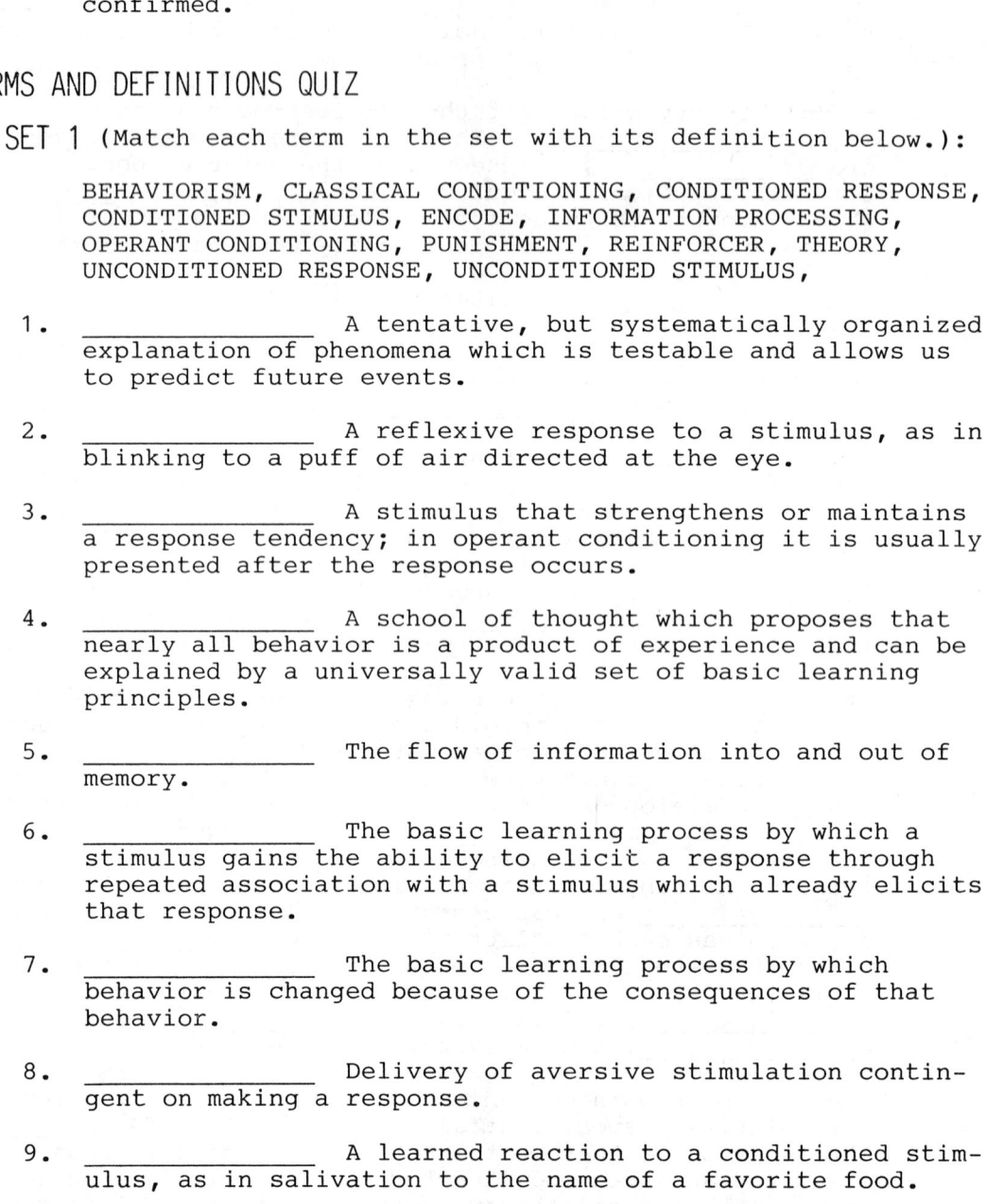

1. _____ A tentative, but systematically organized explanation of phenomena which is testable and allows us to predict future events.

2. _____ A reflexive response to a stimulus, as in blinking to a puff of air directed at the eye.

3. _____ A stimulus that strengthens or maintains a response tendency; in operant conditioning it is usually presented after the response occurs.

4. _____ A school of thought which proposes that nearly all behavior is a product of experience and can be explained by a universally valid set of basic learning principles.

5. _____ The flow of information into and out of memory.

6. _____ The basic learning process by which a stimulus gains the ability to elicit a response through repeated association with a stimulus which already elicits that response.

7. _____ The basic learning process by which behavior is changed because of the consequences of that behavior.

8. _____ Delivery of aversive stimulation contingent on making a response.

9. _____ A learned reaction to a conditioned stimulus, as in salivation to the name of a favorite food.

10. _____ A previously neutral stimulus which, after repeated pairings with an unconditioned stimulus, becomes

capable of eliciting a conditioned response.

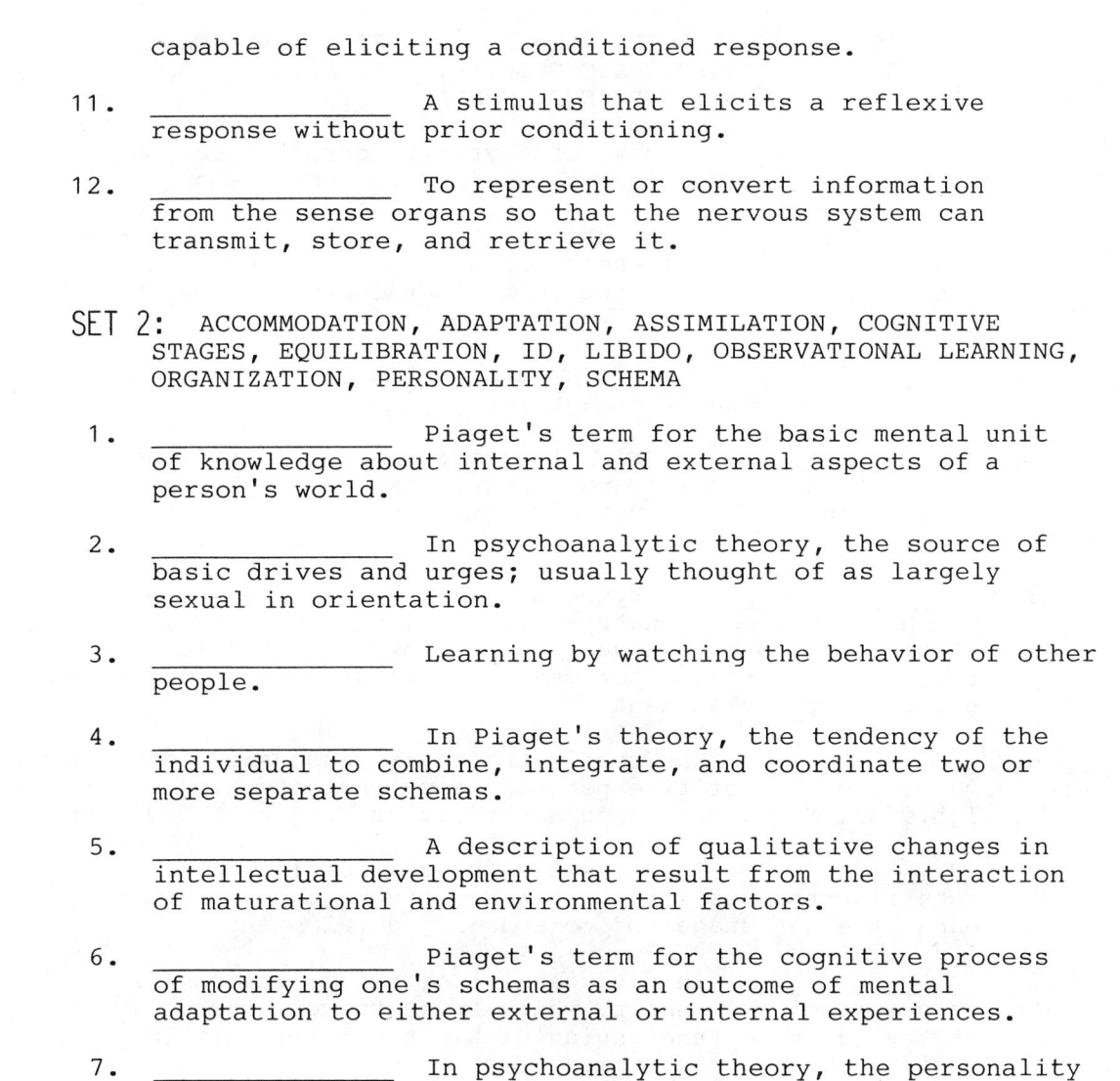

11. _____ A stimulus that elicits a reflexive response without prior conditioning.

12. _____ To represent or convert information from the sense organs so that the nervous system can transmit, store, and retrieve it.

SET 2: ACCOMMODATION, ADAPTATION, ASSIMILATION, COGNITIVE STAGES, EQUILIBRATION, ID, LIBIDO, OBSERVATIONAL LEARNING, ORGANIZATION, PERSONALITY, SCHEMA

1. _____ Piaget's term for the basic mental unit of knowledge about internal and external aspects of a person's world.

2. _____ In psychoanalytic theory, the source of basic drives and urges; usually thought of as largely sexual in orientation.

3. _____ Learning by watching the behavior of other people.

4. _____ In Piaget's theory, the tendency of the individual to combine, integrate, and coordinate two or more separate schemas.

5. _____ A description of qualitative changes in intellectual development that result from the interaction of maturational and environmental factors.

6. _____ Piaget's term for the cognitive process of modifying one's schemas as an outcome of mental adaptation to either external or internal experiences.

7. _____ In psychoanalytic theory, the personality structure where biological instincts are translated into wishes and impulses on an unconscious level.

8. _____ Piaget's term for the process of restoring cognitive states to the status of consistency; also a source of motivation for cognitive growth.

9. _____ Mental interactions and adjustments (e.g., assimilation and accommodation) to internal and external experiences.

10. _____ The underlying processes and broad behavior patterns that characterize the way an individual relates to others.

11. _____ Piaget's term for the cognitive process of incorporating new experiences into one's already existing schemas without modifying these structures.

Chapter 2

SET 3: CRISIS, EGO, ELECTRA COMPLEX, FIXATION, OEDIPUS COMPLEX, PSYCHOSEXUAL STAGES, PSYCHOSOCIAL, SIGN STIMULI, SPECIES-SPECIFIC BEHAVIOR, SUPEREGO, TEMPERAMENTS

1. _____ In psychoanalytic theory, the personality component that functions as one's moral conscience.

2. _____ In psychoanalytic theory, psychological conflict that occurs when a boy in the phallic stage is sexually attracted to the mother but fears harm by the father.

3. _____ Certain events in the environment that evoke species-specific behavior.

4. _____ In Erikson's personality theory, the interaction of social and cultural experiences with maturational forces in the development of the ego through eight stages covering the entire life span.

5. _____ In psychoanalytic theory, the process in which a disproportionate amount of libidinal energy is invested at an early stage of psychosexual development as a result of frustration or over-gratification, thus stunting personality development.

6. _____ In Freud's theory of personality development, a series of five periods, each characterized by libidinal release through a particular erogenous body zone.

7. _____ In Erikson's theory, conflict over acquiring the positive versus negative ego quality at each of eight stages of personality development.

8. _____ In psychoanalytic theory, the conscious component of personality which tries to meet the demands of the id while functioning within the limits set by society and the environment.

9. _____ Inherited basic personality characteristics or dispositions.

10. _____ In ethological theory, distinctive activities of each species that were inherited through biological evolution.

11. _____ In psychoanalytic theory, psychological conflict in girls at the phallic stage that normally results in identification with the mother.

Chapter 2 27

MATCHING QUIZ

Matching Terms and Ideas:

1. _G_ schema
2. _e_ temperament
3. _f_ ethology
4. _b_ social learning theory
5. _a_ information-processing
6. _d_ accommodation
7. _c_ fixated

   a. computer simulations
   b. modeling and imitation
   c. stunted personality growth
   d. changing one's mental organization
   e. inherited personality disposition
   f. sign stimuli
   g. basic unit of knowledge

Matching People and Ideas:

1. _D_ Albert Bandura
2. _G_ Sigmund Freud
3. _e_ Ivan Pavlov
4. _a_ Erik Erikson
5. ___ B. F. Skinner
6. ___ Jean Piaget
7. ___ Robert Gagné
8. ___ John Locke

   a. psychosocial development
   b. knowledge comes through the senses
   c. operant conditioning
   d. observational learning
   e. conditioned reflexes
   f. hierarchy of types of learning
   g. Electra complex
   h. cognitive-stage theory

SELF TEST

1. Theories which propose that development results from the interaction of the child's biological inheritance with the environment are called _____ theories.
   a. heritability
   b. epigenetic
   c. schematic
   d. nature-nurture

2. Early behaviorists were probably LEAST likely to study children's
   a. moral conduct when they could cheat.

    b. reflexes as babies.
    c. reasoning about a logical problem.
    d. incentives for doing their homework.

3. Learning theorists view intellectual development as a maturational process which interacts with the child's experiences.
    a. True
    b. False

4. Pavlov studied _____ connections between stimuli and responses.
    a. operant
    b. reflexive
    c. schematic
    d. species-specific

5. Skinner considered the behavioristic approach to be a well developed theory.
    a. True
    b. False

6. Sounding a loud and sharp noise elicits distress in infants reflexively. If this reflex occurred in a classical conditioning episode, the noise would be the _____; distress would be the _____.
    a. CR; US
    b. UR; CR
    (c.) US; UR
    d. CR; UR

7. In operant conditioning, reinforcement and punishment are _____ of behavior.
    (a.) consequences
    b. respondents
    c. schemas
    d. sign stimuli

8. In Gagné's theory, learning by the process of operant conditioning forms the basis for acquiring increasingly complex skills.
    a. True
    b. False

9. Information-processing theorists describe several types of codes one can use--such as the semantic code, which involves
    a. what the stimuli look like.
    b. what the stimuli sound like.
    c. meanings and associations.
    d. sequences of occurrence or time.

10. In Piaget's theory, cognitive development progresses through four stages: sensorimotor, _____, _____, and _____.
    a. oral; anal; phallic

b. phallic; latency; genital
   c. preoperational; formal operational; concrete operational
   (d.) preoperational; concrete operational; formal operational

11. In Piaget's theory, adaptation is the tendency to combine, integrate, and coordinate separate schemas.
    a. True
    b. False

12. According to Piaget, Lucy uses the process of accommodation when she tries to incorporate new features of the environment into her thinking by modifying what she knows or how she thinks.
    a. True
    b. False

13. The need for theories of cognitive development to include some role for maturational factors is suggested by the
    a. apparent limits to how early a child can learn abstract ideas and complex relationships.
    b. very abrupt stages in thinking that all children pass through.
    c. fact that the brain develops throughout childhood.
    d. both a and c.

14. The stages in cognitive development that Piaget proposed
    a. greatly underestimate young children's thinking abilities.
    b. are incorrect in the description of the order in which cognitive abilities emerge.
    c. correctly predict that training greatly accelerates children's acquisition of logical skills.
    d. all of the above.

15. Detailed task analysis is a principal characteristic of the _____ approach which has made it useful in explaining various types of learning.
    a. Piagetian
    b. learning theory
    c. information-processing
    d. behavioristic

16. The term _____ refers to the underlying processes that account for the broad behavior patterns which characterize the way an individual reacts and relates to others.
    a. information-processing
    b. social learning
    c. personality
    d. libido

17. According to Bandura, personality development can be fully explained by operant and classical conditioning principles.
    a. True
    b. False

18. The likelihood that a model's behavior will be imitated is enhanced if the observer is similar in
    a. age.
    b. sex.
    c. race.
    d. all of the above.

19. According to Bandura, learning is not only an associative process, it also serves a _____ function.
    a. predictive
    b. instinctive
    c. fixating
    d. schematic

20. Psychoanlaytic theories
    a. are epigenetic.
    b. describe development as occurring in stages.
    c. describe certain goals for maturity.
    d. all of the above.

21. Psychoanalysts believe that unconscious thoughts and processes play a dominant role in determining our overt behavior.
    a. True
    b. False

22. Which of the following statements about Freud's theory is TRUE?
    a. Biological instincts are translated into wishes in the libido.
    b. Freud's ideas about unconscious memories grew from his work with people who were drugged.
    c. Freud proposed that the id is present at birth.
    d. The ego is the first personality component to emerge at birth.

23. The sequence of stages in Freud's theory is : oral, anal, phallic, latency, and genital.
    a. True
    b. False

24. According to Freud, the _____ during the period of latency.
    a. Oedipal complex arises
    b. Electra complex arises
    c. libido is dormant
    d. young girl begins to suffer penis envy

25. The neo-Freudian who emphasized the influence of stresses produced by anxiety and insecurity in early childhood was
    a. Adler.
    b. Horney.
    c. Sullivan.
    d. Erikson.

26. Sullivan proposed a neo-Freudian theory consisting of

_____ stages of personality development.
a. four
b. six
c. eight
d. twelve

27. Erikson's neo-Freudian theory describes eight stages in ego development that cover the entire life span.
a. True
b. False

28. Adolescents who go to their guidance counselors to get information about possible majors in college are showing their striving toward a sense of industry.
a. True
b. False

29. The acronym formed by connecting the first letter of each temperament proposed by Buss and Plomin is
a. OAPL.
b. TEMP.
c. TAII.
d. EASI.

30. According to ethologists, the red spot on the bill of a herring gull parent is a(n) _____ stimulus for pecking behavior by newly-hatched chicks.
a. reinforcing
b. fixating
c. encoded
d. sign

IMPORTANT DETAILS TO KNOW

1. Which philosophers proposed that all knowledge is acquired through the senses? (p. 38)

2. Which philosophers proposed (a) inborn logical and perceptual categories and (b) an inborn groundplan for growth through a series of stages? (p. 43)

3. Which social learning theorist emphasized the role of the parents on the child's dependence? (p. 50)

4. Which neo-Freudians emphasized (a) inferiority and superiority, (b) anxieties and insecurities, and (c) zones of interaction? (p. 55)

5. On the basis of the child's age, which of Erikson's stages correspond with Piaget's sensorimotor, concrete operational, and formal operational stages (see Table 2.4). Note that the "ages" and "stages" do not correspond exactly across theories. (p. 63)

TEST YOUR RECALL

1. Describe the characteristics of a "good" theory. (p. 36)

2. What is an epigenetic theory? (p. 36)

3. Briefly describe the process of classical conditioning. (pp. 38-40)

4. Define the term operant conditioning. (p. 41)

5. How does Gagné explain the acquisition of complex learning abilities, such as problem solving? (p. 41)

6. How does information-processing theory attempt to explain children's intellectual development? (p. 42)

7. State the major cognitive characteristics for each of Piaget's stages: sensorimotor, preoperational, concrete operational, and formal operational. (pp. 44-45)

8. What is a schema? (p. 45)

9. Briefly describe the function(s) of the following terms in Piaget's theory: organization, adaptation, and equilibration. (pp. 45-46)

10. Contrast the Piagetian processes of assimilation and accommodation. (pp. 45-46)

11. Explain the contributions and limitations of learning theory toward an understanding of skill and intellectual development. (p. 47-48)

12. Briefly list the contributions and limitations of cognitive-stage theory toward an understanding of skill and intellectual development. (p. 48)

13. Cite two ways social learning theory differs from learning theory. (p. 50)

14. Name the characteristics of models that promote imitation. (p. 51)

15. Define the following Freudian terms: id, ego, and super-ego. (p. 53)

16. To what extent do children have sexual feelings? See Highlight 2.4. (p. 54)

17. List Freud's five psychosexual stages. (pp. 53-54)

18. What is the Oedipus complex? (pp. 54-55)

19. In what major ways is Erikson's theory similar to and different from Freud's theory of personality development?

(p. 56)

20. List in sequential order the opposing ego qualities which Erikson used to characterize his eight psychosocial stages. (p. 57)

21. Name the four temperaments proposed by Buss and Plomin (1975). (p. 59)

22. How does temperament theory differ significantly from learning theory? (p. 60)

23. Briefly describe two species-specific-behaviors. (p. 60)

24. What are the strengths and weaknesses of Freud's theory? (p. 61)

ANSWER SECTION

GUIDED REVIEW:

1. explain; testable; tentative
2. information; cognitive; cognitive-stage
3. Watson; innate; operant
4. hierarchy; problem solving
5. encode; organize
6. concrete; "intuitive"
7. equilibration; accommodation
8. language
9. learning; inborn
10. reinforcers; predictive
11. epigenetic; unconscious
12. sexual; pleasure
13. id; libido; superego; psychosexual; phallic; Electra; fixated
14. social; superiority; zones
15. social; ego; crisis; basic trust; ratio; autonomy; industry; intimacy
16. Temperament; species; sign stimuli
17. maturational (biological); experiences; psychosexual

TERMS AND DEFINITIONS QUIZ:

SET 1:
1. theory
2. unconditioned response
3. reinforcer
4. behaviorism
5. information-processing
6. classical conditioning
7. operant conditioning
8. punishment
9. conditioned response
10. conditioned stimulus
11. unconditioned stimulus

           12. encode

SET 2: 1. schema
        2. libido
        3. observational learning
        4. organization
        5. cognitive stages
        6. accommodation
        7. id
        8. equilibration
        9. adaptation
       10. personality
       11. assimilation

SET 3: 1. superego
        2. Oedipus complex
        3. sign stimuli
        4. psychosocial
        5. fixation
        6. psychosexual stages
        7. crisis
        8. ego
        9. temperaments
       10. species-specific behavior
       11. Electra complex

MATCHING QUIZ:

Matching Terms   Matching People
and Ideas: and Ideas:
1. g (p. 45)   1. d (p. 50)
2. e (p. 59)   2. g (p. 54)
3. f (p. 60)   3. e (p. 38)
4. b (p. 50)   4. a (p. 56)
5. a (p. 42)   5. c (p. 40)
6. d (p. 46)   6. h (p. 44)
7. c (p. 54)   7. f (p. 41)
                         8. b (p. 38)

SELF TEST

 1. b (p. 36)   16. c (p. 50)
 2. c (p. 37)   17. b (p. 50)
 3. b (p. 37)   18. d (p. 51)
 4. b (p. 38)   19. a (p. 51)
 5. b (p. 39)   20. d (p. 51)
 6. c (p. 39)   21. a (p. 52)
 7. a (p. 41)   22. c (p. 53)
 8. a (p. 41)   23. a (p. 53)
 9. c (p. 42)   24. c (p. 54)
10. d (p. 44)   25. b (p. 55)
11. b (p. 45)   26. b (p. 55)
12. a (p. 46)   27. a (p. 56)
13. d (p. 47)   28. b (p. 58)
14. a (p. 48)   29. d (p. 59)
15. c (p. 48)   30. d (p. 60)

CHAPTER 3

Heredity, Prenatal Development, and Birth

SUMMARY IN OUTLINE

<u>PRENATAL DEVELOPMENT</u> (p. 72)

    CONCEPTION
        Egg + sperm = zygote
        Female reproductive system (ovaries, Fallopian tubes, uterus)
        Ovum released; degenerates after 24 hours
        Male reproductive system (testicles, vas deferens, seminal vesicle)
        Sperm in semen expelled through ejaculatory duct

    THREE STAGES OF PRENATAL DEVELOPMENT--human gestation = 266 days or 38 weeks.
        <u>Germinal Stage</u> (0-2 wks.)
            Characterized by rapid cell division (mitosis)
            Blastocyst implants; its layers become the chorion, placenta, amnion, and embryo.
            Multiple births (12/1,000)
                monozygotic (MZ) twins--from one egg ("identical")
                dizygotic (DZ) twins--from two eggs ("fraternal")
        <u>Embryonic Stage</u> (2-8 wks.)
            Differentiation of organ systems
            Embryonic layers:
                ectoderm forms brain, spinal cord, skin, teeth
                mesoderm forms muscles, skeleton, blood vessels
                endoderm forms lungs, liver, digestive system
        <u>Fetal Stage</u> (9 wks. - birth)
            Improvements in organ structure and functioning
            Sexual differentiation
            Quickening and basic movements occur

MATERNAL PHYSIOLOGICAL CHANGES--increases in uterus and breast size, body weight and blood volume

GENETIC DETERMINANTS (p. 80)

GENETIC MATERIALS
Wolff and Darwin
Gametes contain chromosomes; chromosomes contain genes
The DNA Model
Double helix of four pairs of chemical bases: G-C; C-G; A-T; T-A
Meiosis produces gametes (sperm and ova)
Human gametes contain 23 chromosomes; zygote has 23 pairs.
Genetic Sex Differentiation (sex chromosomes--23rd pair)
XX = female; XY = male

GENETIC TRANSMISSION--allele = one gene of a specific pair
Dominant allele can produce a dominant trait.
Recessive allele PAIR produce recessive trait; e.g., Tay-Sachs disease:
NN = homozygous dominant pair; normal phenotype
Nt = heterozygous pair ("carrier"); normal phenotype
tt = homozygous recessive pair; disease
Co-dominant influence; mutation; polygenic inheritance

THE IMPACT OF GENETIC FORCES
Genetic Disorders--sickle-cell anemia, phenylketonuria (PKU), Down's syndrome (nondisjunction), X and Y chromosome aberrations, sex-linked disorders (color blindness, hemophilia, muscular dystrophy)
Genetics and Behavior
Twin studies (MZ and DZ comparisons)
Adoption studies
Intelligence, personality, and mental disorders are influenced by heredity.

ENVIRONMENTAL DETERMINANTS (p. 88)--sensitive periods

MATERNAL NUTRITION--importance of protein

MATERNAL SUBSTANCE INTAKE
Hormones--the "pill"
Nicotine and Caffein
Alcohol and Drugs--fetal alcohol syndrome
Medication

ENVIRONMENTAL POLLUTANTS--X-rays, mercury, lead

Rh INCOMPATIBILITY

INFECTIONS IN THE MOTHER--see Table 3.2

MATERNAL EMOTIONAL STATE

THE BIRTH PROCESS (p. 95)

Chapter 3   37

   GIVING BIRTH--lightening; signs of true labor ("labor pains,"
   "show," amnionic fluid discharge)
      Stages of Labor
         Stage 1: cervix dilation
         Stage 2: delivery of baby
         Stage 3: afterbirth expelled
      Birth Complications--breech position; shoulder
       presentation; cesarean section; anoxia

   PREMATURE BIRTH
      Premature = less than 5½ lbs. and 37 wks. gestation
      "Small for dates" = less than 5½ lbs., but more than 37
       wks. gestation
      Respiratory distress syndrome
      Causes of prematurity

THE NEWBORN BABY: APPEARANCE AND ASSESSMENT (p. 98)

   Lanugo and fontanels
   Apgar Scoring Chart

ISSUES IN ACTION   (p. 100)

   GENETIC COUNSELING
      Pedigree; amniocentesis; chorion biopsy
      Information in "probabilities," not certainties.

   MODERN METHODS OF CHILDBIRTH AND CARE OF THE NEWBORN
      Natural childbirth; "family centered" programs; home
       birth; alternative birth centers
      Birth trauma--Rank and Leboyer
      Early parent/child contact; rooming-in

GUIDED REVIEW

1. Ova, or _____ cells, mature in a follicle within one of two _____. About midway through the menstrual cycle, an ovum is released and begins its journey down the _____ where a sperm can fertilize it, producing a _____. Many millions of sperm are produced and stored in the average adult male's _____, to be released at sexual climax.

2. The zygote undergoes a cell-division process called _____, becomes a blastocyst, and implants itself in the _____ wall at the end of the _____ stage of prenatal development. Genetically identical twins derive from one zygote and are called _____.

3. Once the zygote is implanted, it begins to develop a filterlike system, called the _____--and the _____ stage of prenatal development starts. This stage is characterized by rapid differentiation of organ structures, which develop out of three cell layers:

the _____, the _____, and the endoderm.

4. The fetal stage, lasting from the _____ week to birth is characterized by the beginning and refinement of _____ and muscle functioning. External body parts show considerable development during this stage. A baby born after _____ weeks of gestation has a good chance of survival.

5. For couples who can't conceive, options that allow them to have a child include adoption, _____-tube fertilization, and artificial _____.

6. In 1953 Watson and Crick helped solve the genetic mystery with their model of _____. Today we know that genes and chains of genes, called _____, are made of DNA. Human genes are contained in _____ pairs of chromosomes. The X and Y chromosomes determine a person's _____.

7. When a trait is determined by one allele, the allele is said to be _____. Other traits, such as Tay-Sachs disease, result from two _____ alleles. Carriers of Tay-Sachs have a normal phenotype, but a heterozygous _____. Sometimes a trait results from the joint effect of two alleles; this effect is called _____.

8. Genetic forces can produce severe disorders. Among blacks, _____ leads to oxygen starvation and eventual tissue damage. A disease that usually attacks whites and results in the buildup of a brain-damaging toxin is called _____.

9. Another disorder leading to mental retardation is produced when the child's body cells contain an extra chromosome. This disorder is called _____ syndrome or _____. The extra chromosome results from improper disjunction in the parent's gametes during the process of _____.

10. Scientists are developing gene therapies to eliminate certain genetic disorders. Three kinds of therapies are gene insertion, gene _____, and _____ transduction.

11. Studies that examine differences between monozygotic and dizygotic twins to assess the role of heredity are called _____. Adoption studies provide another approach for assessing genetic influences on development. These approaches have been used to reveal the role of genetics in _____ ability, personality, and _____ disorders.

12. Each organ system is particularly susceptible to harmful

Chapter 3   39

environmental factors during its _____ period. Maternal protein deficiency has been linked to deficiencies in the baby's _____ tissue. Maternal drug use can also harm the baby. Oral contraceptives have been linked to heart defects and _____ abnormalities; smoking may lead to _____ birth; and excessive alcohol use can cause _____ alcohol syndrome.

13. Other environmental factors affecting prenatal development include TORCH infections, _____ from X-rays, Rh-incompatibility, and the mothers' emotional state. In the case of Rh-incompatibility, the mothers' _____ attack and destroy the baby's Rh-_____ blood cells.

14. The birth process consists of three stages which are marked by (1)_____ of the cervix, (2) passage of the baby through the birth canal, and (3) expulsion of the _____. The birth process is complicated when the baby is born rump first, called the _____ position. If normal delivery is risky or impossible, the baby may be removed from the mother's uterus by the _____ procedure. Lack of sufficient oxygen, or _____, during birth can produce brain damage.

15. Premature babies have a higher mortality rate; death often results from the _____ syndrome. The cause of prematurity is unknown, but it has been linked with maternal ill health, smoking, poor nutrition, emotional difficulties, and multiple births, among other factors. Premature babies are often physically and behaviorally _____, but many of these deficits are greatly reduced in later childhood.

16. A neonate in excellent health would recieve a score of 10 on the _____. One who receives a score of 4 or less requires immediate treatment. Eighty percent are born in good condition, and receive a score of _____ or more.

17. The study of genetics has led to the emergence of a new applied field called _____. Here practitioners provide couples with estimates of the likelihood they will have a genetically defective child. Counselors collect data about family traits, or _____, across previous generations. This family history, or _____, helps the counselor estimate the _____ responsible for the family traits.

18. Genetic defects can be detected before birth through a procedure called _____. This procedure has some risk to the fetus, and is usually not attempted until the _____ week of gestation. The _____ biopsy is a new technique that may replace amniocentesis.

19. Americans generally used to believe that mothers would

experience intense and prolonged pain during labor unless they received drugs. Today, partly in an effort to protect the baby from these drugs, many prospective parents are using _____ methods. Other parents are opting to have their babies born at an _____ center or at home, with a _____ attending.

20. Extra mother-infant contact soon after birth seems to be _____ for many babies; as a result, hospitals now offer the option of _____.

TERMS AND DEFINITIONS QUIZ

SET 1 (Match each term in the set with its definition below):

CHORION, EMBRYONIC STAGE, FALLOPIAN TUBES, FETAL STAGE, GERMINAL STAGE, MITOSIS, OVA, OVARIES, SPERM, UTERUS, ZYGOTE

1. _____ Female gametes, or egg cells; in humans they contain 23 single chromosomes.

2. _____ Male gametes; in humans they contain 23 single chromosomes.

3. _____ The first 2 weeks of prenatal development in the human, lasting until uterine implantation; characterized by rapid cell division.

4. _____ The period from about 2 to 8 weeks after conception characterized by structural differentiation of major organs.

5. _____ The single cell formed when the egg and sperm unite at conception.

6. _____ The outermost protective membrane inside of which the embryo and fetus develop.

7. _____ The female organs that store developing egg cells, or ova.

8. _____ Two ducts, each of which connects an ovary with the uterus; ova travel down the ducts and are fertilized there.

9. _____ A reproductive organ in female mammals in which prenatal development occurs.

10. _____ The period from the 9th week of gestation to birth, highlighted by sexual differentiation and organ functioning.

11. _____ Cellular division and duplication of body

cells after a zygote has been formed.

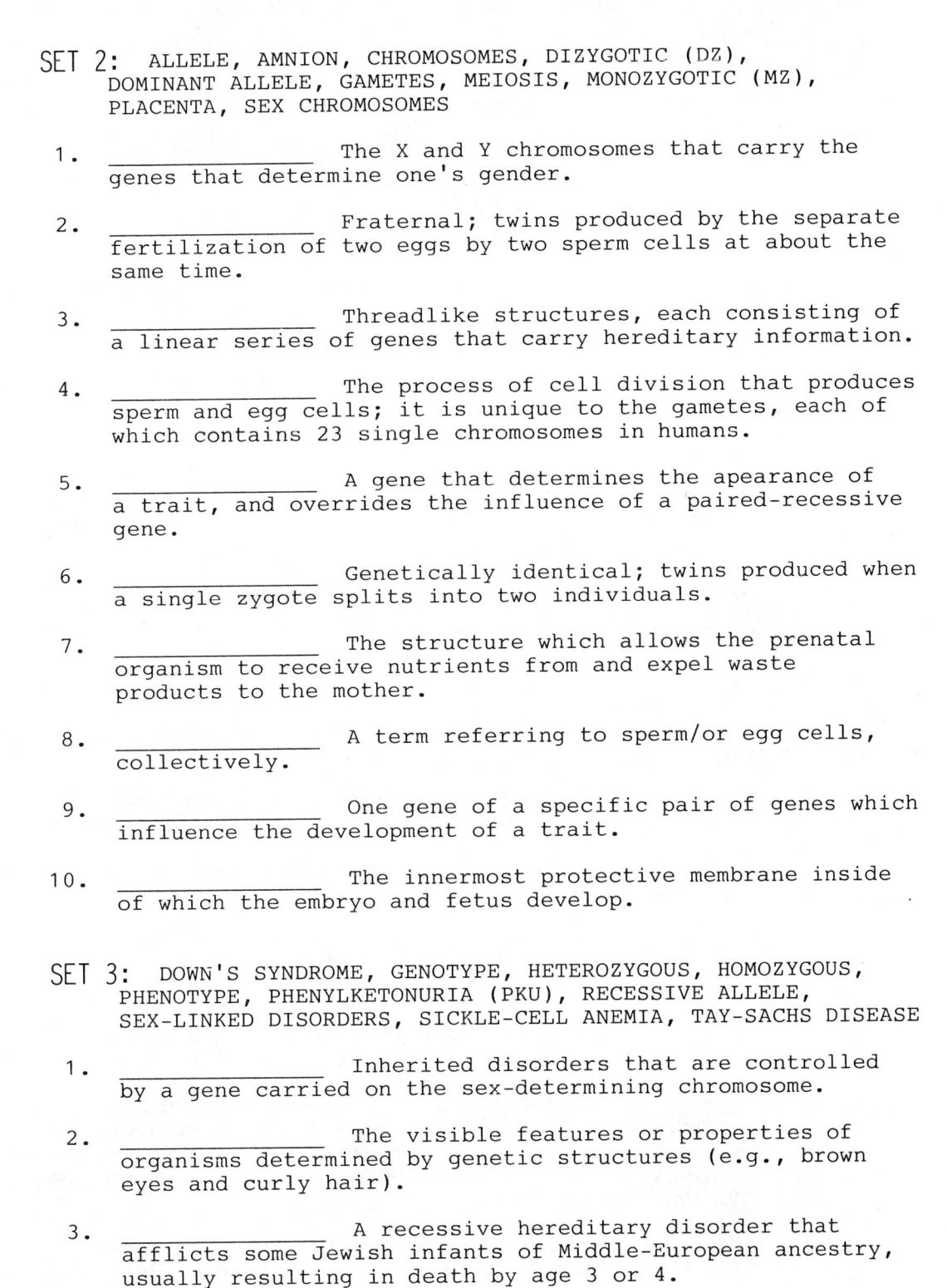

SET 2: ALLELE, AMNION, CHROMOSOMES, DIZYGOTIC (DZ), DOMINANT ALLELE, GAMETES, MEIOSIS, MONOZYGOTIC (MZ), PLACENTA, SEX CHROMOSOMES

1. _____ The X and Y chromosomes that carry the genes that determine one's gender.

2. _____ Fraternal; twins produced by the separate fertilization of two eggs by two sperm cells at about the same time.

3. _____ Threadlike structures, each consisting of a linear series of genes that carry hereditary information.

4. _____ The process of cell division that produces sperm and egg cells; it is unique to the gametes, each of which contains 23 single chromosomes in humans.

5. _____ A gene that determines the apearance of a trait, and overrides the influence of a paired-recessive gene.

6. _____ Genetically identical; twins produced when a single zygote splits into two individuals.

7. _____ The structure which allows the prenatal organism to receive nutrients from and expel waste products to the mother.

8. _____ A term referring to sperm/or egg cells, collectively.

9. _____ One gene of a specific pair of genes which influence the development of a trait.

10. _____ The innermost protective membrane inside of which the embryo and fetus develop.

SET 3: DOWN'S SYNDROME, GENOTYPE, HETEROZYGOUS, HOMOZYGOUS, PHENOTYPE, PHENYLKETONURIA (PKU), RECESSIVE ALLELE, SEX-LINKED DISORDERS, SICKLE-CELL ANEMIA, TAY-SACHS DISEASE

1. _____ Inherited disorders that are controlled by a gene carried on the sex-determining chromosome.

2. _____ The visible features or properties of organisms determined by genetic structures (e.g., brown eyes and curly hair).

3. _____ A recessive hereditary disorder that afflicts some Jewish infants of Middle-European ancestry, usually resulting in death by age 3 or 4.

Chapter 3

4. _____ A gene that produces a particular trait only if it occurs in pairs or in the absence of a dominant gene.

5. _____ Genetic combination involving one dominant and one recessive allele.

6. _____ A specific allele combination; one's genetic makeup.

7. _____ Genetic combination in which both alleles are the same, either dominant or recessive.

8. _____ A recessive hereditary blood disorder that afflicts some black people; causes physical weakness, brain damage, and early death.

9. _____ A recessive hereditary disorder in which the baby's body fails to produce an enzyme that breaks down a toxic substance found in many common foods.

10. _____ A genetic disorder that results when the child's body contains three instead of two of the number 21 chromosomes.

SET 4: AMNIOCENTESIS, ANOXIA, APGAR SCORING CHART, BREECH DELIVERY, CESAREAN SECTION, CHORION BIOPSY, FETAL ALCOHOL SYNDROME, GENETIC COUNSELING, SENSITIVE PERIOD, TORCH

1. _____ Congenital condition involving mental retardation and distinctive physical characteristics of babies born to mothers who drank excessively during pregnancy.

2. _____ A surgical procedure by which a baby is delivered through an incision in the mother's abdomen.

3. _____ Oxygen starvation in the baby during birth which can result in brain damage.

4. _____ A time interval during which development is maximally responsive or vulnerable to environmental influences.

5. _____ A birth complication in which the baby's legs or buttocks emerge from the birth canal first.

6. _____ A technique to test for fetal genetic abnormalities in the ninth week; guided by ultrasound, a narrow tube is inserted into the uterus through the cervical opening, and a sample of fetal material is drawn from the chorion for analysis.

7. _____ A set of five harmful infections or diseases that a mother may contract during pregnancy

Chapter 3   43

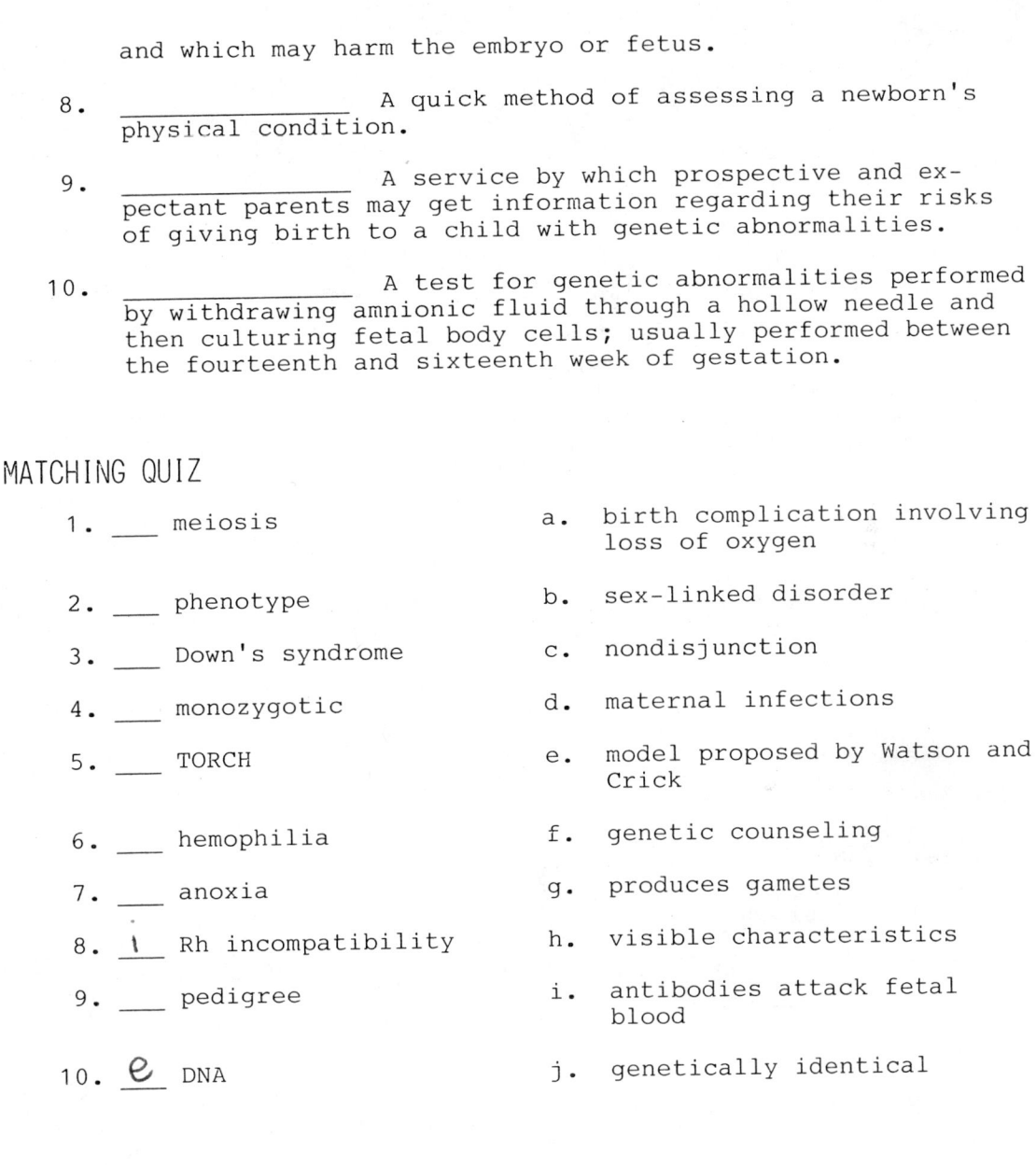

and which may harm the embryo or fetus.

8. _____ A quick method of assessing a newborn's physical condition.

9. _____ A service by which prospective and expectant parents may get information regarding their risks of giving birth to a child with genetic abnormalities.

10. _____ A test for genetic abnormalities performed by withdrawing amnionic fluid through a hollow needle and then culturing fetal body cells; usually performed between the fourteenth and sixteenth week of gestation.

MATCHING QUIZ

1. ___ meiosis
2. ___ phenotype
3. ___ Down's syndrome
4. ___ monozygotic
5. ___ TORCH
6. ___ hemophilia
7. ___ anoxia
8. _i_ Rh incompatibility
9. ___ pedigree
10. _e_ DNA

a. birth complication involving loss of oxygen
b. sex-linked disorder
c. nondisjunction
d. maternal infections
e. model proposed by Watson and Crick
f. genetic counseling
g. produces gametes
h. visible characteristics
i. antibodies attack fetal blood
j. genetically identical

SELF TEST

1. The female reproductive system contains the uterus, two _____ tubes, and two _____, which store eggs before they mature.
   a. follicle; zygotes
   b. vesicle; deferens
   c. Fallopian; ovaries
   d. fertilization; ovollicles

2. About _____ hours after being released from a follicle of an ovary, the egg degenerates.
   a. 10

      b. 15
      c. 24
      d. 48

3. Ova are continuously produced after puberty at the rate of 500 per day.
   a. True
   b. False

4. When a male ejaculates, _____ from the testicles travel through the _____ to the seminal vesicle, and are eventually expelled from the penis.
   a. sperm; vas deferens
   b. ova; vas deferens
   c. ova; ejaculatory duct
   d. sperm; ejaculatory duct

5. Once the blastocyst is implanted in the uterine wall, two structures are formed: the _____, which is a protective membrane, and the placenta, which is a _____ system.
   a. amnion; filterlike
   b. amnion; germinal
   c. chorion; germinal
   d. chorion; filterlike

6. Identical twins are also called "monozygotic" because they are formed when one zygote splits into two.
   a. True
   b. False

7. The germinal stage of prenatal development is characterized by differentiation of major organ structures.
   a. True
   b. False

8. Tanner has estimated that perhaps _____ of all pregnancies end in _____.
   a. 50%; spontaneous abortion
   b. 50%; miscarriage
   c. 30%; spontaneous abortion
   d. 30%; miscarriage

9. Although some mothers lose weight in the first few months of pregnancy, it is normal and desirable to gain
   a. about 25 pounds, including the fetus, placenta, etc.
   b. not more than 15 pounds, including the fetus, etc.
   c. 30 pounds over and above the fetus, etc.
   d. weight and any amount of weight is medically acceptable.

10. Darwin discovered by looking through his microscope that sperm do not contain fully formed people; instead he saw individual alleles and suggested that they control development.
    a. True
    b. False

Chapter 3   45

11. The human zygote contains 46 chromosomes, having received
    a. all of them from the same-sex parent.
    b. all of them from the opposite-sex parent.
    c. half of them from each parent.
    d. 46 from each parent, but at fertilization pairs of chromosomes unite so that only 46 remain.

12. In the process of cell division called meiosis, the
    a. first division is like mitosis and simply replicates the original cell.
    b. second division "double replicates" and makes four cells, each with 46 chromosomes.
    c. third division produces eight gametes.
    d. third division produces both eggs and sperm.

13. The mother cannot contribute a Y chromosome to her offspring.
    a. True
    b. False

14. If one parent is homozygous dominant (normal) for PKU and the other parent has the PKU phenotype, the probability that their next child will have PKU is _____%.
    a. 100
    b. 75
    c. 25
    d. 0

15. Two hereditary diseases tend to afflict specific ethnic groups: Tay-Sachs afflicts _____, sickle-cell anemia afflicts _____.
    a. Hispanics; Blacks
    b. Blacks; Jews
    c. Jews; Blacks
    d. Hispanics; Jews

16. Down's syndrome occurs when the child receives three instead of two of the number 21 chromosomes; this results from nondisjunction which involves
    a. improper mitosis during the germinal stage of prenatal development.
    b. improper separation of chromosomes in the parent's gametes during meiosis.
    c. uncontrolled meiosis during the embryonic stage of prenatal development.
    d. none of the above.

17. Researchers conducting twin studies could measure the influence of heredity by subtracting the differences between MZ pairs from the differences between DZ pairs if each MZ and DZ pair had equal environmental experiences.
    a. True
    b. False

18. Research with animals has found that offspring have deficits in brain neurons and learning if their mothers had

diets deficient in _____ during pregnancy.
   a. carbohydrates
   b. protein
   c. vitamin A
   d. iron

19. Research has consistently found that mood-changing drugs (LSD, marijuana, etc.) cause serious defects in the developing human fetus.
   a. True
   b. False

20. The TORCH infections are grouped into five categories: Toxoplasmosis, Other diseases, _____, Cytomegalovirus, and _____.
   a. Rh-factor; Hepatitis
   b. Rh-factor; Herpes simplex
   c. Rubella; Hepatitis
   d. Rubella; Herpes simplex

21. The signs of true labor include labor pains, the "show," and the _____.
   a. discharge of menstrual material
   b. appearance of the baby's head at the vaginal opening
   c. discharge of amniotic fluid
   d. full dilation of the cervix

22. The placenta is discharged after the entire birth process--all three stages--have been completed.
   a. True
   b. False

23. The birth complication in which the baby lies crosswise in the uterus is called the _____ presentation.
   a. breech
   b. cesarean
   c. rump
   d. shoulder

24. Which of the following statements about anoxia is TRUE?
   a. It is usually caused by the placenta detaching too late.
   b. Researchers have found that sedation of the mother reduces its occurrence.
   c. It produces brain damage which can impair the child's motor functioning.
   d. Both a and c are correct.

25. Respiratory distress syndrome
   a. rarely occurs among premature babies.
   b. primarily afflicts "small for dates" infants during the second week after birth.
   c. causes spontaneous abortions.
   d. none of the above.

26. Babies are more likely to be born prematurely if their

Chapter 3   47

mothers smoke cigarettes, are poor and undernourished, and have received little or no prenatal care.
a. True
b. False

27. Newborns have soft areas of the skull, called _____, and may have skin blemishes and fine body hair, called _____.
a. fontanels; lanugo
b. lanugoes; fontanel
c. cesarean sections; down
d. cranial sections; celia

28. Apgar scoring ranges from _____ to 10; babies with a score of _____ or below require immediate attention and treatment.
a. -10; 0
b. 0; 4
c. 0; 7
d. -10; -4

29. The following inherited disorders are NOT due to a homozygous recessive genotype: Down's syndrome, Duchenne muscular dystrophy, hemophilia, Klinefelter's syndrome, and Turner's syndrome.
a. True
b. False

30. Lamaze and Dick-Read proposed
a. a procedure to reduce "birth trauma."
b. the midwife method for home birth.
c. the method of "natural childbirth."
d. the rooming-in procedure for hospitals.

IMPORTANT DETAILS TO KNOW

1. How long is the egg viable for fertilization after ovulation? (p. 72)

2. What is the average length of human gestation? (p. 73)

3. The interior and exterior cells of the blastocyst form into what structures? (p. 74)

4. What percentage of all twin births result in fraternal twins? (p. 75)

5. How many chromosomes does a zygote have? (p. 82)

6. Name the chemical bases in DNA. (p. 81)

7. Which two organ systems begin their sensitive period earliest in gestation? Which two are latest? (p. 89)

8. The onset of true labor is marked by which three signs?

(p. 95)

9. How are the definitions of PREMATURE and SMALL FOR DATES babies different? (p. 97)

10. When is the risk of death greatest for an infant? (p. 99)

11. Name the obstetricians who developed modern methods of childbirth. (p. 103)

TEST YOUR RECALL

1. Diagram and name the major structures of the female reproductive system. (p. 72)

2. Describe the journey of the ovum from ovulation, to conception, to implantation in the uterus. (pp. 72-75)

3. Draw and label the major parts of the male reproductive system. (p. 73)

4. Outline the course of development during the germinal stage. (p. 74)

5. In what ways are MZ and DZ twins different? (pp. 74-75)

6. Describe the changes that occur during the embryonic stage. (pp. 75-76)

7. List the highlights of development during the fetal stage. (pp. 77-78)

8. How does the mother's body change during pregnancy? (p. 78)

9. Specify the historical contributions of Wolff, Darwin, and Watson and Crick to our understanding of genetic materials. (pp. 80-81)

10. Describe the DNA model. (p. 81)

11. Define the term meiosis. (p. 82)

12. Make a chart showing how a recessive trait can be transmitted to offspring by parents who are both heterozygous for that trait? (pp. 83-84)

13. Distinguish between a genotype and a phenotype. (p. 83)

14. List the symptoms that describe a person with sickle-cell anemia, PKU, and Down's syndrome. (p. 85)

15. What is a sex-linked disorder? (p. 86.)

16. Explain how twin and adoption studies provide knowledge about hereditary influences. (pp. 86-87)

17. List those human traits (exclude disorders) for which there is evidence of genetic influence. (p. 87)

18. Describe the effects of maternal malnutrition on prenatal development. (p. 89)

19. Make a list of substances that pregnant women sometimes consume that can have a harmful effect on their gestating offspring. Next to the substance's name state the harmful effects. (pp. 90-92)

20. Name several environmental pollutants that could harm the gestating baby. (p. 92)

21. Explain how the Rh factor in the mother's blood could pose risks to her fetus. (p. 92)

22. What does the acronym TORCH mean? (p. 93)

23. How can the mother's emotional state affect her unborn child? (p. 94)

24. Describe the three stages of birth. (pp. 95-96)

25. Briefly discuss three types of birth complications. (p. 96)

26. What are some of the special problems faced by premature infants? (pp. 97-98)

27. Describe the physical appearance of the newborn. (pp. 98-99)

28. What is the Apgar Scoring Chart? (pp. 99-100)

29. Explain how genetic counseling attempts to help prospective parents understand the likelihood of producing a child with genetic defects. (pp. 100-101)

30. Define the term chorion biopsy. (pp. 101-102)

31. Describe the method of "natural childbirth" and alternatives to the standard hospital delivery. (pp. 103-104)

ANSWER SECTION

GUIDED REVIEW:

1. egg; ovaries; Fallopian tube; zygote; testicles
2. mitosis; uterine; germinal; monozygotic
3. placenta; embryonic; ectoderm; mesoderm
4. nineth; organ; 28

50   Chapter 3

          5. test; insemination
          6. DNA; chromosomes; 23; sex
          7. dominant; recessive; genotype; co-dominance
          8. sickle-cell anemia; PKU
          9. Down's; mongolism; meiosis
         10. replacement; viral
         11. twin studies; intellectual; mental
         12. sensitive; brain; chromosome; premature; fetal
         13. irradiation; antibodies; positive
         14. dilation; afterbirth; breech; cesarean section; anoxia
         15. respiratory distress; retarded (deficient)
         16. Apgar Scoring Chart; 7
         17. genetic counseling; phenotypes; pedigree; genotypes
         18. amniocentesis; fourteenth to sixteenth; chorion
         19. natural childbirth; alternative birth; midwife
         20. beneficial; rooming-in

TERMS AND DEFINITIONS QUIZ:

          SET 1: 1. ova
                  2. sperm
                  3. germinal stage
                  4. embryonic stage
                  5. zygote
                  6. chorion
                  7. ovaries
                  8. Fallopian tubes
                  9. uterus
                 10. fetal stage
                 11. mitosis

          SET 2: 1. sex chromosomes
                  2. dizygotic (DZ)
                  3. chromosomes
                  4. meiosis
                  5. dominant allele
                  6. monozygotic (MZ)
                  7. placenta
                  8. gametes
                  9. allele
                 10. amnion

          SET 3: 1. sex-linked disorders
                  2. phenotype
                  3. Tay-Sachs disease
                  4. recessive allele
                  5. heterozygous
                  6. genotype
                  7. homozygous
                  8. sickle-cell anemia
                  9. phenylketonuria (PKU)
                 10. Down's syndrome

          SET 4: 1. Fetal alcohol syndrome
                  2. cesarean section
                  3. anoxia

Chapter 3

4. sensitive period
5. breech delivery
6. chorion biopsy
7. TORCH
8. Apgar Scoring Chart
9. genetic counseling
10. amniocentesis

MATCHING QUIZ:

1. g (p. 82)
2. h (p. 83)
3. c (p. 85)
4. j (p. 74)
5. d (p. 93)
6. b (p. 86)
7. a (p. 96)
8. i (p. 92)
9. f (p. 101)
10. e (p. 81)

SELF TEST:

1. c (p. 72)
2. c (p. 72)
3. b (p. 72)
4. a (p. 73)
5. d (p. 74)
6. a (p. 74)
7. b (p. 75)
8. c (p. 77)
9. a (p. 78)
10. b (p. 81)
11. c (p. 82)
12. a (p. 82)
13. a (p. 82)
14. d (p. 83)
15. c (p. 83)
16. b (p. 85)
17. a (p. 86)
18. b (p. 89)
19. b (p. 91)
20. d (p. 93)
21. c (p. 95)
22. b (p. 96)
23. d (p. 96)
24. c (p. 96)
25. d (p. 97)
26. a (p. 98)
27. a (p. 99)
28. b (p. 100)
29. a (p. 102)
30. c (p. 103)

CHAPTER 4

Infant Physical, Cognitive, and Language Development

SUMMARY IN OUTLINE

    THE NEWBORN BABY (p. 110)

        BODILY FUNCTIONS
           Respiration--rapid, shallow, noisy
           Nutrition, Digestion, and Elimination--colostrum
           Temperature Regulation
           Circulation--heart rate is 140 beats per minute
           Brain Function--cortical and subcortical areas

        BEHAVIORAL CAPACITIES
           Survival Reflexes--rooting, sucking, coughing, sneezing,
             yawning, withdrawal, pupillary, and blinking
           Nonessential Reflexes--swimming, Babinski, grasping,
             startle (Moro reflex), and knee jerk

        SENSORY CAPACITIES
           Hearing
               Can detect differences in length, volume, and pitch
               Can recognize their own mother's voice
           Vision
               Best acuity at about 9 inches (between 7 and 15 inches)
                 from object.
               Poor accommodation and convergence
           Taste, Touch, and Smell

        ASSESSING HOW THE NEWBORN IS DOING--the Brazelton Neonatal
          Behavioral Assessment Scale

    INFANT PHYSICAL AND MOTOR DEVELOPMENT (p. 115)

BODY GROWTH
    Height, weight, body proportions, and teeth
    Immunological defenses develop

BRAIN GROWTH
    Increases in glial cells, myelin, dendrites and axons
    Sequence of brain area maturation (motor, sensory, visual)
    Nerves in upper areas of the body mature before those in
      lower regions.

MOTOR DEVELOPMENT
    Many reflexes are replaced with voluntary behavior.
    Natural progression in gross motor skills--see Fig. 4.4
    Crawling, hitching or scooting, creeping, and stand-alone
      walking (12-14 months)
    Fine motor control parallels neural growth.
    Experience influences motor development.

DAILY RHYTHMS
    Sleep needs decrease during infancy.
    Proportion of REM ("active") to non-REM ("quiet") sleep
      declines with age.

SENSORY AND PERCEPTUAL DEVELOPMENT   (p. 121)

HEARING AND VISION
    Hearing
        Sensitivity and discrimination of sounds improves.
        Hearing helps babies locate people and acquire language.
    Vision
        Accommodation nears adult performance by age 4 months.
        Visual acuity improves to 20/100 by 6 months.
        Visual scanning begins early and focuses on edges.
        Depth perception
        Infants can coordinate visual and auditory events by
          by age 3 weeks.

ATTENTION AND EXPLORATION
    Visual pattern preferences--faces are preferred the most.
    Attention and habituation are influenced by novelty,
      discrepancy, and complexity.
    Exploration and play aid cognitive development.

INFANT LEARNING AND MEMORY   (p. 127)

CLASSICAL CONDITIONING
    Watson and Rayner (1920) condition fear in "Little Albert."
    Stimulus generalization, stimulus discrimination,
      extinction
    Classical conditioning may occur in utero. Infants learn
      CS-CR connections more easily with age.

OPERANT CONDITIONING--behavioral consequences produce
  learning.
    Positive Reinforcement
        Basic (primary) reinforcers

Chapter 4   55

        Conditioned (secondary) reinforcers
    <u>Extinction</u>--weakens the behavior
    <u>Punishment</u>--should be used infrequently, very cautiously
    and with other procedures.
    <u>Negative Reinforcement</u>--reduction or removal of an
    aversive stimulus
    <u>Age and Operant Conditioning</u>

COMBINING CLASSICAL AND OPERANT CONDITIONING

INFANT IMITATION--MONKEY SEE, MONKEY DO--young infants show
  very immature imitation.

INFANT MEMORY--recognition memory functions in young infants,
  recall memory probably does not.

MENTAL ORGANIZATION
    Newborns recognize that objects belong to categories.
    Infants (7 months) have some "counting" knowledge.
    Babies (3-4 months) can detect differences in facial
    expressions.

<u>THE DEVELOPMENT OF THINKING AND INTELLIGENCE</u>   (p. 135)

    PIAGET'S VIEW OF SENSORIMOTOR DEVELOPMENT
        Substage 1:   Reflex activity (1 month)
        Substage 2:   Primary circular reactions (1-4 months)
        Substage 3:   Secondary circular reactions (4-8 months)
        Substage 4:   Coordinating secondary circular reactions
        (8-12 months)
        Substage 5:   Tertiary circular reactions (12-18 months)
        Substage 6:   Mental combinations and representations
        (18-24 months)

    OBJECT PERMANENCE
        Development of the object permanence concept parallels
        the sequence of sensorimotor substages--see Table 4.3.
        Object permanence is fully formed by 18 to 24 months.
        Infants have more knowledge of object permanence than
        Piaget claimed.

    TESTING MENTAL ABILITY: IQs FOR INFANTS?
        Low scores are useful for diagnosis and prediction; but
        moderate or high scores do not correlate well with later
        IQ scores.

<u>LANGUAGE DEVELOPMENT</u>   (p. 140)

    PREVERBAL INTERACTION
        <u>Attention to Speech</u>
        <u>Preverbal Sounds</u>
            Crying--anger cry, pain cry, rhythmical cry
            Cooing is followed by babbling
            Motherese may promote the baby's language development.

    FIRST WORDS

Chapter 4

One-word sentences
Intonation, context, and body language aid comprehension.

ISSUES IN ACTION (p. 143)

SUDDEN INFANT DEATH SYNDROME (SIDS)
One theory is that apnea causes SIDS.
SIDS victims and their mothers are different from others.

PARENTING AND TOYS TO ENCOURAGE INFANT COMPETENCE

GUIDED REVIEW

1. Typical neonates sleep 15 to 20 hours a day, but require much care because they feed and eliminate frequently, and cannot regulate their own body _____ well. They can perform involuntary or reflex behaviors, since _____ areas of the brain are fairly mature. Breast milk contains _____ which protect the baby from illnesses.

2. Reflexes that help maintain life functions are called _____ reflexes. One that helps the baby find the nipple is the _____ reflex; this reflex is typically followed by the _____ reflex. The reflex that protects the baby's eyes from intense light is the _____ reflex. Many other reflexes are relatively nonessential. For example, stroking the baby's foot elicits the _____ reflex. By the end of the first year, all nonessential reflexes, except the _____ reflex, have disappeared.

3. All sensory systems function at birth. Neonates seem to hear fairly well, and can distinguish between changes in pitch, length, and _____. They also attend and respond selectively to the _____ of different people, such as their mother's versus another woman's.

4. Newborns can detect visual movement and brightness, but they cannot focus, or _____, well to objects more than 1½ feet away. The ability to direct both eyes at an object, which is called visual _____, is also lacking.

5. Tests of the newborn's behavioral functioning, such as the _____ Neonatal Behavioral Assessment Scale, give a profile of current functioning but do not _____ later behaviors or abilities.

6. The body grows rapidly in infancy. By 18 months of age babies have gained about _____% in height, and their weight has more than tripled. "Baby" teeth start to come in between _____ and _____

Chapter 4　　　　57

months.

7. The brain more than doubles in weight during infancy. Most of this gain is from increased number of _____ cells and a white fatty substance, called _____, that insulates nerves.

8. Different areas of the brain tend to mature in the following order: motor, _____, visual, and then _____.

9. During infancy many reflexive responses are replaced by _____ responses.

10. A highlight of motor development is locomotion which starts when the baby _____. Then, at around 8 to 9 months, infants begin to _____, or move on hands and knees.

11. During infancy the amount of time babies sleep each day decreases from about 16 to 17 hours to _____, and the percentage of this time that is in the "active" or _____ sleep stage declines from about 50% to _____%.

12. By filming the body movements of babies while they listened to tape-recorded adult speech, Condon and Sander (1974) found that newborns pay close attention to speech sounds and _____ their movements with these sounds.

13. The baby's visual capabilities develop quickly. Six-month-olds have a visual _____ of about 20/100. At first, young infants shown a triangle will visually _____ only one area of it, later they scan the whole perimeter. Young infants appear to perceive depth. When placed on the deep side of the visual cliff, their heart rates became _____.

14. Fantz (1961) found that infants have attentional preferences for different visual stimuli. The _____-like patterns were preferred most, and the solid _____ stimuli were preferred least.

15. Two processes governing exploration are attention and its opposite, _____. Both processes are influenced by stimulus novelty, discrepancy, and _____.

16. "The acquisition of a relatively permanent behavioral tendency as a result of experience" is the definition of _____. Since this process cannot be directly observed, we infer from changes in _____ that learning has occurred.

17. Classical conditioning is often involved in learning _____ behaviors, such as love and fear. Watson

and Rayner (1920) conditioned Little Albert to fear a white rat by pairing it with a _____. When Albert was presented with objects somewhat similar to the rat, his fear demonstrated the process of stimulus _____. In the presence of highly dissimilar objects, such as blocks, Albert's lack of fear reflected stimulus _____.

18. The basic learning process whereby behavior changes because of its consequences is called _____. Consequences that strengthen a response are called _____. Those consequences which satisfy basic physiological needs are called _____, while those that are learned are called _____ reinforcers.

19. Once operant conditioning has been established, the response rate can be reduced by withholding reinforcement. This process is called _____. However, if an aversive condition exists and the child makes a response which reduces or removes the aversive condition, this is called _____.

20. Young infants can imitate _____ expressions, but they do not begin to copy arm and hand movements until about _____ months. Infants perform better on tasks of recognition memory than _____ memory.

21. Memory is already becoming organized in infancy; and by 6 to 9 months of age, babies begin to show their knowledge that objects belong to different _____. At even earlier ages, infants seem to discriminate between the facial expressions of others in that they look longer at emotional expressions of _____ than of anger.

22. According to Piaget, infant cognition is at the _____ stage of development. This stage consists of _____ substages, beginning with _____ activity and ending with mental combinations and _____.

23. As infants develop, they become more competent in searching for hidden objects. This reflects their growing awareness of the _____ concept.

24. Language development begins with preverbal interactions and sounds. Wolff (1969) discovered that babies produce three types of cries: rhythmical, pain, and _____ cries. Vowel-like sounds produced at around 7 weeks of age are called _____. Later, as consonants appear, babies begin to form _____ sounds.

25. The baby's first words function as one-word _____ which are given clarity through context, body language, and _____.

26. SIDS tends to strike _____- to _____-

Chapter 4 59

month-old boys from low-income and _____ group families. A promising theory is that SIDS results when a normal episode of not breathing, called _____, becomes prolonged.

TERMS AND DEFINITIONS QUIZ

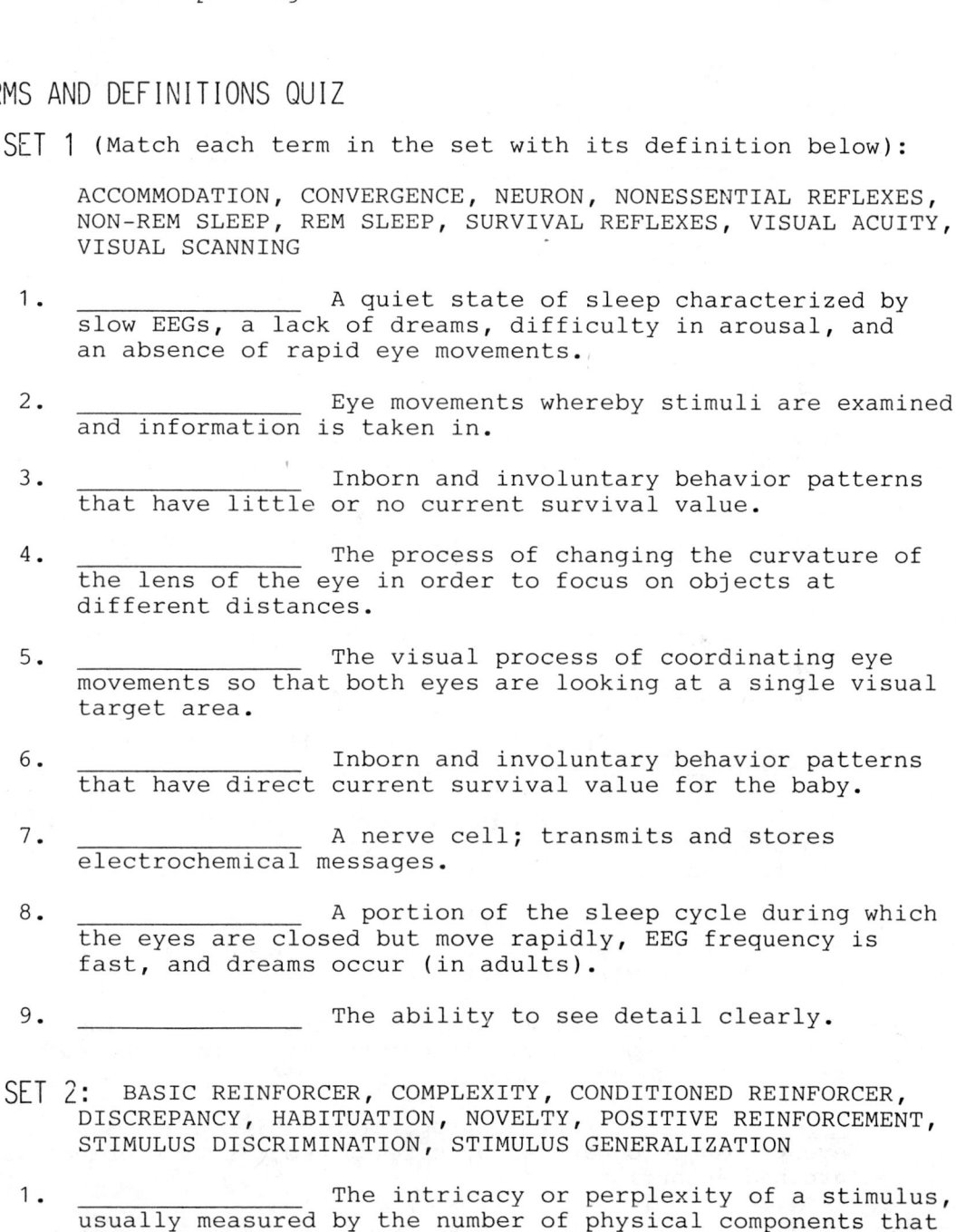

SET 1 (Match each term in the set with its definition below):

ACCOMMODATION, CONVERGENCE, NEURON, NONESSENTIAL REFLEXES, NON-REM SLEEP, REM SLEEP, SURVIVAL REFLEXES, VISUAL ACUITY, VISUAL SCANNING

1. _____ A quiet state of sleep characterized by slow EEGs, a lack of dreams, difficulty in arousal, and an absence of rapid eye movements.

2. _____ Eye movements whereby stimuli are examined and information is taken in.

3. _____ Inborn and involuntary behavior patterns that have little or no current survival value.

4. _____ The process of changing the curvature of the lens of the eye in order to focus on objects at different distances.

5. _____ The visual process of coordinating eye movements so that both eyes are looking at a single visual target area.

6. _____ Inborn and involuntary behavior patterns that have direct current survival value for the baby.

7. _____ A nerve cell; transmits and stores electrochemical messages.

8. _____ A portion of the sleep cycle during which the eyes are closed but move rapidly, EEG frequency is fast, and dreams occur (in adults).

9. _____ The ability to see detail clearly.

SET 2: BASIC REINFORCER, COMPLEXITY, CONDITIONED REINFORCER, DISCREPANCY, HABITUATION, NOVELTY, POSITIVE REINFORCEMENT, STIMULUS DISCRIMINATION, STIMULUS GENERALIZATION

1. _____ The intricacy or perplexity of a stimulus, usually measured by the number of physical components that make up a stimulus pattern.

2. _____ The stimulus attribute of being different from or inconsistent with one's expectations.

3. _____ The tendency to respond in the same way to different stimuli; the greater the similarity of the stimuli, the greater the tendency to respond the same to them.

4. _____ Stimulus that satisfies basic physiological needs, such as hunger and thirst, and strengthens or maintains a response tendency.

5. _____ Distinguishing between stimuli and responding differently to them.

6. _____ The process in which attention decreases to a stimulus that has been presented frequently or over a long period of time.

7. _____ The stimulus quality of not having been experienced before.

8. _____ Any stimulus that has acquired the ability to strengthen or maintain a behavior through association with an established reinforcer.

9. _____ The process by which the tendency to repeat a behavior is increased by a consequence that involves adding a pleasant stimulus to the situation.

SET 3: ATTRIBUTE, DIMENSION, EXTINCTION, NEGATIVE REINFORCEMENT, PRIMARY CIRCULAR REACTIONS, RECALL MEMORY, RECOGNITION MEMORY, SECONDARY CIRCULAR REACTIONS, SENSORIMOTOR STAGE

1. _____ Remembering simply that an object, event, or image has been experienced before.

2. _____ In Piaget's theory, the substage of the sensorimotor stage in which the baby repeats actions that are focused on or around the body.

3. _____ In Piaget's theory, the substage of the sensorimotor stage in which the baby repeats actions that are focused toward the external world.

4. _____ Remembering something by retrieving information from memory without the item being currently present in the environment.

5. _____ A broad property by which objects and events can be organized or categorized, as when objects are grouped according to size.

6. _____ Level or value of a stimulus within a dimension: red and green are values within the dimension of color.

7. _____ Piaget's first stage of cognitive growth,

Chapter 4   61

lasting from birth to 2 years, during which the infant learns to coordinate sensory experience with motor activity.

8. _____ The process whereby a behavioral tendency is weakened or eliminated by withholding the stimuli (e.g., reinforcer or US) that maintained it.

9. _____ Reduction or removal of aversive stimulation contingent on performance of an appropriate response.

SET 4: BABBLING, BODY LANGUAGE, COOING, INTONATION, MOTHERESE, OBJECT PERMANENCE, ONE-WORD SENTENCES, SUDDEN INFANT DEATH SYNDROME (SIDS), TERTIARY CIRCULAR REACTIONS

1. _____ A single word intended to communicate a complete thought; commonly used by older infants and young children.

2. _____ Bodily gestures and facial expressions that convey meaning.

3. _____ The sudden and unexplained death of seemingly healthy babies; also called CRIB DEATH.

4. _____ The vocalization of vowel-like sounds, characteristic of very young infants.

5. _____ The vocalization of consonant-vowel combinations, such as "gaga" or "baba," shown by normal babies between 3 and 6 months of age.

6. _____ In Piaget's theory, the substage of the sensorimotor stage in which infants try to discover how and why things happen.

7. _____ Variation in the pitch of language sounds that conveys meaning.

8. _____ Piaget's term for the concept that objects and events have a separate existence from the mind of the perceiver and, therefore, exist outside of one's immediate sensory range.

9. _____ Baby talk; a simple form of language used by adults when speaking with infants.

MATCHING QUIZ

1. ___ REM
2. ___ discrepancy
3. ___ stimulus generalization
4. ___ colostrum
5. ___ apnea
6. ___ accommodation
7. ___ myelin
8. ___ tertiary circular reactions
9. ___ intonation
10. ___ object permanence

a. affects habituation
b. milklike fluid
c. ability to focus
d. may be related to neural growth
e. crucial to the use of symbols
f. may be a cause of SIDS
g. useful aspect of vocalization
h. increases the speed of nerve impulses
i. miniature "experiments"
j. CR "spreads" to other CSs

SELF TEST

1. Which of the following can be a disadvantage of breast-feeding?
   a. The mother's mobility and freedom may be reduced.
   b. The mother's milk can become contaminated by drugs or other substances that may harm the baby.
   c. The mother's milk contains fewer antibodies to protect the baby from illness than formulas do.
   d. both a and b

2. Temperature regulation in neonates is
   a. almost as consistent and stable as in adults.
   b. easily accomplished because they have high blood pressure.
   c. difficult partly because the physiological systems that regulate body temperature do not function well.
   d. difficult because they gain heat too easily.

3. Reflexes that have clear utility for feeding, maintaining physiological functioning, and protecting the baby against injury include the Babinski and Moro reflexes.
   a. True
   b. False

4. The ability to focus the lens of the eye is called
   a. accommodation.

b. convergence.
   c. habituation.
   d. scanning.

5. Which of the following brain tissues is(are) thought to service and maintain neurons?
   a. myelin
   b. glial cells
   c. axons
   d. dendrites

6. At birth, which two areas of the brain are the LEAST maturationally advanced?
   a. motor and sensory
   b. visual and auditory
   c. auditory and motor
   d. sensory and visual

7. The average baby can roll over at about 3 months, sit without support at _____ months, and stand alone well by _____ months.
   a. $3\frac{1}{2}$; 5
   b. $4\frac{1}{2}$; 9
   c. $5\frac{1}{2}$; 12
   d. $7\frac{1}{2}$; 9

8. Locomotion from a sitting position by pushing with the arms and legs is called hitching or scooting.
   a. True
   b. False

9. Films of body movements showed that neonates moved in synchrony with tape-recorded adult speech just as readily for Chinese speech as for English.
   a. True
   b. False

10. Which statement about infant perception is TRUE?
    a. Visual acuity is about 20/800 at 1 month of age.
    b. Babies cannot distinguish between spoken sounds until they are 6 months old.
    c. Babies do not listen to speech sounds until they begin to babble.
    d. Both b and c are true.

11. Research using the "visual cliff" apparatus found that
    a. infants do not perceive depth until 1 month of age.
    b. babies increased their heart rates when placed on the "deep side."
    c. very few 6- to 14-month-olds crept onto the "deep side" even when their mother coaxed them.
    d. by 11 months of age babies understand that the "deep side" is not dangerous and readily cross it.

12. Aronson and Rosenbloom (1971) found that the typical young baby was at first curious, and then delighted, when the

research apparatus displaced the mother's voice 3 feet from her mouth.
   a. True
   b. False

13. When looking at a person's face, newborns look mostly at the
    a. eyes.
    b. mouth.
    c. nose.
    d. periphery.

14. The process by which our attention declines with continued exposure to the same stimulus is called
    a. discrepancy.
    b. stimulus generalization.
    c. stimulus discrimination.
    d. habituation.

15. Learning is a(n)
    a. relatively permanent change in behavior.
    b. product of experience.
    c. inferred process based on performance.
    d. all of the above.

16. Watson and Rayner's (1920) study with "Little Albert" demonstrated that a child can learn a fear reaction by classical conditioning.
    a. True
    b. False

17. There is some evidence to suggest that the earliest time that classical conditioning can occur is
    a. in the embryonic stage of prenatal development.
    b. during the last couple of months before birth.
    c. after 1 month of age.
    d. after 3 months of age.

18. An example of a conditioned reinforcer is
    a. food.
    b. water.
    c. money.
    d. all of the above.

19. Spanking a child to stop his/her misbehavior is an example of negative reinforcement of that behavior.
    a. True
    b. False

20. Newborns have the capacity to imitate certain
    a. hand movements.
    b. finger movements.
    c. leg movements.
    d. facial gestures.

21. Memory that involves retrieving or bringing up information

in the absence of relevant stimuli is called
a. convergence.
b. habituation.
c. recognition.
d. recall.

22. When given the task of classifying objects, such as blue blocks and red blocks, most 6-month-olds do not show an awareness of the categories.
a. True
b. False

23. In Piaget's theory, infant behavior that is focused on or around the body and is repeated over and over is called a
a. reflex activity.
b. primary circular reaction.
c. secondary circular reaction.
d. tertiary circular reaction.

24. According to Piaget, infants at Substage 4 (Coordinating Secondary Circular Reactions) begin to combine previously acquired behaviors to achieve a desired or intended goal.
a. True
b. False

25. Piaget reported that when 8- to 12-month-old (Substage 4) infants see something hidden in one place and find it there, and then see it moved to another hiding place, they tend to look for the object in the original hiding place by mistake. More recent studies have disconfirmed this finding and Piaget's interpretation.
a. True
b. False

26. Infants show three principal patterns of crying: the anger, _____, and _____ cries.
a. survival; nonessential
b. generalization; discrimination
c. pain; rhythmical
d. secondary; tertiary

27. Infant preverbal sounds include cooing by 2 months of age, _____ by 6 months, and _____ by 12 months.
a. motherese; one-word sentences
b. one-word sentences; motherese
c. intonation; babbling
d. babbling; intonation

28. Evidence for the influence of biological factors in the onset of preverbal vocal behavior includes the finding that
a. at birth language areas of the brain function differently to speech sounds than to nonspeech sounds.
b. preverbal milestones are achieved at about the same age by infants around the world.
c. deaf babies begin to babble at about the same age as

        babies with normal hearing.
    d. all of the above.

29. As a group, SIDS victims tend to
    a. be between 2 and 4 months of age.
    b. have faster growth rates than non-SIDS babies.
    c. suffer from biochemical imbalances, especially the lack of adrenalin.
    d. suffer from overventilation of the lungs.

30. Recommended toys for infants include crib devices and mirrors between 2 and 6 months of age, balls and stuffed toys between 6 and 12, and battery operated toys and picture books after 12 months.
    a. True
    b. False

IMPORTANT DETAILS TO KNOW

1. The distance for optimal visual clarity is _____ inches for most newborns. (p. 113)

2. What factors determine a young infant's immunity to disease? (p. 115)

3. What percentage of the adult's brain weight does the child's brain reach at 6 and 24 months of age? See Table 4.1. (p. 115)

4. When can infants roll over in their cribs, walk well without support, and walk up stairs? See Figure 4.4. (pp. 117-118)

5. How are crawling, creeping, hitching, and scooting different from each other? (p. 117)

6. What effect does swaddling have on infant development? (p. 119)

7. How much do infants sleep and nap at 6 and 18 months of age? (p. 120)

8. What percentage of total sleep is devoted to REM in neonates and older infants? (p. 120)

9. At what age is the infant's visual acuity 20/800 and 20/100? (p. 122)

10. According to Piaget, how do infants perform on a standard object permanence task at 10 and 15 months of age? (pp. 137-138)

11. At what age does infant babbling show intonation? (p. 141)

12. What toys do babies usually like to play with between 2-6 and 6-12 months of age? (pp. 145-146)

TEST YOUR RECALL

1. List the unique bodily functions that characterize newborns. (pp. 110-111)
2. Cite the pros and cons of breast and bottle feeding. (p. 111)
3. Describe the newborn's sucking reflex. (p. 112)
4. Which reflexes are important to the newborn's survival? (p. 112)
5. Name five nonessential reflexes of the newborn. (p. 112)
6. Describe the newborn's hearing capabilities. (p. 113)
7. How well can a newborn see? (p. 113)
8. What functions does the Brazelton Neonatal Behavioral Assessment Scale measure? (p. 114)
9. Outline the changes in body growth that occur in infancy. (p. 115)
10. Describe the growth of the infant's brain. (pp. 115-116)
11. List sequentially the gross motor accomplishments of infancy. (pp. 117-119)
12. Give an example of how gross motor development can be accelerated by experience. (p. 119)
13. How does the baby's sleep change throughout infancy? (p. 120)
14. Describe how hearing is important in infant development. (pp. 121-122)
15. Explain how researchers have studied depth perception in infants. Cite their findings. (pp. 122-123)
16. What types of visual preferences have researchers found in babies? Were there any developmental trends? (p. 124)
17. Describe the role of novelty, discrepancy, and complexity in infant perception. (p. 125)
18. Write a brief proposal for showing how classical conditioning could produce learning in infants. (p. 127)

19. Contrast the processes of positive and negative reinforcement. (pp. 129-130)

20. Specify the abilities and limitations of infant memory. (p. 132)

21. Describe the method and results of the study by D. Starkey (1981) on infant mental organization. (p. 133)

22. Outline the major achievement that occurs in each of Piaget's substages of sensorimotor development. (pp. 135-136)

23. Cite three criticisms of Piaget's views on sensorimotor development. (p. 137)

24. Describe the procedure and findings of the Bjork and Cummings (1984) study on object permanence. (p. 139)

25. What "messages" do babies communicate with their different types of crys? (p. 141)

26. Outline the sequence of preverbal vocalizations made by infants. (p. 141)

27. What factors influence the development of infant vocalizations? (p. 142)

28. What factors contribute to an adult's comprehension of an infant's one-word sentences? (p. 142)

29. How are the victims of SIDS different from nonvictims? (p. 144)

ANSWER SECTION

GUIDED REVIEW:

1. temperature; subcortical; antibodies
2. survival; rooting; sucking; pupillary; Babinski; knee jerk
3. volume; voices
4. accommodate; convergence
5. Brazelton; predict
6. 50; 6; 9
7. glial; myelin
8. sensory; auditory
9. voluntary
10. crawls; creep
11. 13; REM; 30
12. synchronize
13. acuity; scan; slower
14. face; color
15. habituation; complexity

Chapter 4   69

16. learning; performance (behavior)
17. emotional; loud noise; generalization; discrimination
18. operant conditioning; reinforcers; basic (primary); conditioned (secondary)
19. extinction; negative reinforcement
20. facial; 6; recall
21. categories (classes); joy
22. sensorimotor; six; reflex; representations
23. object permanence
24. anger; cooing; babbling
25. sentences; intonation
26. 2; 4; minority; apnea

TERMS AND DEFINITIONS QUIZ

SET 1:
1. non-REM sleep
2. visual scanning
3. nonessential reflexes
4. accommodation
5. convergence
6. survival reflexes
7. neuron
8. REM sleep
9. visual acuity

SET 2:
1. complexity
2. discrepancy
3. stimulus generalization
4. basic (primary) reinforcer
5. stimulus discrimination
6. habituation
7. novelty
8. conditioned (secondary) reinforcer
9. positive reinforcement

SET 3:
1. recognition memory
2. primary circular reactions
3. secondary circular reactions
4. recall memory
5. dimension
6. attribute
7. sensorimotor stage
8. extinction
9. negative reinforcement

SET 4:
1. one-word sentence
2. body language
3. sudden infant death syndrome (SIDS)
4. cooing
5. babbling
6. tertiary circular reactions
7. intonation
8. object permanence
9. motherese

Chapter 4

MATCHING QUIZ:

1. d (p. 120)   6. c (p. 113)
2. a (p. 125)   7. h (p. 116)
3. j (p. 128)   8. i (p. 136)
4. b (p. 110)   9. g (p. 141)
5. f (p. 144)   10. e (p. 138)

SELF TEST

1. d (p. 111)   16. a (p. 127)
2. c (p. 110)   17. b (p. 128)
3. b (p. 112)   18. c (p. 129)
4. a (p. 113)   19. b (p. 130)
5. b (p. 116)   20. d (p. 131)
6. b (p. 116)   21. d (p. 132)
7. c (p. 118)   22. a (p. 133)
8. a (p. 117)   23. b (p. 136)
9. a (pp. 121-122)   24. a (p. 136)
10. a (p. 122)   25. a (p. 139)
11. c (p. 123)   26. c (p. 141)
12. b (p. 124)   27. d (p. 141)
13. d (p. 124)   28. d (p. 142)
14. d (p. 125)   29. a (p. 144)
15. d (p. 127)   30. a (pp. 145-146)

CHAPTER 5

Infant Social, Emotional, and Personality Development

SUMMARY IN OUTLINE

<u>ATTACHMENT: THE INFANT/PARENT BOND</u> (p. 152)

    THE DEVELOPMENT OF ATTACHMENT--4 stages
        1st stage: reacts similarly toward all adults
        2nd stage: directs signals and attention to a few recognized adults (age 2-6 months)
        3rd stage: more expressive and assertive in social relationships after age 6 months
        4th stage: "partnership" forms by age 3 years

    HOW DOES THE BABY BECOME ATTACHED?
        Lorenz, imprinting, sensitive period
        Sensitive period between $1\frac{1}{2}$ to 24 months of age in humans.
        Harlow's studies on "mother love" and social deprivation in monkeys
        Infant attachment is influenced by cognitive development.

    ATTACHMENT IN OTHER CULTURES
        Soviet Union, Japan, and the Israeli kibbutz

    THE QUALITY OF ATTACHMENT
        Securely attached infants
        Anxiously attached infants--anxious-avoidant and anxious-resistant

    PARENTING AND ATTACHMENT QUALITY
        Most babies from middle-class homes are securely attached.
        The quality of a bond is influenced by the mother's life circumstances and personality.

THE CHANGING ROLE OF THE FATHER
Fathers spend less than half as much time with their infants as mothers do.
Father/infant interactions are more likely to involve play, rather than caretaking activities.

RECIPROCAL ROLES OF INFANT AND PARENT
"Turn-taking"
The baby's personality and temperaments influence attachment.

SEPARATION DISTRESS
The presence of familiar people and objects reduce distress.
Securely attached infants cope better with separation than do anxiously attached infants.
Bowlby's stages of distress in long-term separation--protest, despair, and detachment.

THE BABY'S RELATIONS WITH OTHER PEOPLE (p. 165)

REACTION TO STRANGERS
Less than a majority of infants experience "fear of strangers."
Factors influencing fear of strangers include social experience, presence of parent, familiarity of the environment

INFANTS PLAYING SOCIALLY TOGETHER
Infants usually have limited opportunities to interact.
In the first year infants gaze, gesture, and touch one another; interactions are brief, two-unit sequences (one turn per baby)
In the second year, turn-taking, communication, and social behaviors become more complex.

INFANT EMOTIONS (p. 168)

Emotional expressions of newborns are disgust, distress, startle, interest, and neonatal smile.
Biological and experiential factors influence the development of emotional expressions.

POSITIVE EMOTIONS: PUTTING ON A HAPPY FACE
Social smiles appear at age 3-4 weeks; laughing, at 4 months.
Events that evoke laughter shift from tactile to visual stimulation with development.

NEGATIVE EMOTIONS: EXPRESSING DISCOMFORT
Sadness, anger, and fear develop later than disgust and distress.

MIXING AND JUDGING EMOTIONS
Mixed emotional expressions begin to emerge around age 6 months.

Chapter 5   73

    Infants at age 3 months can judge some emotional expressions of adults.

PERSONALITY DEVELOPMENT   (p. 173)

THE BEGINNING OF A SELF CONCEPT
Infants at 6 months don't differentiate between mirror images of themselves and others.
Recognition of one's own physical features occurs at about age 15 months.

BUILDING TRUST AND AUTONOMY
Infant competence is linked with developing a sense of "basic trust."

DEVELOPING SELF-CONTROL
Self-control makes important but limited progress during infancy.

INDIVIDUAL DIFFERENCES IN TEMPERAMENTS
Five temperamental characteristics that identify "easy" and "difficult" babies are adaptability, approach-withdrawal, intensity of reaction, quality of mood, and rhythmicity--see Table 5.5.
Children with different temperaments should be handled differently by caretakers.

ISSUES IN ACTION   (p. 178)

REDUCING PARENT/INFANT CONFLICT IN TOILET TRAINING
Maturational readiness occurs between 1 and 2 years of age.
Parental warmth and rewards aid toilet training.

INFANT DAY CARE
Infants in day care prefer their mothers to other caregivers.
High quality day care appears to have no negative effect on attachment if it begins in the second year or starts in the first year on a part-time basis.

GUIDED REVIEW

1. An affectional interpersonal bond that ties people together is called _____. In forming attachments infants at first do not _____ between adults; they react similarly to all adults.

2. Lorenz (1952) discovered that goslings would follow him about right after hatching. He called this process _____. Imprinting forms easiest during time intervals called _____.

3. Harlow's work with mother-deprived monkeys showed that

_____ covered surrogate mothers had a calming effect thus illustrating the importance of contact _____ in attachment.

4. Some babies become "anxiously" attached, and others become _____ attached. Ainsworth believes that there are two types of anxious attachment: rejecting and angry mothers produce an anxious-avoidant bond; inept or insensitive mothers produce an anxious-_____ bond.

5. About 60 to 70% of infants from middle-class homes develop a _____ attachment. The quality of attachment seems to depend on the mother's life _____ and the way she cares for her baby. For instance, Egeland and Farber (1984) found that mothers whose attitudes about motherhood changed from being negative--and became positive--had babies whose attachment quality changed from _____ to _____.

6. Fathers generally spend less than _____ as much time with their infants than mothers do, usually spending time _____ with their babies. Infants develop attachments to both parents; the bond to the _____ is usually more dominant--a preference babies show when _____.

7. Parent/child attachments form via mutual or _____ interaction. The baby's particular personality dispositions, or _____, can affect the kinds of interactions they experience. Likewise the quality and intensity of parental responsiveness can affect attachment.

8. When removed from their attachment figures, babies may endure separation _____. The intensity of their distress is related to the length of separation and _____ of the environment. When separation is protracted, children pass through a sequence of reactions starting with _____, then despair, and finally, _____.

9. Between 5 and 12 months, many babies show a distinct _____ of strangers. This fear reaction appears (greater/lesser) when the mother is absent, when the environment is unfamiliar, or when the baby has only one _____.

10. Very young infants show interest in other babies by _____ at and touching one another. True social intent and interaction among infants begins at about _____ months when they gesture and smile at each other. After 12 months of age, _____ become increasingly important in promoting social contact between infants.

11. Orphaned infants in institutions with unstimulating

environments suffer retardation in _____ development and show symptoms of psychological disorder. Today institutional settings are more stimulating and homelike. Yet, infants who spend more than a few months in these institutions often show poor _____ with other children and teachers in childhood. The effects on the child depend on the richness of the experience in the institution, the time spent there, and the _____ at entry.

12. Neonates display five emotional expressions: disgust, _____, startle, interest, and the neonatal _____. Anger emerges a few months later, followed by _____ after about 6 months of age. Other emotions, such as shame and guilt, emerge in the _____ and _____ years.

13. Young infants react negatively when their mothers display an unhappy expression. By 1 year of age infants look to the facial expressions of others to determine whether a situation is _____.

14. The knowledge each of us has of our unique personal identity is called the _____. Although infants show some degree of self awareness at 6 months of age, they do not recognize their own facial features and distinguish themselves from others until after _____ months.

15. The infant's primary concern is with acquiring a sense of basic trust according to _____. An important part of this trust is a sense of _____.

16. Some babies have temperaments that can be classified as "easy" or "difficult." Thomas et al. (1970) found in a follow-up of "difficult" infants that eventually 70% needed _____ attention, as compared to 18% of the "easy" infants.

17. Maturational _____ for toilet training generally occurs between 1 and 2 years of age. Parents can reduce toileting problems by waiting until the second year to start training, showing warmth and concern, and giving the child _____ for successful toileting.

18. High-quality day care seems to have no negative effect on attachment if it begins in the _____ year, or starts earlier on a _____ basis.

TERMS AND DEFINITIONS QUIZ

SET 1: (Match each term in the set with its definition below):

ANXIOUSLY ATTACHED, ATTACHMENT, DEPENDENCY, IMPRINTING, KIBBUTZ, RECIPROCAL ROLES, SECURELY ATTACHED, SENSITIVE PERIOD, SEPARATION DISTRESS, SPECIES-SPECIFIC BEHAVIOR, TURN-TAKING

1. _____ Mutual social contributions made by the parent and child to their relationship.

2. _____ A time interval during which development is maximally responsive or vulnerable to environmental influences.

3. _____ A qualitative type of parent/child bond; after a brief separation, the child either avoids the parent or approaches but resists contact or interaction with the parent.

4. _____ Distinctive activities of each species that were inherited through biological evolution.

5. _____ Each party to a social interaction making contributions and expecting reactions in alternation.

6. _____ Emotional upset sometimes shown by infants and children when separated from a person (typically a parent) with whom they have formed an attachment bond.

7. _____ An Israeli collective farming community where children are often reared in communal nurseries.

8. _____ An affectional bond which disposes parent and child to interact with each other in mutually supportive ways.

9. _____ Reliance upon other people for aid and affection.

10. _____ A qualitative type of parent/child bond; the child shows moderate distress at the parent's absence and happily greets and stays near the parent upon return.

11. _____ The process by which young animals rapidly form a following response to a moving object during a sensitive period after birth; an attachment process.

SET 2: ADAPTABILITY, APPROACH-WITHDRAWAL, BASIC TRUST, DESPAIR REACTION, DETACHMENT REACTION, FEAR OF STRANGERS, INTENSITY OF REACTION, PROTEST REACTION, QUALITY OF MOOD, RHYTHMICITY, SELF-CONCEPT

1. _____ Emotional upset shown by many 5- to 12-

Chapter 5

month-old infants to unfamiliar adults.

2. _____ A temperamental characteristic; amount of pleasant versus negative emotional expression.

3. _____ A temperamental characteristic; regularity of hunger, sleep, wakefulness, and elimination of wastes.

4. _____ The organized internal or personal idea we have about our own characteristics; it includes the self-image and self-esteem.

5. _____ In Erikson's theory, the positive ego quality of the crisis in the first stage of personality development; it involves the infant's trust in other people and in oneself.

6. _____ A temperamental characteristic; ease with which a child adapts to changes in the environment.

7. _____ Initial reaction to long-term separation; child cries, calls, and searches often for parents; may last for 1 or more days.

8. _____ A temperamental characteristic; ease in approaching new objects or people.

9. _____ Following the protest reaction to long-term separation from parents, the child becomes quiet and withdrawn.

10. _____ Following the despair reaction to long-term separation from parents, the child seems on the surface to be back to normal; if reunited with parents, the child seems to reject them.

11. _____ A temperamental characteristic; energy of response, regardless of quality or direction.

MATCHING QUIZ

1. ___ attachment   a. turn-taking
2. ___ separation distress   b. Konrad Lorenz
3. ___ reciprocal roles   c. mirror-image research
4. ___ emotions   d. Mary Ainsworth
5. ___ imprinting   e. possible effect of hospitalization
6. ___ self-concept   f. Carroll Izard

7. ___ temperament   g. slow-to-warm-up

8. ___ "surrogate" mothers   h. Harry Harlow

SELF TEST

1. The development of attachment begins with the baby reacting similarly to all adults, and by the third stage the
   a. infant shows increased initiative and expressiveness.
   b. basic bond of affection toward specific persons may be established.
   c. attachment relationship becomes a "partnership."
   d. both a and b.

2. Which of the following statements about imprinting is FALSE?
   a. Imprinting occurs in a wide variety of animals.
   b. Once imprinting has occurred, the following response is quite persistent.
   c. The goslings imprinted to Lorenz would leave him to spend the night at their usual riverbank habitat.
   d. Imprinting can occur to any active or salient object-- even a flashing light.

3. When Harlow initially separated young monkeys from their mothers, removing them was difficult, development became abnormal, and some of the young died.
   a. True
   b. False

4. In Harlow's classic research using wire and cloth covered "mothers," the young monkeys
   a. became attached to whichever "mother" provided food.
   b. sought out and clung to the wire mother when stressed.
   c. spend more and more time with the wire mother as they got older.
   d. had great difficulty establishing peer relationships.

5. According to Ainsworth (1979), mothers who are inept or insensitive tend to have babies who develop an _____ attachment.
   a. approach-withdrawal
   b. imprinted
   c. anxious-resistent
   d. independent

6. About 60 to 70% of infants from middle-class homes develop a(n) _____ attachment to their mother by 12 months of age.
   a. anxious-resistant
   b. anxious-avoidant
   c. secure
   d. dependent

7. Once an attachment has formed, the quality of the bond is

Chapter 5   79

not affected by the mother's life circumstances or attitudes about the baby.
a. True
b. False

8. According to ethologists, some features of babies' faces evoke an inborn reaction, or _____ behavior, to provide attention and care.
   a. reciprocal
   b. turn-taking
   c. dependency
   d. species-specific

9. Belsky, Gilstrap, and Rovine's (1984) longitudinal study of parent-child interaction found that mothers and fathers _____ as their baby got older.
   a. decreased caregiving
   b. decreased affection
   c. showed no change in reading or TV watching while with the baby
   d. all of the above

10. Difficult babies are more likely to cry when their diapers are wet than easy babies are.
    a. True
    b. False

11. Separation distress reaches its peak at 15 months of age, and is likely to be pronounced if the baby
    a. is in a familiar setting.
    b. is in an unfamiliar setting.
    c. has had day care experience.
    d. is securely (rather than anxiously) attached.

12. According to Bowlby, when long-term separation distress has run its course, the child's reaction is one of detachment from the mother.
    a. True
    b. False

13. Yarrow et al. (1971) found that adopted children who had the greatest social deficits were those who had been placed from the institution with a foster mother and then separated, after less than 6 months, to be adopted.
    a. True
    b. False

14. The fear of strangers shows great variation in the
    a. age of onset.
    b. age when it reaches maximum strength.
    c. occasions when a particular child may show it.
    d. all of the above.

15. During the second year, interactions between infants
    a. are not yet affected by toys.
    b. are mostly brief, with little or no turn-taking.

c. become increasingly complex, involving longer sequences of turn-taking.
d. consist mostly of offering and taking toys.

16. According to Izard (1978), newborns display five emotional expressions, including
    a. anger.
    b. wariness.
    c. the pleasure smile.
    d. none of the above.

17. Which of the following emotions is not displayed by infants in the first year?
    a. surprise
    b. the social smile
    c. shame
    d. all of the above

18. The role of biological factors in emotional development is supported by the facts that (a) babies show several emotions right from birth, (b) people around the world express many emotions in similar ways, and (c) blind babies start to show brief social smiles at about the same age as sighted babies do.
    a. True
    b. False

19. Malatesta and Haviland (1982) studied the facial expressions of infants and their mothers and found that babies apparently learn to control the expression of emotion through the frequent exchange of facial expressions with the parents.
    a. True
    b. False

20. Infants begin to show brief social smiles at 2 months of age, but don't begin to laugh until 7 months.
    a. True
    b. False

21. Research on infant emotions has found that
    a. 3-month-olds seem not to notice when their mothers look unhappy.
    b. babies cannot discriminate smiles and frowns of adults until 6 months of age.
    c. 6-month-olds can mix two emotions simultaneously in their facial expressions.
    d. both a and b are correct.

22. Researchers using the visual cliff apparatus to study the ability of 12-month-olds to assess the emotional expressions of their mothers found that the babies
    a. did not look at their mother because they were so frightened by the deep side.
    b. recognized the mother's anger expression, but not her surprise expression.

c. crossed the "deep side" to comfort their mother if she looked worried.
d. used their mother's expression to determine whether the situation was dangerous.

23. Prior to about _____ months of age, infants do not use mirror reflections correctly and respond to videotaped images of themselves and of other babies in the same way.
    a. 9
    b. 12
    c. 15
    d. 18

24. Wenar (1976) studied infant competence longitudinally, beginning at 12 months of age, and found that
    a. competent infants typically became less competent over time.
    b. infants who were restricted at home in playpens showed large gains in competence over time.
    c. some low-competence infants improved over time, but others did not.
    d. virtually all low-competence infants improved greatly.

25. The ability to govern one's own actions is called
    a. basic trust.
    b. detachment.
    c. self-control.
    d. adaptability.

26. In Thomas, Chess, and Birch's (1970) research on temperaments, they found that about _____ % of the children they studied could be classified as "easy."
    a. 10
    b. 18
    c. 40
    d. 60

27. The temperamental characteristics that are especially useful for classifying a child as "easy" or "difficult" are: adaptability, approach-withdrawal, intensity of reaction, quality of mood, and rhythmicity.
    a. True
    b. False

28. The temperamental characteristic termed _____ refers to the ease with which a child adjusts to changes in his/her environment.
    a. approach-withdrawal
    b. adaptability
    c. rhythmicity
    d. quality of mood

29. The temperamental characteristic termed _____ refers to the amount of pleasant versus unpleasant behavior the child generally shows.
    a. adaptability

b. approach-withdrawal
c. intensity of reaction
d. quality of mood

30. Some evidence suggests that children in day care may appear to be somewhat less securely attached to the mother than home-reared children if attendance at day care began in the
   a. second year.
   b. first year on a part-time basis.
   c. first year on a full-time basis.
   d. all of the above.

IMPORTANT DETAILS TO KNOW

1. When does the sensitive period for attachment seem to occur in humans? (p. 153)

2. What types of stimuli elicit laughter in young and older infants? (p. 171)

3. What proportion of babies may be classified as "difficult," "easy," and "slow-to-warm-up?" (p. 176)

4. If you wanted to spend the least amount of time toilet training an infant, when would be the best age to start? (p. 178)

TEST YOUR RECALL

1. Trace the four stages of infant attachment. (p. 152)

2. Explain the process of imprinting and the importance of the sensitive period. (p. 153)

3. Describe the findings of Harlow's work on maternal deprivation in monkeys. (p. 154)

4. How is the attachment process different for kibbutzniks in contrast with American children? (p. 155)

5. Contrast the likely outcomes for securely and anxiously attached infants during their early childhood years. (p. 156)

6. What did Egeland and Farber (1984) find concerning the quality of attachment and changes in mothers' life circumstances. (p. 157)

7. Speculate on how the features of infant faces might affect the quality of parental care and affection. See Highlight 5.1. (p. 159)

8. What have recent studies found concerning the role of the father in the attachment process? (pp. 159-160)

9. Describe what is meant by "reciprocal roles of infant and parent." (pp. 161-162)

10. Give an example of how temperament could affect the quality of bonding. (p. 162)

11. Discuss factors that have been shown to affect separation distress. (pp. 162-163)

12. Describe Bowlby's (1960) portrayal of infant reactions to long-term separation. (pp. 163-164)

13. What have studies on orphaned infants living in institutions revealed? See Highlight 5.2. (p. 164)

14. Summarize the factors that influence the infant's "fear of strangers." (p. 166)

15. Characterize the development of infant social interactions during play. (p. 167)

16. List the five emotional expressions Izard has observed in newborns. (p. 168)

17. How do emotional expressions change with development? (pp. 168-172)

18. Discuss the evidence supporting the view that emotional expressions are influenced by biological factors. (p. 169)

19. Outline the developmental sequence of infant smiling at facelike stimuli. (p. 170)

20. How do infant emotional expressions to pain change with development? (p. 171)

21. Describe the development of infant self-awareness. (p. 174)

22. What factors aid infants in forming a basic sense of trust? (p. 175)

23. What improvements do babies exhibit toward self-control during infancy? (pp. 175-176)

24. Discuss the research findings of Thomas, Chess, and Birch (1970) on temperaments. (p. 176)

25. Suggest several factors parents should keep in mind in order to reduce conflict during toilet training. (pp. 178-179)

26. What advice and cautions would you offer parents who were

thinking of placing infants in day care? (pp. 179-180)

ANSWER SECTION

GUIDED REVIEW:

1. attachment; discriminate
2. imprinting; sensitive periods
3. cloth; comfort
4. "securely"; resistent
5. secure; circumstances; anxious; secure
6. half; playing; mother; distressed (upset)
7. reciprocal; temperaments
8. distress; familiarity; protest; detachment
9. fear; greater; caretaker (parent)
10. gazing (looking); 6; toys
11. language, relationships; age
12. distress; smile; fear; second; third
13. dangerous
14. self concept; 15
15. Erikson; competence (self trust)
16. psychiatric
17. readiness; rewards
18. second; part-time

TERMS AND DEFINITIONS QUIZ:

SET 1:
1. reciprocal roles
2. sensitive period
3. anxiously attached
4. species-specific behavior
5. turn-taking
6. separation distress
7. kibbutz
8. attachment
9. dependency
10. securely attached
11. imprinting

SET 2:
1. fear of strangers
2. quality of mood
3. rhythmicity
4. self-concept
5. basic trust
6. adaptability
7. protest
8. approach-withdrawal
9. despair
10. detachment
11. intensity of reaction

MATCHING QUIZ:

1. d (p. 152)
2. e (p. 163)
3. a (p. 161)
4. f (p. 168)
5. b (p. 153)
6. c (p. 174)
7. g (p. 176)
8. h (p. 154)

SELF TEST

1. d (p. 152)
2. c (p. 153)
3. a (p. 154)
4. d (p. 154)
5. c (p. 156)
6. c (p. 157)
7. b (p. 157)
8. d (p. 159)
9. d (p. 161)
10. a (p. 162)
11. b (p. 162)
12. a (p. 164)
13. b (p. 164)
14. d (p. 166)
15. c (p. 167)
16. d (p. 168)
17. c (p. 168)
18. a (p. 169)
19. a (p. 170)
20. b (pp. 170-171)
21. c (p. 171)
22. d (p. 172)
23. a (p. 174)
24. c (p. 175)
25. c (p. 176)
26. c (p. 176)
27. a (p. 176)
28. b (p. 177)
29. d (p. 177)
30. c (p. 179)

CHAPTER 6

Physical and Motor Development in Childhood

SUMMARY IN OUTLINE

PHYSICAL DEVELOPMENT (p. 188)

General characteristics of growth include asynchronous growth, cephalocaudal and proximodistal patterns, differentiation, integration, and hierarchical integration.

BODY GROWTH: CHANGING SIZE AND SHAPE
   The rapid growth of infancy slows down in childhood.
   Changes in body proportions
   Cross-cultural differences in growth

INNER ORGANS: GROWTH YOU CAN'T SEE--different organ systems have distinctive growth curves.

THE DEVELOPING BRAIN
   Percentage of adult brain weight at age 6 months = 50%; at 2 years = 75%; 5 years = 90%; and 10 years = 95%.
   Myelination slows after early childhood.
   Right- and left-hemisphere differences
   Neural sprouting and recovery of lost function after aphasia

NUTRITION, DIET, AND HEALTH
   Malnutrition
      Marasmas and kwashiorkor
      Animal and human studies
   Obesity
      Role of biological processes--endocrine glands and twin studies
      Role of convenience foods and exercise

Fat cells and obesity

DAILY SLEEP NEEDS
Sleep time and napping decline with age.
REM remains fairly constant after 3 years of age.

DEVELOPING MOTOR ABILITIES (p. 196)

PATTERNS OF MOTOR DEVELOPMENT
Walking and throwing
Developing strength, speed, flexibility, and coordination

THE IMPORTANCE OF MOTIVATION AND EXPERIENCE
Intrinsic and extrinsic motivation
Motor development is influenced by rewards, opportunities, practice, and guidance.

GROSS MOTOR SKILLS
<u>Running and Climbing</u>
<u>Jumping, Hopping, and Skipping</u>
<u>From Tricycles to Bicycles</u>

SPORTS AND PLAY: ADVANCED MOTOR SKILLS--the most popular sports outside the school are baseball, softball, and swimming.

FINE MOTOR SKILLS
Feeding and dressing skills
Use of marking tools
Kellogg's four stages in the development of drawing: (1) scribbles, (2) shapes, (3) designs, and (4) pictures.

HANDEDNESS
By 4 years of age, 90% show right hand preference.
Congruent versus cross dominant preferences
No relationship between handedness and reading disabilities

ISSUES IN ACTION (p. 205)

HEALTH PROBLEMS--decline in mortality rate due to improved nutrition, health care, and immunization.
<u>Accidents</u>--highest rate of accidental death involves automobiles.
<u>The Sick Child</u>--special care for children

PHYSICALLY IMPAIRED CHILDREN--incidence and types of impairments
<u>Reactions of Other People</u>
<u>Special Problems for Parents</u>
<u>Helping the Handicapped Child</u>
Spock's advise to caregivers
Mainstreaming

CHILD ABUSE--incidence of abuse; failure to thrive
<u>The Abused Child</u>

Chapter 6   89

>   Differences between abused and nonabused children
>   Usually one child in a family becomes a target.
>   Perceived "immaturity" and attractiveness are important
>   <u>The Abusing Parent</u>--four conditions associated with abuse
>   <u>Controlling Child Abuse</u>--psychotherapy, parent training,
>   hotlines, crisis nurseries, Parents Anonymous, etc.

GUIDED REVIEW

1. Because different parts of the body grow at different rates, this pattern of growth is described as _____. Physical maturation of motor control spreads in a head-to-tail, or _____, direction and outward from the center in a _____ direction. As maturation proceeds, the small muscle groups come under control through the process of _____. In time, differentiated fine movements are integrated into complex skills like walking, through the process Werner (1948) called _____.

2. Body growth is steady in childhood--height and weight increase by about _____ inches and _____ pounds each year. Although the timing and magnitude of growth varies for children from different _____, the _____ of the growth patterns is universal. Cultural variations are related to levels of prosperity. In Hong Kong, for example, children in _____ SES groups have smaller body heights than those in higher classes.

3. The heart, lungs, and muscles have the same growth pattern as _____; it begins with rapid growth in infancy, _____ growth in childhood, followed by a growth spurt.

4. The last organ system to mature is the _____ system. The _____ system matures very early in life, and the _____ system, which includes the tonsils, has a highly accelerated growth rate until adolescence.

5. The _____ hemisphere of the brain has areas that process language, and the _____ hemisphere handles nonverbal processes. This differentiation has been found in 3-month-old babies. Language disabilities, called _____, are usually temporary if they result from damage to the left hemisphere before _____ years of age.

6. Malnutrition retards growth. An extreme form of starvation in the first year of life is called _____. Another extreme form of malnutrition occurs in early childhood; it is called _____ and results from a severe lack of _____.

7. Animal studies have revealed the alarming effects of severe malnutrition. Malnourished pregnant rats gave birth to offspring that had undersized _____ with fewer and smaller cells and low levels of _____ and _____ proteins. Similar defects were noted during autopsies of infants who suffered from _____.

8. Malnutrition can also lower resistance to _____ or infection, intensify and prolong physical disease, and increase the likelihood of dehydration and further malnutrition through the effects of _____.

9. Obesity is considered a health problem because it is associated with _____ blood pressure, heart disease, and early _____ in adults.

10. Obese children often eat less than slim children, but they also _____ much less. Very few cases of obesity are due to _____ disorders, but genetic factors may play a role. Some infants are overfed, which results in an increase in the (number/size) of their fat cells.

11. Sleep requirements decrease with age, but the proportion of sleep time to REM time _____ in childhood. Two-year-olds sleep about 12 hours a day, including a daytime nap. Napping usually stops around age _____.

12. Motor development parallels growth of the nervous system and is accompanied by increased strength, speed, _____, balance, and coordination.

13. Motor development is influenced by physical readiness, motivation, and opportunities to learn and _____. Without guidance and appropriate practice, children can develop _____ movements, like swimming by dog paddling.

14. Gross motor skills, such as running and climbing, are mastered in early childhood. Most children can learn to ride tricycles by _____ years of age, and bicycles between _____ and _____ years.

15. Many children enter the competitiion of o_____ kid sports at ages 4 or 5. Simon and Martin (1979) found that precompetition _____ in team sports was the same as that experienced in taking a school test.

16. Fine motor skills, such as eating and dressing, are acquired during childhood. Children can feed themselves with a spoon at age _____, and slicing meat with a knife is mastered by age 8.

17. According to Kellogg (1967), children's drawing progresses through _____ stages. Infantile scribbling advances to the drawing of simple _____ forms, which are later combined to make various designs. At

_____ years of age children make various designs. By _____ years of age children make drawings that look something like the objects they represent.

18. Uniform left- or right-sided preference for two or more parts of the body is called _____ preference; opposite-side preference is called _____.

19. A serious hazard to children's lives comes from accidents, particularly those involving _____. The second, third, and fourth leading forms of fatal accidents are drowning, burns, and _____.

20. Physically impaired children must not only learn to adjust to their handicap, but to handle the _____ reactions of others. Parents, likewise, must learn to accept their child's limitations by setting _____ challenges and by offering warm support. Integrating handicapped children in regular classrooms is called _____.

21. Child abuse can result from adult acts of comission or _____ that lead to physical injury. Abused children tend to be more a_____ toward age-mates, less socially mature, and less willing to learn than non-abused children are. Children who are at special risk for abuse are those who were born _____, are physically unattractive, and show high levels of disagreeable behavior.

22. Abusing parents can be found in _____ social strata. They do not seem to have a typical _____ profile, but they often expect their children to live up to _____ standards.

23. Acts of battering often occur at times of family _____. Many services are available to help abusive parents, such as some programs designed to teach anger control and non-_____ methods of child discipline. Other programs encourage social contacts in order to break up patterns of _____. They also provide "_____ nurseries" and emergency telephone numbers or "_____."

TERMS AND DEFINITIONS QUIZ

SET 1: (Match each term in the set with its definition below.):

APHASIA, ASYNCHRONOUS GROWTH, CATCH-UP GROWTH, CEPHALO-CAUDAL, CEREBRUM, DIFFERENTIATION, HIERARCHICAL INTEGRATION, INTEGRATION, LEFT-HEMISPHERE, PROXIMODISTAL, RIGHT HEMISPHERE

1. _____ The right half of the brain; controls

movement on the left side of the body and processes visual imagery, emotions, and pattern perception.

2. _____ The pattern of physical maturation that begins in the head region and proceeds toward the lower extremities.

3. _____ The pattern of physical growth that starts in the spinal region and proceeds toward the body extremities.

4. _____ A concept that applies to both physical growth and motor development; the process by which one's anatomy and motor movements become increasingly specialized, individual, and subject to voluntary control.

5. _____ A general term indicating difficulty in understanding or using speech.

6. _____ A concept that applies to both physical growth and motor development; the process of organizing differentiated components of anatomy and motor movements into increasingly complex and smoothly coordinated arrangements as the child develops.

7. _____ The process in motor development resulting from the continuing interaction between differentiation and integration; it leads to higher levels of complex and finely coordinated skills, such as those involved in performing gymnastic routines or playing a musical instrument.

8. _____ The pattern of physical maturation typified by different growth rates in different parts of the body.

9. _____ The accelerated physical growth that occurs when the child's health has been restored after a period of illness or malnutrition.

10. _____ The highly convoluted hemispheres of the brain where higher cognitive functions, such as language and spatial operations, are carried out.

11. _____ The left half of the brain; controls movement by the right side of the body and contains the areas that handle language processes.

SET 2: CONGRUENT PREFERENCE, CROSS DOMINANCE, FAILURE TO THRIVE, FINE MOTOR SKILLS, GROSS MOTOR SKILLS, HANDEDNESS, KWASHIORKOR, MAINSTREAMING, MARASMUS, OBESITY

1. _____ A term applied to infants and young children who are slow to develop physically and socially; may result from lack of proper nutrition and emotional support by caregivers.

2. _____ The coordinated use of large muscle groups, as in running, jumping, or climbing.

3. _____ The coordinated use of small muscle groups, such as those in the hands and face.

4. _____ A person's preference for using one hand over the other in certain activities.

5. _____ A severe form of infant malnutrition resulting in a variety of symptoms including physical and motor retardation and abdominal protrusion.

6. _____ Severe protein deficiency in young children, which may produce various symptoms ranging from general physical retardation to death.

7. _____ Uniform left- or right-sided preference for two or more parts of the body; same-side preference for hand and eye, for instance.

8. _____ Different left-right preferences in different parts of the body; for example, right-hand and left-eye preference in the same individual.

9. _____ The state of being substantially overweight due to excessive body fat.

10. _____ The integration of physically impaired or handicapped children into regular classrooms and the social life of the nonhandicapped.

MATCHING QUIZ

1. ___ aphasia   a. a predictable pattern of growth
2. ___ marasmus   b. for the physically impaired
3. ___ mainstreaming   c. Parents Anonymous
4. ___ lymphatic system   d. a form of starvation
5. ___ child abuse   e. protects against disease
6. ___ flexibility   f. language deficit
7. ___ cephalocaudal   g. girls perform better than boys

SELF TEST

1. The pattern of asynchronous growth in which the child gains control of movement in the head, then trunk, legs, and then feet is called _____ development.
   a. differentiation
   b. proximodistal
   c. cephalocaudal
   d. hierarchical

2. A child combines simple movements of the arm and hand into the smoothly coordinated act of writing. This demonstrates the process called
   a. cross dominance.
   b. integration.
   c. differentiation.
   d. congruence.

3. After birth, a child's fastest rate of growth in height occurs in infancy; the second fastest growth occurs at about _____ years of age.
   a. 2-5
   b. 6-9
   c. 11-14
   d. 16-19

4. Which statement concerning changes in body proportions is TRUE?
   a. Children acquire their full set of baby teeth between 4 and 5 years of age.
   b. The arms reach adult proportions after the legs do.
   c. The jaw becomes narrower and the forehead becomes more prominent with age.
   d. At about 11 years, children's arms and legs appear disproportionately long and spindly.

5. In terms of average heights across cultures, rural Mexico has the shortest 9-year-olds and the United States has the tallest.
   a. True
   b. False

6. At _____ years of age, the child's brain reaches 90% of the average adult's brain weight.
   a. 2
   b. 5
   c. 10
   d. 15

7. The cerebrum
   a. is where complex mental activity occurs.
   b. includes the cortex, which is convoluted.
   c. is almost the adult size at about age 5.
   d. all of the above.

8. For aphasias occurring after the age of 3, recovery is very

difficult and often incomplete.
a. True
b. False

9. Severe protein deficiency in infants often causes marasmus, which includes
   a. muscular atrophy.
   b. protruding stomachs.
   c. retarded physical and motor development.
   d. all of the above.

10. The effects of malnutrition are deepened by diarrhea.
    a. True
    b. False

11. Obese individuals generally _____ than slim people do.
    a. have higher blood pressure
    b. get more exercise
    c. have slimmer parents
    d. none of the above

12. On average, toddlers nap _____ per day; by age _____, napping is quite brief or absent.
    a. once; 4
    b. twice; 5
    c. three times; 4
    d. four times; 5

13. The proportion of REM sleep experienced in one's total daily sleep
    a. constitutes about 90% for 5-year olds.
    b. increases sharply throughout childhood.
    c. declines from infancy to early childhood.
    d. increases sharply in adolescence.

14. Children's dreams tend to reflect the everyday events and concerns of their lives; their nightmares generally don't require professional treatment.
    a. True
    b. False

15. Sleepwalking occurs frequently in about 15% of children; an episode usually involves acting out a dream the child is having.
    a. True
    b. False

16. Intrinsic motivation is exemplified by a child who
    a. performs well in school to earn a gold star.
    b. promises to be good while shopping so he will have an ice cream later.
    c. cleans her room to earn her allowance.
    d. none of the above.

17. Teachers can provide the uidance needed to prevent chil-

dren from acquiring poor motor habits.
a. True
b. False

18. Children in competitive sports suffer more precompetition anxiety than children who play instruments in musical competitions.
a. True
b. False

19. Although children make crude representations of real objects, such as "stick people," at about 5 years of age, they begin to include linear perspective at about age
a. 7.
b. 9.
c. 12.
d. 15.

20. Which statement about the development of fine motor skills is TRUE?
a. Most children cannot feed themselves with a spoon until 3 years of age.
b. Toddlers are more skillful at putting clothes on than taking them off.
c. A 4-year-old generally prints letters very small and almost always places them in the center of a page.
d. At 9 years of age children usually give up printing in favor of handwriting.

21. A preference for using parts of the body involving opposite sides, such as left-ear and right-eye, is called a _____ preference.
a. cross dominant
b. congruent
c. proximodistal
d. asynchronous

22. Childhood illnesses that CANNOT be controlled by immunization include
a. tetanus.
b. rubella.
c. tuberculosis.
d. whooping cough.

23. About 7% of all persons under age 21 have serious sensory impairments or crippling health impairments.
a. True
b. False

24. Which statement about physically impaired children is TRUE?
a. Handicapped children almost always have only a single and isolated area of retarded functioning.
b. Parents should try to ignore the handicap and give the child many special privileges.
c. Nonhandicapped children tend to exclude handicapped classmates from social activities.

d. none of the above.

25. The process of integrating handicapped children into regular classes is called
    a. mainstreaming.
    b. hierarchical integration.
    c. cross dominance.
    d. canalizing.

26. Failure to thrive is a syndrome in which children are slow to develop physically and socially, which may result from a lack of proper nutrition and emotional support by the parents.
    a. True
    b. False

27. Most experts believe that the actual yearly incidence of child abuse in the United States is two or three times the _____ cases reported to the American Humane Society.
    a. 231,000
    b. 397,000
    c. 624,000
    d. 851,000

28. Because abuse causes a physical effect on the child, it is easy to detect.
    a. True
    b. False

29. In the study by Main and George (1985), observations of abused and nonabused preschoolers revealed that _____ children typically responded to a child's distress with _____.
    a. abused; concern
    b. abused; sadness
    c. nonabused; concern or interest
    d. nonabused; fear or distress

30. Which statement about child abuse is TRUE?
    a. Abused children often look younger than their actual age.
    b. Being physically unattractive may make a child more vulnerable to abuse.
    c. Most abused children are fearless and outgoing.
    d. Premature babies are almost never abused because their parents recognize how delicate they are.

IMPORTANT DETAILS TO KNOW

1. At what age is the rate of growth (in inches per year) the greatest? See Figure 6.2. (p. 188)

2. Which two countries have the shortest 9-year-olds, and which two have the tallest? (p. 189)

3. Which two organ systems develop fastest in childhood? (pp. 189-190)

4. What percentage of the adult's brain weight does the child's brain reach at age 10 years? (p. 190)

5. What physical effects result from dietary deficiencies in protein? (p. 192)

6. How common is sleepwalking in childhood and adolescence? See Highlight 6.1. (p. 195)

7. When can most children ride tricycles and bicycles? (p. 200)

8. When can children use a fork, a knife, and lace their shoes? (p. 201)

9. When can children draw circles and triangles, and three-dimensional forms? (p. 202)

10. When do children print their names, and then give up printing in favor of handwriting? (p. 203)

11. What percentage of persons between 3 and 21 years are physically impaired? (p. 207)

TEST YOUR RECALL

1. Name six general and highly predictable patterns of physical development. (p. 188)

2. Diagram the rates of change in height from infancy through adolescence. See Figure 6.2. (p. 188)

3. Describe the changes in body proportions that occur during childhood. (p. 189)

4. What factors may account for the height differences between children of the same age in different parts of the world? (p. 189)

5. Draw the growth curves, from infancy through adolescence, for the brain, lymphoid system, and reproductive system. See Figure 6.4. (p. 190)

6. What role does melatonin appear to play in development? (p. 190)

7. Describe the functions and development of myelin during childhood. (p. 190)

8. Contrast the functional differences between the left and right hemispheres of the brain. (p. 190)

9. How does malnutrition affect child development in cases of marasmus and kwashiorkor? (p. 192)

10. Discuss the findings on the effects of malnutrition in animal studies. (p. 192)

11. Describe the study by Costanzo and Woody (1979) on convenience foods and obesity in children. (p. 193)

12. Explain how fat cells may play a role in child and adult obesity. (p. 194)

13. Outline the developmental changes in daily sleep needs. (p. 194)

14. Explain how throwing an object illustrates the sequential pattern of motor development. (p. 197)

15. Make a list of the differences between girls and boys in strength, speed, flexibility, and coordination. (p. 198)

16. Give two examples each of extrinsic and intrinsic sources of motivation. (pp. 198-199)

17. Describe the development of running and climbing. (pp. 199-200)

18. List the age at which various fine motor tasks in eating and dressing are mastered. (p. 201)

19. Outline Kellogg's four stages in the development of drawing. (p. 202)

20. List in rank order the three most frequent sources of accidental death among children. (p. 206)

21. Discuss the special problems of parents with handicapped children and provide suggestions for helpful parenting. (p. 208)

22. Describe how abused and nonabused children differ. (pp. 209-210)

23. What four conditions has Kempe described as usually present when battering occurs? (pp. 211-212)

24. What approaches have been introduced to control child abuse? (pp. 212-213)

Chapter 6

ANSWER SECTION

GUIDED REVIEW:

1. asynchronous; cephalocaudal; proximodistal; differentiation; hierarchical integration
2. 2 or 3; 5 or 6; cultures; sequence; lower
3. height; moderate
4. reproductive; central nervous (brain); lymphatic
5. left; right; aphasias; 3
6. marasmus; kwashiorkor; protein
7. brains; DNA; RNA; marasmus
8. illnesses; diarrhea
9. high; death
10. exercise; glandular (endocrine), number
11. remains constant; 4
12. flexibility
13. practice; incorrect (inefficient)
14. 3; 5; 7
15. organized; anxiety
16. 2
17. four; geometric; 3 or 4; 5 to 7
18. congruent; cross dominance
19. automobiles; poisoning
20. negative; realistic (appropriate); mainstreaming
21. omission; aggressive; prematurely
22. every; personality; unrealistic
23. crisis; punitive; isolation; crisis; hotlines

TERMS AND DEFINITIONS QUIZ:

SET 1:
1. right hemisphere
2. cephalocaudal
3. proximodistal
4. differentiation
5. aphasia
6. integration
7. hierarchical integration
8. asynchronous growth
9. catch-up growth
10. cerebrum
11. left-hemisphere

SET 2:
1. failure to thrive
2. gross motor skills
3. fine motor skills
4. handedness
5. marasmus
6. kwashiorkor
7. congruent preference
8. cross dominance
9. obesity
10. mainstreaming

MATCHING QUIZ:

1. f (p. 190)
2. d (p. 192)
3. b (p. 208)
4. e (p. 190)
5. c (p. 213)
6. g (p. 198)
7. a (p. 188)

SELF TEST:

1. c (p. 188)
2. b (p. 188)
3. c (p. 188)
4. d (p. 189)
5. b (p. 189)
6. b (p. 190)
7. d (p. 190)
8. a (p. 190)
9. d (p. 192)
10. a (p. 193)
11. a (p. 194)
12. a (p. 194)
13. c (p. 194)
14. a (p. 195)
15. b (p. 195)
16. d (p. 199)
17. a (p. 199)
18. b (p. 202)
19. c (p. 203)
20. d (p. 203)
21. a (p. 204)
22. c (p. 206)
23. b (p. 207)
24. c (p. 208)
25. a (p. 208)
26. a (p. 209)
27. d (p. 209)
28. b (p. 209)
29. c (p. 210)
30. b (p. 211)

CHAPTER 7

Child Cognition I: Perception, Learning, and Memory

SUMMARY IN OUTLINE

<u>PERCEPTUAL DEVELOPMENT</u>   (p. 218)

    PERCEPTUAL PROCESSES
       <u>Attention</u>
          Younger children are more easily distracted than older ones.
          Children prefer increasingly complex stimuli through age 12.
          Visual scanning becomes more efficient with age.
       <u>Discrimination</u>--older children scan more systematically and focus more on details than younger ones do.
       <u>Perceiving Constancy</u>--size constancy improves at least until age 8; shape constancy is acquired earlier.
       <u>Integrating Perceptual Systems</u>--improvement is greatest between ages 3 and 6.
       <u>Perceiving with Incomplete Information</u>

    GIBSON'S DIFFERENTIATION THEORY
       Reduction of perceptual uncertainty through differentiation.
       Perceptual skills are acquired by (1) attending to distinctive features, (2) detecting invariant properties, and (3) forming higher order structures or rules.

    WHEN LEARNING TO READ, HEARING IS IMPORTANT TOO

<u>HOW CHILDREN LEARN</u>   (p. 224)

    TYPES OF LEARNING--Gagné's hierarchy
       <u>Signal and Stimulus-Response Learning</u>

Classical (signal) conditioning
Operant (stimulus-response) conditioning
Immediate reinforcement is important
<u>Chaining</u>
A sequence of responses (links) form a chain.
Backward chaining
<u>Verbal Associations</u>
<u>Multiple Discrimination Learning</u>
<u>Concept Learning</u>
<u>Rule Learning</u>--relations between two or more concepts
<u>Problem Solving</u>--two or more rules applied to a problem

IMITATION: OBSERVATIONAL LEARNING
<u>The Observation "Method"</u>--all of Gagné's types of learning can occur by observation
<u>The Role of Consequences on Imitation</u>

TEACHING AND LEARNING
The Montessori method--multisensory training
Gagné's hierarchy implies that lower-order skills should be mastered before more complex ones.

<u>THE DEVELOPMENT OF MEMORY</u>   (p. 230)

A MODEL OF MEMORY STORAGE--control processes regulate the transfer of information within the memory system.

DEVELOPMENTAL CHANGES IN MEMORY
<u>Sensory Storage</u>
Holds sensory impressions for less than one second
Storage capacity is constant between ages 5 and 21.
<u>Short-Term Storage</u>
Limited to about seven "chunks" of information in adults
Short-term capacity and speed improve with age.
Rehearsal aids memory.
<u>Long-Term Storage and Information Processing from Short-Term Storage</u>
How is Memory Organized?
"Free recall" technique
Clusters, subjective organization, and scripts
What Makes Information "Salient?"--imagery; questions

DO CHILDREN UNDERSTAND HOW MEMORY WORKS?--metamemory

<u>MOTIVATION: "PUSHES" AND "PULLS" IN COGNITION</u>   (p. 235)

Competence motivation is an internal desire to be effective.
Children use speed, effort, and authoritative feedback to evaluate their own competence.
Impulsive and reflective cognitive styles

<u>PLAYFUL COGNITIVE ACTIVITIES</u>   (p. 236)

EXPLORATION AND PLAY
"Overt" and "covert" exploration

Chapter 7   105

Pretend play and dramatic play

HUMOR: WHAT'S FUNNY TO KIDS--cognitive incongruity

ISSUES IN ACTION (p. 240)

LEARNING DISABILITIES--dyscalculia, dyslexia, hyperactivity, and receptive and expressive aphasia
   Possible Causes of Learning Disabilities
      Brain disorders; maturational lag
      Faulty information processing
   Experiences of the Learning-Disabled Child
      Poor social relations with parents and peers
      Diminished self-confidence; behavioral problems

USING LEARNING PRINCIPLES TO IMPROVE CHILD BEHAVIOR
   Teaching a Child to Print--shaping, prompting, and fading
   Bedwetting--enuresis
   Doing Household Chores
   Classroom Conduct--token economy

GUIDED REVIEW

1. The development of perceptual skills depends on learning and maturation of our s_____ systems. Compared to older children, the young child's _____ is shorter and more distractable. Attention is affected by characteristics of the stimulus; children prefer increasingly _____ stimuli as they get older.

2. The ability to detect differences between stimuli is called _____. Older children's improved visual _____ while exploring a novel object aids their discrimination ability.

3. Children try to construct a stable world by perceiving constancies. Two examples of constancy are _____ and _____ constancy.

4. Eleanor Gibson has proposed a theory of perceptual development based on the process of _____. She states that perceptual skills become more proficient as children learn to make fine discriminations between stimuli by (1) attending to _____, (2) detecting _____ properties of stimuli, and (3) discovering higher order _____ and _____ that describe relationships between stimuli.

5. Gagné has proposed a _____ of learning composed of eight types of learning arranged in a hierarchy. All learning progresses from the simpler types to the more complex. Operant conditioning links combine to form _____. Later, children acquire concepts and _____ which they use in problem solving.

6. Sometimes rewards can "backfire" and _____ motivation, especially if the rewards are tangible, _____, and normally not given for the activity.

7. Chains that link two or more words are called _____. Learning to distingusih between more than two stimuli among a larger set, such as letters of the alphabet, is called _____ learning.

8. Copying other people's behavior after watching them illustrates _____ learning. Imitation is generally enhanced when the model or observer receives a _____. Punishment _____ imitation, but does not prevent observational learning.

9. Knowledge of perceptual and cognitive development has been applied to the classroom. The Montessori method focuses on training the _____; Gibson stresses the _____ features of letters at the prereading level; and Gagné emphasizes that prerequisite learning must be mastered before a child attempts higher order learning.

10. A useful approach to the study of memory views the memory system as consisting of three storage mechanisms. The processing of sensory impressions, which usually vanish in less than a second, occurs in the _____. From about age _____ to 21, the capacity of the sensory store remains fairly constant. The sensory store sends information to the _____ store, where adults can process about _____ units or chunks at one time. As children get older, they can retain more items in short-term memory largely because they spontaneously _____ the items more extensively. The third memory mechanism, which holds most of our knowledge of the world, is called the _____ store. Here, material is stored in an organized fashion that is like a _____ system.

11. Free recall tasks show that as children get older, their clustering and _____ organization improves. Long-term memory is aided by imagery and asking _____. Knowledge about your own memory and how it works is called _____.

12. The notion that children strive to master tasks is captured by the concept of _____ motivation. Children's anxiety and cognitive styles can influence their problem-solving efficiency. Children who generate quick and inaccurate solutions are said to be _____, and those who deliberate are called _____.

13. Children explore stimuli that are, for them, moderately _____ and complex. Thus, younger children are usually more interested in simpler stimuli than very complex ones. Younger children tend to explore more _____ objects and events; older children explore

Chapter 7   107

at a more mental (covert) and abstract level.

14. When toddlers make believe they are feeding a doll, they are engaging in _____ play. "Cops and robbers" is a social activity in which each person plays a role; this game is an example of _____ play.

15. Children's humor often derives from cognitive _____ in jokes and riddles. With advances in cognitive skills, old incongruities are resolved, and humor is less dependent on them.

16. When children have a fairly specific learning disorder, they are classified as _____. About 3% of American school children receive special education for learning disabilities. Some children have great difficulty performing math calculations, which is called _____. Others have severe disabilities in learning the components of words or sentences, a disorder called _____. A disability in understanding or using speech is referred to as _____.

17. Another learning disability involves high motor activity and poor attentional processes; it is called _____. Paradoxically, this disorder is often treated with _____ drugs. The exact causes of these disabilities is unknown, but it seems likely that these defects are a product of both maturational and learning factors.

18. Parents and teachers can use _____ principles to improve child behavior. The procedure, called shaping, in which rewards are given for _____ approximations to the correct behavior, is very useful in teaching motor responses, such as printing. Learning principles can also be used to reduce bedwetting, encourage doing household chores, and improve _____ conduct.

TERMS AND DEFINITIONS QUIZ

SET 1: (Match each term in the set with its definition below.):

CHAINS, DIFFERENTIATION THEORY, DISTINCTIVE FEATURES, HIGHER ORDER STRUCTURES, INVARIANT PROPERTIES, MULTIPLE DISCRIMINATION LEARNING, SHAPE CONSTANCY, SIZE CONSTANCY, VERBAL ASSOCIATIONS

1. _____ Gibson's explanation of perceptual development which involves the capacity to identify, classify, and organize stimuli into meaningful arrangements by attending to distinctive features, detecting invariant properties, and discovering the rules that describe relationships among stimuli.

2. _____ In Gagné's taxonomy, the ability to

distinguish between more than two stimuli among a larger set.

3. _____ The attributes of stimuli which permit them to be distinguished from one another, such as the shape differences between geometric figures.

4. _____ Attributes of a stimulus which, because they remain stable or constant, enable one to recognize the stimulus despite alternations in its other features or characteristics.

5. _____ Rules which facilitate people's perceptions of and reactions to stimuli.

6. _____ The ability to judge the size of an object accurately, regardless of its distance from the viewer.

7. _____ In Gagné's taxonomy, behaviors composed of a sequence of simple operant motor responses (called links).

8. _____ The ability to judge the shape of an object accurately, regardless of its orientation in space.

9. _____ In Gagné's taxonomy, chains of two or more words linked together.

SET 2: CLUSTERS, CONTROL PROCESSES, LONG-TERM STORAGE, MONTESSORI METHOD, REHEARSAL, SCRIPT, SENSORY STORAGE, SHORT-TERM STORAGE, SUBJECTIVE ORGANIZATION

1. _____ The memory mechanism which takes in information, holds as much as seven "chunks" temporarily, and transfers some to the long-term storage.

2. _____ The individual's unique scheme or pattern for retrieving items from memory, such as by using a personalized mnemonic device.

3. _____ A mental representation of a sequence of expected events for a commonly experienced situation, like eating at a restaurant.

4. _____ The large-capacity memory mechanism that contains most of the individual's knowledge of the world.

5. _____ A teaching method with a set of materials to emphasize perceptual integration and learning among preschool children.

6. _____ Cognitive operations, such as rehearsal and retrieval, which regulate the flow of information in the memory system.

Chapter 7   109

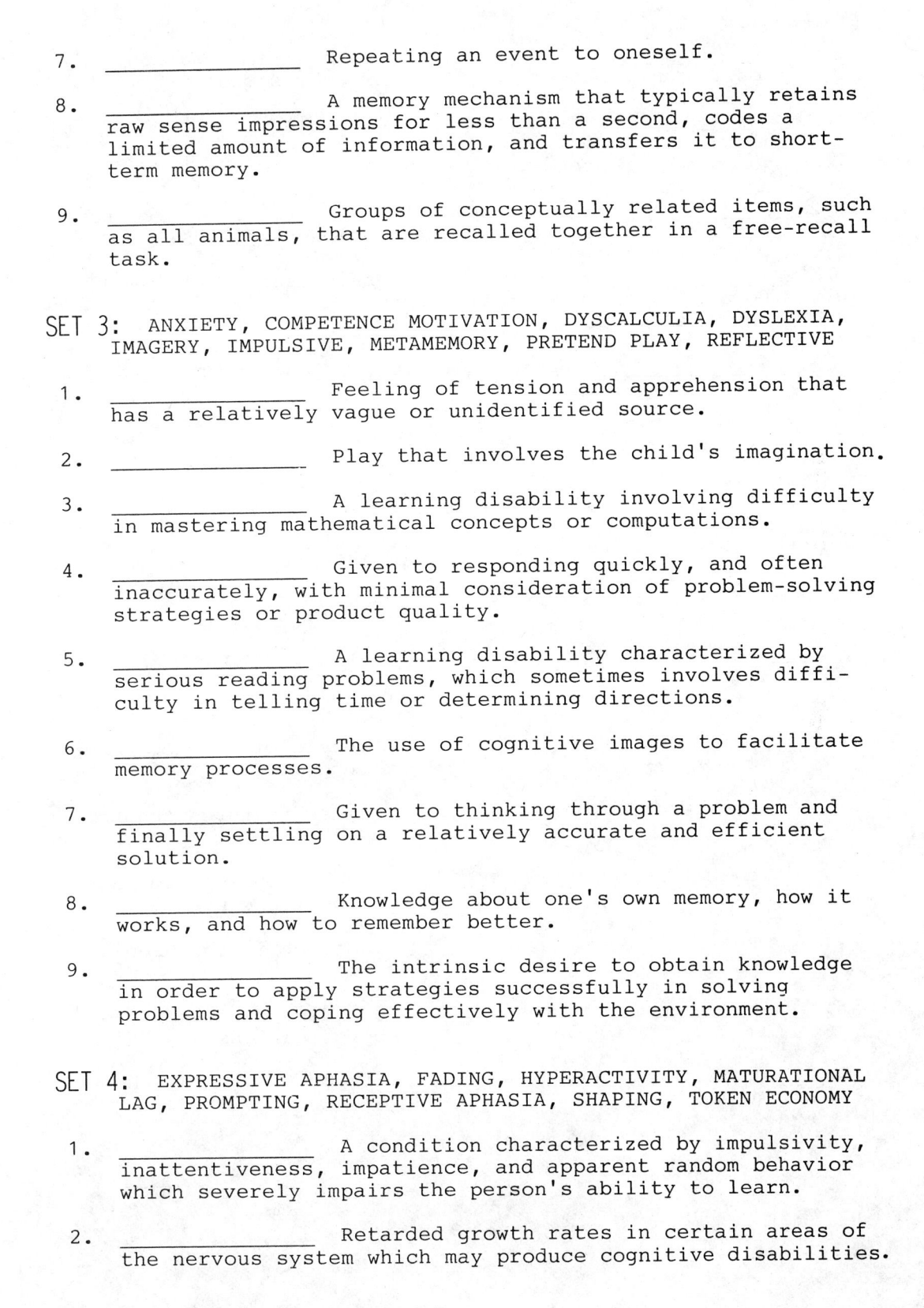

7. _____ Repeating an event to oneself.

8. _____ A memory mechanism that typically retains raw sense impressions for less than a second, codes a limited amount of information, and transfers it to short-term memory.

9. _____ Groups of conceptually related items, such as all animals, that are recalled together in a free-recall task.

SET 3: ANXIETY, COMPETENCE MOTIVATION, DYSCALCULIA, DYSLEXIA, IMAGERY, IMPULSIVE, METAMEMORY, PRETEND PLAY, REFLECTIVE

1. _____ Feeling of tension and apprehension that has a relatively vague or unidentified source.

2. _____ Play that involves the child's imagination.

3. _____ A learning disability involving difficulty in mastering mathematical concepts or computations.

4. _____ Given to responding quickly, and often inaccurately, with minimal consideration of problem-solving strategies or product quality.

5. _____ A learning disability characterized by serious reading problems, which sometimes involves difficulty in telling time or determining directions.

6. _____ The use of cognitive images to facilitate memory processes.

7. _____ Given to thinking through a problem and finally settling on a relatively accurate and efficient solution.

8. _____ Knowledge about one's own memory, how it works, and how to remember better.

9. _____ The intrinsic desire to obtain knowledge in order to apply strategies successfully in solving problems and coping effectively with the environment.

SET 4: EXPRESSIVE APHASIA, FADING, HYPERACTIVITY, MATURATIONAL LAG, PROMPTING, RECEPTIVE APHASIA, SHAPING, TOKEN ECONOMY

1. _____ A condition characterized by impulsivity, inattentiveness, impatience, and apparent random behavior which severely impairs the person's ability to learn.

2. _____ Retarded growth rates in certain areas of the nervous system which may produce cognitive disabilities.

3. _____ The process of reinforcing successively closer approximations to the correct response.

4. _____ In operant conditioning, the process of guiding or helping individuals as they try to make an appropriate response.

5. _____ Severe difficulty in talking, even though the person can easily make the component sounds.

6. _____ The process whereby assistance (prompting) that was given to help a person make appropriate responses is gradually reduced.

7. _____ Serious difficulty in comprehending speech.

8. _____ A method of teaching and maintaining appropriate behavior by awarding tokens which can be exchanged later for desired goods or activities.

MATCHING QUIZ

1. ___ operant conditioning   a. learned sequence of motor responses
2. ___ chain   b. stimulus-response learning
3. ___ rule   c. Eleanor Gibson
4. ___ differentiation theory   d. emphasis of the Montessori method
5. ___ short-term memory   e. limited to three chunks in preschoolers
6. ___ dyscalculia   f. a relationship between two or more concepts
7. ___ shaping   g. important in children's humor
8. ___ multisensory approach   h. rewarding successive approximations
9. ___ cognitive incongruity   i. difficulty with arithmatic

SELF TEST

1. Which statement about perceptual development is TRUE?
    a. Vision and hearing equal adult levels by 3 years of age.
    b. Vision and hearing improve for several years after infancy.
    c. Distracting stimuli are more disruptive for older children because they perceive stimuli more easily than younger children do.
    d. Children's preference for stimulus complexity increases until age 5 but not thereafter.

2. Which of the following characteristics of visual scanning does NOT help children to make fine discriminations, such as between a 0, a 6, and a 9?
    a. Focusing on only one part, such as the upper right side of each number.
    b. Paying attention to critical features.
    c. Scanning systematically.
    d. Examining several details of each stimulus.

3. The ability to judge that a square window you see from an angle is, in fact, square is called
    a. cognitive congruity.
    b. metamemory.
    c. dyscalculia.
    d. shape constancy.

4. Gibson's differentiation theory proposes that children acquire perceptual skills primarily to satisfy the challenges and demands of parents and teachers.
    a. True
    b. False

5. In Gibson's theory, the relevant characteristics a child must perceive to make accurate differentiations between stimuli are called
    a. invariant properties.
    b. control processes.
    c. distinctive features.
    d. scripts.

6. Young children rely on both vision and hearing when learning to read.
    a. True
    b. False

7. In Gagné's hierarchy of learning, multiple discriminations are prerequisites for learning _____, followed by rule learning.
    a. chains
    b. verbal associations
    c. to solve problems
    d. concepts

8. A sure-fire way to maintain a child's high interest in a task is to give the child rewards for engaging in the task.
    a. True
    b. False

9. Rewards are most likely to enhance behavior when
    a. the child's interest in the task is already high.
    b. reinforcement is immediate.
    c. reinforcement is delayed.
    d. they are not things the child really likes.

10. In chain learning the stimulus in each link functions as _____ and as a _____ for the next link.
    a. reinforcement; rule
    b. prompting; concept
    c. feedback; cue
    d. rehearsal; multiple discrimination

11. A child who learns that "round things roll" is engaging in _____ learning.
    a. signal
    b. multiple discrimination
    c. concept
    d. rule

12. Children who try to learn things by observing another person and then practicing the task in their heads find that this is a very inefficient method of learning.
    a. True
    b. False

13. Which of the following statements is FALSE?
    a. Montessori proposes that the systematic training of the child's senses aids cognitive growth.
    b. Piaget has described a hierarchy of learning in which mastering simpler tasks enable the child to learn increasingly complex skills.
    c. Gagné proposes that teachers need to map out each learning task in terms of the prerequisite skills the child will need.
    d. Gibson has described training techniques for the teaching of reading.

14. The mechanism in Atkinson and Shiffrin's (1971) model of memory that holds information for less than 1 second is called the _____ store.
    a. sensory
    b. short-term
    c. long-term
    d. control processing

15. Which of the following is NOT a control process?
    a. attention
    b. rehearsal
    c. organization
    d. differentiation

16. Short-term memory in 7-year-olds is limited to about five "chunks" of information.
    a. True
    b. False

17. Which of the following statments is TRUE?
    a. The difference between younger and older children in their use of control processes cannot be reduced by training.
    b. Older children show better short-term memory than younger children do because older children rehearse items as isolated units.
    c. Older children show better short-term memory than younger children do because older children have a larger memory capacity in sensory store.
    d. Older children encode and identify stimuli, such as digits, faster than younger children do.

18. A cluster in a child's free recall is better represented in "knife, fork, spoon" than in "tree, bulb, hat."
    a. True
    b. False

19. To organize memory, children store an experience as a sequence of events, or cognitive
    a. cluster.
    b. chain.
    c. script.
    d. association.

20. Asking questions, answering questions, and using imagery make material easier to remember by making it more salient.
    a. True
    b. False

21. Knowing that it is easier to remember recent events than distant ones and that imagery helps in learning and remembering are examples of
    a. invariant properties.
    b. multiple discrimination learning.
    c. metamemory.
    d. prompting.

22. Children can use their speed of performing tasks to assess their competence in cognitive skills, but they cannot take into account the amount of effort they put into the tasks.
    a. True
    b. False

23. As children get older, their exploration involves things that are increasingly novel, _____, and _____.
    a. simple; social
    b. complex; covert
    c. complex; abstract
    d. both b and c are correct

24. When 2-year-old Geraldo uses a shoe to represent an airplane flying overhead, he is engaging in _____ play.
    a. pretend
    b. congruent
    c. token
    d. receptive

25. The use of _____ in humor involves putting words, ideas, or images together in an unexpected or unconventional manner.
    a. cognitive incongruity
    b. metamemory
    c. distinctive features
    d. subjective organization

26. A learning disability is essentially the same thing as mental retardation.
    a. True
    b. False

27. Dyslexia involves difficulty in learning arithmetic computations or concepts.
    a. True
    b. False

28. Joan's inability to say the word CAMERA, even though she can make the component sounds, reflects the learning disability called
    a. dyslexia
    b. dyscalculia
    c. expressive aphasia
    d. receptive aphasia

29. The operant technique called fading involves
    a. the rewarding of successively better approximations to the correct behavior.
    b. a gradual reduction in the size of rewards.
    c. the reduction of physical assistance given by the teacher.
    d. the introduction of a token economy.

30. About 16% of 6-year-olds have bedwetting problems.
    a. True
    b. False

IMPORTANT DETAILS TO KNOW

1. Until what age does children's preference for greater complexity increase? (p. 218)

2. Intersensory communication increases very rapidly during what age range? (p. 220)

3. In Gagné's hierarchy, which types of learning are prereq-

uisites for each higher form of learning? (pp. 224-229)

4. The amount of information the sensory store can process remains constant between what ages? (p. 231)

5. How long is information held in sensory store and short-term memory? (p. 230)

6. How many chunks of information can be retained in the short-term memory by the average adult, 7-year-old, and preschooler? (p. 232)

TEST YOUR RECALL

1. What characteristics of stimuli are important in attracting children's attention. (p. 218)

2. Describe the development of attentional processes during childhood. (p. 218)

3. State the findings of the Nodine and Simmon's (1974) study. (p. 219)

4. Give an example to explain why it is important for children to learn to integrate perceptual systems. (p. 220)

5. Name the three proficiencies that aid perceptual development according to Gibson. (pp. 221-222)

6. Describe the outcomes of the experiment by Gibson and her colleagues (1963) on higher order structures. (pp. 222-223)

7. Explain the role of hearing in learning to read. (p. 223)

8. Draw a diagram of Gagné's hierarchy of types of learning. (p. 225)

9. Under what three conditions can rewards undermine motivation. See Highlight 7.1. (p. 226)

10. Use an example not in the text to describe the process of chaining. (p. 225)

11. How are concept and rule learning related to problem solving? (p. 227)

12. What did Bandura's (1965b) study reveal about the role of consequences on imitation? (p. 228)

13. Discuss how principles of the Montessori method are consistent with recent research findings. (p. 229)

14. How could Gagné's hierarchy be applied in teaching academic

116   Chapter 7

skills. (p. 229)

15. Diagram the flow of information through Atkinson and Shiffrin's memory model. (p. 231)

16. Outline the developmental changes in (a) sensory storage and (b) short-term storage. (pp. 231-232)

17. How is long-term memory organized? (p. 233)

18. List four specific mnemonic techniques that could be used to aid memory. See Highlight 7.2. (p. 234)

19. How do children with impulsive and reflective cognitive styles differ? (p. 236)

20. Cite the differences between pretend and dramatic play. (pp. 237-238)

21. Describe how children's sense of humor changes with age. (pp. 238-239)

22. Explain the difference between receptive and expressive aphasia. (p. 241)

23. List the possible causes of learning disabilities. (p. 242)

24. Describe how shaping could be used to teach a child to print letters. (p. 244)

25. Explain how a token economy can help control classroom behavior? (p. 245)

ANSWER SECTION

GUIDED REVIEW:

1. sensory; attention; complex
2. discrimination; scanning
3. size; shape
4. differentiation; distinctive features; invariant; structures; rules
5. taxonomy; chains; rules
6. undermine; salient
7. verbal associations; multiple discrimination
8. observational; reward; suppresses
9. senses; distinctive
10. sensory storage; 5; short-term; seven; rehearse; long-term; file
11. subjective; questions; metamemory
12. competence; impulsive; reflective
13. novel; concrete (physical)
14. pretend; dramatic

Chapter 7

15. incongruity
16. learning disabled; dyscalculia; dyslexia; aphasia
17. hyperactivity; stimulant
18. learning; successive; classroom

TERMS AND DEFINITIONS QUIZ:

SET 1:
1. differentiation theory
2. multiple discrimination learning
3. distinctive features
4. invariant properties
5. higher-order structures
6. size constancy
7. chains
8. shape constancy
9. verbal associations

SET 2:
1. short-term storage
2. subjective organization
3. script
4. long-term storage
5. Montessori method
6. control processes
7. rehearsal
8. sensory storage
9. clusters

SET 3:
1. anxiety
2. pretend play
3. dyscalculia
4. impulsive
5. dyslexia
6. imagery
7. reflective
8. metamemory
9. competence motivation

SET 4:
1. hyperactivity
2. maturational lag
3. shaping
4. prompting
5. expressive aphasia
6. fading
7. receptive aphasia
8. token economy

MATCHING QUIZ:

1. b (p. 224)
2. a (p. 225)
3. f (p. 227)
4. c (p. 221)
5. e (p. 232)
6. i (p. 241)
7. h (p. 244)
8. d (p. 229)
9. g (p. 238)

Chapter 7

SELF TEST:

1.	b	(p. 218)	16.	a	(p. 232)
2.	a	(p. 219)	17.	d	(p. 232)
3.	d	(p. 220)	18.	a	(p. 233)
4.	b	(p. 221)	19.	c	(p. 233)
5.	c	(p. 222)	20.	a	(p. 234)
6.	a	(p. 223)	21.	c	(p. 235)
7.	d	(p. 227)	22.	b	(p. 235)
8.	b	(p. 226)	23.	d	(p. 237)
9.	b	(p. 226)	24.	a	(p. 237)
10.	c	(p. 226)	25.	a	(p. 238)
11.	d	(p. 227)	26.	b	(p. 240)
12.	b	(p. 228)	27.	b	(p. 241)
13.	b	(p. 229)	28.	c	(p. 241)
14.	a	(p. 230)	29.	c	(p. 244)
15.	d	(p. 230)	30.	a	(p. 244)

CHAPTER 8

Child Cognition II: Thinking, Reasoning, and Intelligence

SUMMARY IN OUTLINE

    PROLOGUE (p. 251)

        Thinking involves the use of mental representations (symbols and images).
        Reasoning involves planning and problem solving in a logical manner.

    FORMING AND USING MENTAL REPRESENTATIONS (p. 252)

        CONCEPT LEARNING
            Concrete and abstract concepts
            Broad concepts ("tree") can be divided into basic-level categories ("evergreen"), and then further divided into specific-level concepts ("pine").
            Number Concepts--preschoolers understand something about the magnitude of numbers and can detect counting errors.
            Relational concepts--development of the concepts for "front" and "back," and "same" and "different"
            Space Concepts--skilled use of maps increases with age.
            Speed, Distance, and Time
            Causality

        LEARNING COGNITIVE RULES
            Older children learn rules more easily than younger ones do.
            Learning sets or "learning to learn"
            Preschoolers learn a nonreversal shift more easily than a reversal shift; older children find the reversal shift easier.

Chapter 8

FORMING STRATEGIES AND SOLVING PROBLEMS

PREOPERATIONAL THINKING: PIAGET'S VIEW (p. 260)

SYMBOLIC FUNCTIONS--mental ability to make one thing represent something else which is not present

INTUITIVE OR "SEMILOGICAL" THINKING--because young children lack the needed operations, thinking is largely determined by what is currently seen and heard.
- Incomplete Understanding of Classes--failure to use the operation called class inclusion
- Transductive Thinking
  - Inferences are made based on individual cases or characteristics
  - Animism--attributing life to inanimate objects
- Centration--focus on only one aspect of a multifaceted problem; preoperational thinkers cannot decenter
- Irreversibility--inability to think through a sequence of mental actions in reverse order
- Egocentrism--self-centered thinking; cannot consider another's perspective

IS PRESCHOOL THINKING REALLY SO INTUITIVE?
- Classification: Is a Yam a Hamburger?
  - Young children show better classification skills when they know about relevant concepts.
  - The phrasing of a question can impair younger children's performance.
- Is Preschool Thinking "Centered?"--young children can attend to two dimensions, but they apply the wrong rule.
- How Egocentric is Preschool Thinking?--young children are less egocentric than Piaget claimed.

CONCRETE OPERATIONAL THINKING: PIAGET'S VIEW (p. 268)

According to Piaget, children can perform mental operations after about 7 years of age. These early mental operations involve concrete objects (tangible) and events (here-and-now).

SOLVING CONSERVATION PROBLEMS--different problems are typically solved at different ages--see Table 8.4

SERIATION: ARRANGING THINGS IN SEQUENCE

CAN TRAINING SPEED UP COGNITIVE DEVELOPMENT?
- Training results in cognitive advances; skills generalize.
- There is a limit to the amount that training can speed up cognitive development.

CONCLUDING REMARKS ON PIAGET'S VIEW
- His overview of sensorimotor development seems to be valid.
- Underestimated children's cognitive abilities
- Overall sequence of mental development is basically correct

Stimulated much theorizing and research

INTELLIGENCE (p. 273)

Intelligence is a set of many different abilities which are continually changing.

DEFINITIONS OF INTELLIGENCE
Intelligence can be seen as a hierarchy of abilities with general intelligence at the top.
Guilford's cubical model of intelligence has 120 different mental abilities arranged within three dimensions: (1) contents, (2) operations, and (3) products.

INTELLIGENCE TESTING
<u>Stanford-Binet Intelligence Test</u>
  Binet and Terman
  Basal age, ceiling age, and mental age
<u>Wechsler Intelligence Tests</u>--WISC-R and WPPSI
  WISC-R has a verbal and a performance scale.

IQ DIFFERENCES
Standardization sample and normal curve
"Exceptional" children--see Highlight 8.3
<u>The Stability and Predictive Ability of the IQ</u>
  IQs are used to assess relatively current abilities.
  Correlation between school performance and IQ scores is about +0.50.
<u>Social Class, Culture, and the IQ</u>--SES; culture fair tests
<u>Genetics and IQ</u>
  Correlations between identical twins average about +0.90; for fraternal twins the correlation is less than +0.60.

CREATIVE THINKING (p. 281)

GENERATING CREATIVE IDEAS
<u>Measuring Creative Thinking</u>--divergent thinking
<u>Talent and Creative Thinking</u>--importance of early training, significant teachers, and parent characteristics

ISSUES IN ACTION (p. 283)

IMPROVING THE CHILD'S COGNITIVE SKILLS
Computers can be useful at school and home.
Hobbies, books, games, and outings can aid cognitive development.

RACE AND IQ
Black Americans score about 15 IQ points below whites.
The social environment has a dominant role in determining the average IQ level of black children.

Chapter 8

GUIDED REVIEW

1. The process of using mental representations of our knowledge--mostly in the form of symbols and images--is called _____. When we _____ we use mental representations in a logical manner to solve problems.

2. Children learn concrete concepts before advancing to _____ concepts. When learning concrete concepts, children generally acquire basic-level categories first, then the broad category, and then the _____ concepts. Relational concepts, like "front" and "back," are first understood by children when used to refer to their own _____; later, these concepts are used to refer to other objects.

3. Preschool-age children acquire a fundamental knowledge of many abstract concepts, such as those of number, space, and time. And they are aware that events in their world have _____. Young children determine causality quite well if the forces are clear; if the forces are not clear, preschoolers tend to decide that the event _____ the effect is the cause.

4. Children's knowledge about where babies come from develops throughout childhood--at first they have no idea, so they often say what they've been _____, as in "Babies come from God." Once children know that babies come from the mother's belly, they assume that the newborn emerges from the _____.

5. Developmental trends in rule learning can be illustrated by the process of "learning to learn" or _____, and in learning the reversal and _____ shift task. Young children found it easier to perform the _____ shift task, implying that they were not using a rule; older children found it easier to _____ a rule than to change it.

6. According to Piaget's theory of cognitive development, children's thinking is at the preoperational stage between _____ and _____ years of age. By "preoperational" Piaget means that the necessary logical _____, or mental actions, are lacking at this stage. Young children's thinking is semilogical or _____.

7. Piaget's theory describes several limitation's of preoperational thinking, such as transductive thinking, irreversibility, cen_____, and the inability to perform the operation of class _____. Another limitation, that preoperational thinking cannot assume the role or veiwpoint of another person, is called _____.

8. Research has shown that preschoolers' thinking is much

_____ logical than Piaget claimed. For instance their thinking is not centered; they can and do consider more than one _____ when trying to solve a problem. And even 2-year-olds are not completely egocentric; they understand at least _____ another person has a different view.

9. Piaget described the thinking of children between 7 and 12 years of age as _____. During this stage, children acquire the necessary mental _____ to solve concrete problems in the here-and-now.

10. To study logical thinking, Piaget used a type of task called _____ problems. Contrary to Piaget's view, research has shown that _____ can enhance preschoolers' logical problem solving, and these new skills can _____ to other problems.

11. Intelligence is a difficult concept to define. Some psychologists see it as a hierarchy of abilities that begins with an overall factor called _____ intelligence, which can be subdivided into specific ones. Others, such as Guilford, view intelligence as a matrix of many separate and distinct skills.

12. Intelligence is inferred from a person's _____ on a test and is usually expressed as an _____ score. The first such test was developed by the Frenchman Alfred _____, and was later modified by Terman to become the _____-Binet Intelligence Scale. This test is individually administered, and it primarily measures _____ ability. The Wechsler intelligence tests were developed later and have two scales: a verbal scale and a _____ scale.

13. Children with either very low or very high IQs are called _____ children. Those whose IQs are below 70 are classed as mentally retarded, and those above 130 are _____. Retardates are classified by IQ as profoundly, severely, _____, and mildly retarded. The vast majority of these children are mildly retarded, probably because of _____ deprivation. Special educational programs can help these individuals to become self-supporting.

14. Gifted children, contrary to some old myths, typically have _____ physiques, health, academic achievement, and social adjustment in comparison with children of average intelligence.

15. For many children, IQ scores are not very stable over _____ time intervals. But IQs are very useful in assessing relatively _____ intellectual abilities.

16. Children from the lower classes and some ethnic minorities

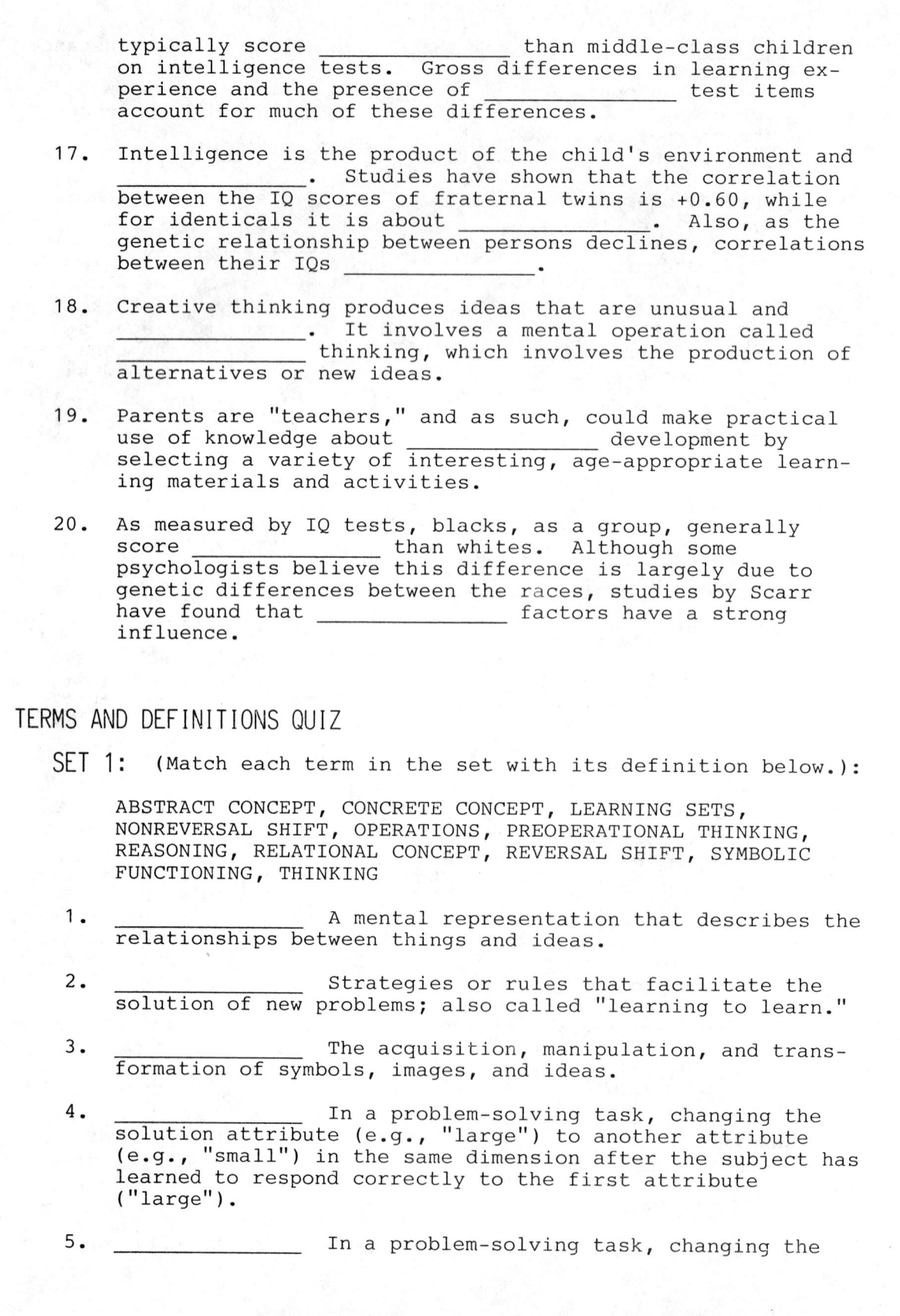

typically score _____ than middle-class children on intelligence tests. Gross differences in learning experience and the presence of _____ test items account for much of these differences.

17. Intelligence is the product of the child's environment and _____. Studies have shown that the correlation between the IQ scores of fraternal twins is +0.60, while for identicals it is about _____. Also, as the genetic relationship between persons declines, correlations between their IQs _____.

18. Creative thinking produces ideas that are unusual and _____. It involves a mental operation called _____ thinking, which involves the production of alternatives or new ideas.

19. Parents are "teachers," and as such, could make practical use of knowledge about _____ development by selecting a variety of interesting, age-appropriate learning materials and activities.

20. As measured by IQ tests, blacks, as a group, generally score _____ than whites. Although some psychologists believe this difference is largely due to genetic differences between the races, studies by Scarr have found that _____ factors have a strong influence.

TERMS AND DEFINITIONS QUIZ

SET 1: (Match each term in the set with its definition below.):

ABSTRACT CONCEPT, CONCRETE CONCEPT, LEARNING SETS, NONREVERSAL SHIFT, OPERATIONS, PREOPERATIONAL THINKING, REASONING, RELATIONAL CONCEPT, REVERSAL SHIFT, SYMBOLIC FUNCTIONING, THINKING

1. _____ A mental representation that describes the relationships between things and ideas.

2. _____ Strategies or rules that facilitate the solution of new problems; also called "learning to learn."

3. _____ The acquisition, manipulation, and transformation of symbols, images, and ideas.

4. _____ In a problem-solving task, changing the solution attribute (e.g., "large") to another attribute (e.g., "small") in the same dimension after the subject has learned to respond correctly to the first attribute ("large").

5. _____ In a problem-solving task, changing the

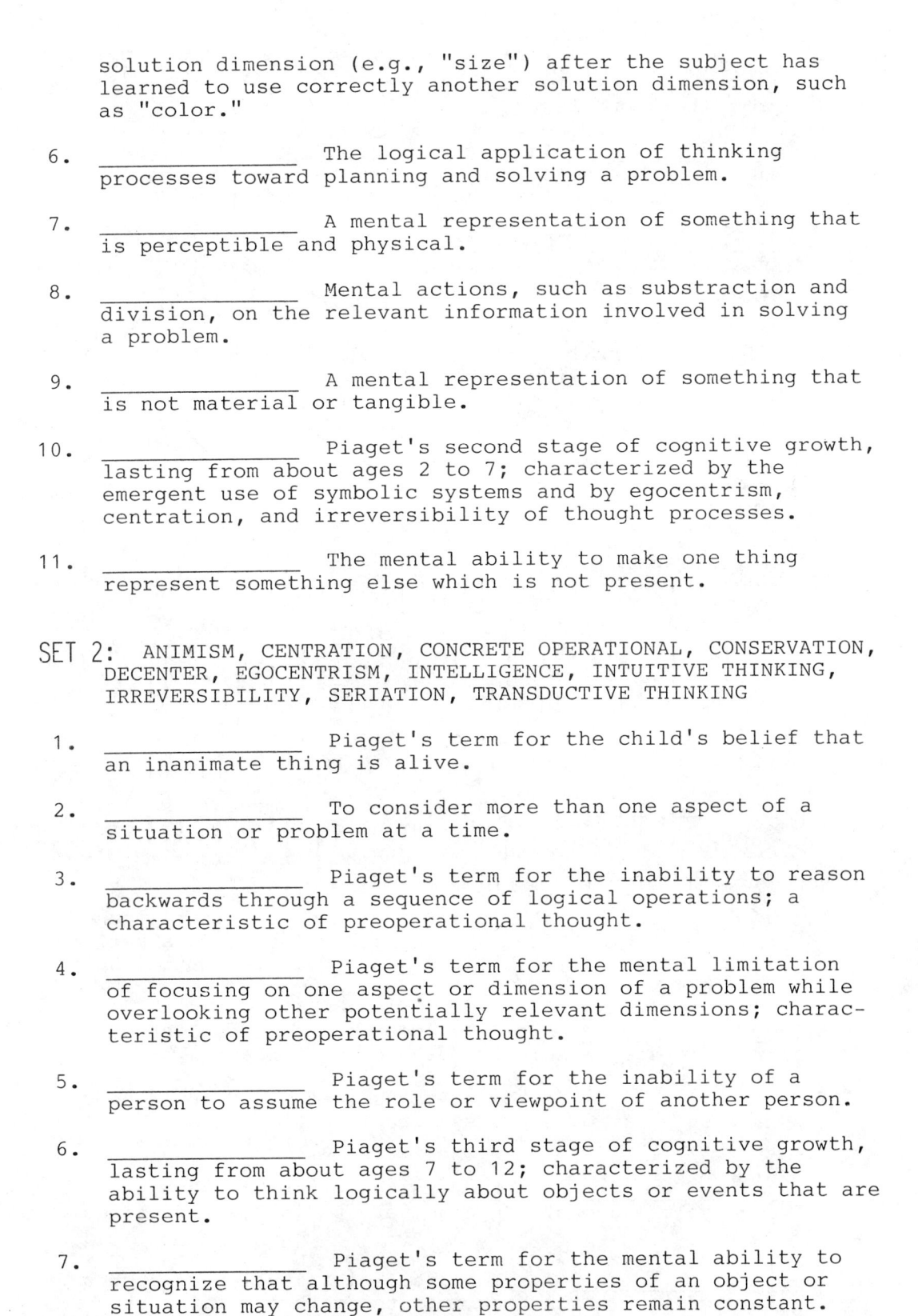

solution dimension (e.g., "size") after the subject has learned to use correctly another solution dimension, such as "color."

6. _____ The logical application of thinking processes toward planning and solving a problem.

7. _____ A mental representation of something that is perceptible and physical.

8. _____ Mental actions, such as substraction and division, on the relevant information involved in solving a problem.

9. _____ A mental representation of something that is not material or tangible.

10. _____ Piaget's second stage of cognitive growth, lasting from about ages 2 to 7; characterized by the emergent use of symbolic systems and by egocentrism, centration, and irreversibility of thought processes.

11. _____ The mental ability to make one thing represent something else which is not present.

SET 2: ANIMISM, CENTRATION, CONCRETE OPERATIONAL, CONSERVATION, DECENTER, EGOCENTRISM, INTELLIGENCE, INTUITIVE THINKING, IRREVERSIBILITY, SERIATION, TRANSDUCTIVE THINKING

1. _____ Piaget's term for the child's belief that an inanimate thing is alive.

2. _____ To consider more than one aspect of a situation or problem at a time.

3. _____ Piaget's term for the inability to reason backwards through a sequence of logical operations; a characteristic of preoperational thought.

4. _____ Piaget's term for the mental limitation of focusing on one aspect or dimension of a problem while overlooking other potentially relevant dimensions; characteristic of preoperational thought.

5. _____ Piaget's term for the inability of a person to assume the role or viewpoint of another person.

6. _____ Piaget's third stage of cognitive growth, lasting from about ages 7 to 12; characterized by the ability to think logically about objects or events that are present.

7. _____ Piaget's term for the mental ability to recognize that although some properties of an object or situation may change, other properties remain constant.

Chapter 8

8. _____ In Piaget's theory, thinking by children in the preoperational stage, applying only a partial logic to solve a problem.

9. _____ In Piaget's theory, preoperational thought in which the child draws inferences about objects or events by considering only individual cases or characteristics.

10. _____ Piaget's term for the ability to arrange objects according to some quantitative dimension on which they vary.

11. _____ A set of complex cognitive abilities, including verbal, perceptual-spatial, memory, and reasoning skills; the ability to profit from experience.

SET 3: BASAL AGE, CEILING AGE, DIVERGENT THINKING, MENTAL AGE, NORMAL CURVE, PERFORMANCE SCALE, SOCIOECONOMIC STATUS (SES), STANFORD-BINET INTELLIGENCE SCALE, VERBAL SCALE, WECHSLER INTELLIGENCE TESTS

1. _____ A single index that summarizes such factors as income, education, and occupational status; approximately equivalent to social class.

2. _____ The mental age assigned to a set of questions on the Stanford-Binet test, all of which were answered incorrectly by the testee.

3. _____ Mental operations that generate alternatives or new ideas; an important feature of creativity.

4. _____ The child's level of mental skills as expressed in terms of the chronological age of a group of children whose average test scores are closest to his or her own.

5. _____ Widely accepted and used intelligence tests; the WISC-R includes a verbal scale and a performance scale to tap three abilities: verbal, perceptual-spatial, and memory.

6. _____ A widely accepted and used test of intelligence, originally developed in France.

7. _____ A set of tasks in the WISC-R in which knowledge of words plays a crucial role in the child's performance.

8. _____ A set of tasks in the WISC-R that does not involve the use of language, except in the directions given to the child.

9. _____ A symmetrical distribution of scores from low to high, which describes the mathematically expected

variability of scores around the mean.

10. _____ The mental age assigned to a set of questions on the Stanford-Binet test, all of which were correctly answered by the testee.

MATCHING QUIZ

1. ___ class inclusion   a. inferences based on individual cases
2. ___ general intelligence   b. Lewis Terman
3. ___ WISC-R   c. exceptional children
4. ___ divergent thinking   d. used as a test of creativity
5. ___ learning sets   e. understanding how to use categories
6. ___ profoundly retarded   f. taps perceptual-spatial and memory abilities
7. ___ transductive thinking   g. hierarchical model
8. ___ Stanford-Binet test   h. involve learning how to learn

SELF TEST

1. Thinking involves the use of mental representations, mostly in the form of _____ and ideas.
   a. operations
   b. seriations
   c. centrations
   d. symbols

2. Which of the following is NOT an example of a concrete concept?
   a. truck
   b. morality
   c. cloud
   d. dictionary

3. Concepts are based on the regularity of relationships among objects, events, or ideas.
   a. True
   b. False

4. Although the number concepts young children acquire are generally incomplete, preschoolers
   a. can typically count 25 items in a large display.

b. show high accuracy when counting more than 10 items.
c. understand something about the magnitudes of the numbers that range from 5 to 20.
d. do not notice when someone makes a mistake in counting.

5. Seventh graders who see two toy trains moving in the same direction along parallel tracks can make correct judgments about the relative _____ of travel of the trains.
   a. speeds
   b. distances
   c. durations
   d. all of the above

6. When preschool children see two things happen in sequence, they usually
   a. evaluate causality by deciding that the first event caused the second event.
   b. ascribe a cause based on their own needs and experiences, rather than on what they see.
   c. guess randomly as to what caused what.
   d. try to apply abstract concepts to explain what caused what.

7. A strategy or rule for solving logical problems is called a
   a. relational concept.
   b. learning set.
   c. reversal shift.
   d. nonreversal shift.

8. In Kendler and Kendler's classic research on reversal and nonreversal shifts, a NONREVERSAL shift required the children to select the correct stimulus based on a different attribute within the same dimension of the one they learned to choose before the shift occurred.
   a. True
   b. False

9. Although preschoolers can learn rules, they do not perform as well as older children in solving logical problems.
   a. True
   b. False

10. Which of the following statements is representative of Piaget's theory?
    a. An operation is an inborn schema.
    b. Symbolic functioning is a term that describes cognitive functioning that uses false logic.
    c. Preoperational thinking is intuitive or semilogical.
    d. Mental actions used to solve problems are called reversal shifts.

11. In Piaget's theory, the operation for simultaneously holding a class and its subclass in mind and moving back and forth between them is called
    a. class inclusion.

    b. a learning set.
    c. a nonreversal shift.
    d. divergent thinking.

12. According to Piaget, _____ in children's thinking is shown by their belief that psychological events, such as dreams, are real and tangible entities.
    a. centration
    b. conservation
    c. rationalization
    d. realism

13. In Piaget's theory, the child's tendency to focus on one aspect or dimension of a problem, thereby overlooking other important factors, is called
    a. learning sets.
    b. irreversibility.
    c. centration.
    d. conservation.

14. Five-year-olds try to apply a strategy to solve a classification problem; but, because it is usually wrong, they sometimes perform worse than 3-year-olds.
    a. True
    b. False

15. Fewer than half of the 3- to 5-year-olds in the Hughes (1975) study of egocentrism were successful at hiding the boy doll from the police-officer doll.
    a. True
    b. False

16. Children usually can solve the conservation of number problem by _____ years of age, and the conservation of displaced volume by age _____.
    a. 4; 7
    b. 6; 7
    c. 4; 12
    d. 6; 12

17. When Betty organizes her marbles by size, she demonstrates the ability called
    a. nonreversal shifting.
    b. intuitive thinking.
    c. seriation.
    d. irreversibility.

18. The training in conservation rules Field (1981) provided for preschoolers enhanced their performance on conservation tasks and was more successful for the 4-year-olds than the 3-year-olds.
    a. True
    b. False

19. Psychologists today generally view intelligence as a
    a. single general ability that is exactly measured by IQ

tests.
b. set of many abilities that continually change.
c. score on a test that has no relation to ability.
d. set of a few abilities that remain fixed throughout development.

20. According to Guilford's cubical model, intelligence consists of 120 abilities within three major dimensions: _____, operations, and _____.
a. contents; products
b. centration; conservation
c. verbal scale; performance scale
d. intuition; reversals

21. In the products dimension of Guilford's model of intelligence, the _____ aspect involves simply stating a fact.
a. unit
b. figural
c. class
d. symbolic

22. Lewis Terman constructed the first major intelligence test.
a. True
b. False

23. To determine the child's _____ age on the Stanford-Binet test, the examiner gives the child progressively _____ items.
a. basal; difficult
b. basal; easy
c. verbal; difficult
d. verbal; easy

24. Taken together, about _____% of the total population are classified as exceptional (gifted and mentally retarded).
a. 2
b. 5
c. 10
d. 20

25. Most mentally retarded children are classified as "trainable" (IQ = 25 to 39).
a. True
b. False

26. Retarded children who are most likely to require life-long custodial care are _____ retarded.
a. mildly
b. moderately
c. severely
d. profoundly

27. Terman's longitudinal study of gifted children confirmed the general idea that the gifted are physical weaklings, unpopular, and socially awkward.

a. True
b. False

28. The stability of a child's IQ generally is greatest if the child is _____ years of age and retesting is done after a _____ period of time.
    a. younger than 10; short
    b. younger than 10; long
    c. older than 10; short
    d. older than 10; long

29. Scores on IQ and on creativity tests are only somewhat related, the correlation being about +0.25.
    a. True
    b. False

30. Racial differences in studies of performance on IQ tests probably resulted from
    a. bias in the tests which favored middle-class over lower-class children.
    b. having been tested by a white examiner.
    c. the different environments under which the children are raised.
    d. all of the above.

IMPORTANT DETAILS TO KNOW

1. What changes in the concepts of front, back, and side occur when the child is about 3 years of age? (p. 254)

2. At what age can most children answer the following questions: What day is it? What time is it? What year is it? (p. 255)

3. What age group did better on Kendler and Kendler's (1962) nonreversal shifts than on reversal shifts? (p. 257)

4. Which two conservation tasks are mastered earliest by children, and which two are mastered latest? See Table 8.4. (p. 269)

5. Describe the hierarchical model of intellectual abilities. See Figure 8.10(a). (p. 274)

6. Name and define Guilford's (1967) overall dimension of intelligence. See Figure 8.10(b). (p. 274)

7. Who developed the first major intelligence test? (p. 275)

8. What is the percentage of children classified as "exceptional?" See Highlight 8.3. (p. 278)

9. Distinguish between "educable," "trainable," moderately, severely, and profoundly retarded in terms of IQs and

abilities. See Highlight 8.3. (p. 278)

TEST YOUR RECALL

1. Describe how concept learning changes with development? (pp. 252-253)

2. How did Gelman and Meck (1983) show that preschoolers have some understanding of the concept of number? (p. 254)

3. Trace the development of the concepts of "front" and "back" between 2 and 4 years of age. (p. 254)

4. Recount the developmental progression of children's knowledge about where babies come from. See Highlight 8.1. (p. 256)

5. State the results of the Kendler and Kendler (1961, 1962, 1967) studies on reversal and nonreversal shifts. (p. 257)

6. What did the Eimas (1970) study reveal about the development of problem solving strategies? (p. 258)

7. According to Piaget, how does a preoperational thinker demonstrate an incomplete understanding of categories? (p. 262)

8. Give an example illustrating Piaget's concept of centration. (p. 263)

9. Cite two examples Piaget and other writers have described of egocentric thinking at the preoperational stage. (p. 264)

10. Why do children sometimes have difficulty with classification tasks? (pp. 265-266)

11. Cite evidence that preschoolers are NOT as egocentric as Piaget claimed. (pp. 266-267)

12. Describe the conservation of liquid task. According to Piaget, why can children at the concrete operational stage solve the task? (p. 268)

13. Discuss the method and results of Field's (1981) study to see if training can speed up cognitive development. (pp. 270-271)

14. List contributions and limitations of Piaget's views on cognitive development during childhood. (p. 272)

15. List four definitions of intelligence once held by psychologists. (p. 273)

Chapter 8   133

16. Describe the hierarchical model of intelligence. (p. 274)

17. According to Guilford (1967), intelligence is composed of which three dimensions? (p. 274)

18. Outline the procedures for administering the Stanford-Binet Intelligence Scale. (p. 275)

19. How do the WISC-R and Stanford-Binet tests differ? (p. 276)

20. List the four classifications of mental retardation and their corresponding IQ ranges. See Highlight 8.3. (p. 278)

21. Discuss the relationship between social class and IQ. (pp. 277-278)

22. Cite evidence supporting the view that intelligence is influenced by heredity. (pp. 279-280)

23. Characterize the parents of creative individuals. (p. 282)

24. Cite a common myth concerning creative people. (p. 283)

25. List several ways that parents can enhance their children's cognitive skills. (pp. 283-285)

26. Describe the work of Sandra Scarr and her colleagues on the relation between racial differences and IQ. (p. 286)

ANSWER SECTION

GUIDED REVIEW:

1. thinking; reason
2. abstract; specific-level; bodies
3. causes; preceding
4. told; belly button
5. learning sets; nonreversal; nonreversal; reverse
6. 2; 7; operations; intuitive
7. centration; inclusion; egocentrism
8. more; dimension; whether
9. concrete operational; operations
10. conservation; training; generalize
11. general
12. performance; IQ; Binet; Stanford; verbal; performance
13. exceptional; gifted; moderately; environmental
14. superior (better)
15. long; current
16. lower; biased
17. heredity (genetics); +0.90; decrease
18. useful; divergent
19. cognitive

20. lower; environmental

TERMS AND DEFINITIONS QUIZ:

SET 1:
1. relational concept
2. learning sets
3. thinking
4. reversal shift
5. nonreversal shift
6. reasoning
7. concrete concept
8. operations
9. abstract concept
10. preoperational stage
11. symbolic functioning

SET 2:
1. animism
2. decenter
3. irreversibility
4. centration
5. egocentrism
6. concrete operational stage
7. conservation
8. intuitive thinking
9. transductive thinking
10. seriation
11. intelligence

SET 3:
1. socioeconomic status (SES)
2. ceiling age
3. divergent thinking
4. mental age
5. Wechsler intelligence tests
6. Stanford-Binet Intelligence Scale
7. verbal scale
8. performance scale
9. normal curve
10. basal age

MATCHING QUIZ:

1. e (p. 262)
2. g (p. 274)
3. f (p. 276)
4. d (p. 282)
5. h (p. 256)
6. c (p. 278)
7. a (p. 262)
8. b (p. 275)

Chapter 8

SELF TEST:

1.	d	(p. 251)	16.	d	(p. 269)
2.	b	(p. 252)	17.	c	(p. 270)
3.	a	(p. 252)	18.	a	(p. 271)
4.	c	(p. 254)	19.	b	(p. 273)
5.	d	(p. 255)	20.	a	(p. 274)
6.	a	(p. 255)	21.	a	(p. 274)
7.	b	(p. 256)	22.	b	(p. 275)
8.	b	(p. 257)	23.	b	(p. 275)
9.	a	(p. 258)	24.	b	(p. 278)
10.	c	(p. 261)	25.	b	(p. 278)
11.	a	(p. 262)	26.	d	(p. 278)
12.	d	(p. 263)	27.	b	(p. 279)
13.	c	(p. 262)	28.	c	(p. 277)
14.	a	(p. 265)	29.	a	(p. 282)
15.	b	(p. 266)	30.	d	(pp. 285-286)

CHAPTER 9

Language Development in Childhood

SUMMARY IN OUTLINE

   THE DEVELOPMENTAL COURSE OF LANGUAGE (p. 292)

      EARLY WORDS
         Phonemes are the basic sounds of a language.
         Morphemes are the smallest units of meaning in a language.
         Mean length of utterance (MLU) is a measure of language development.
         Vocabulary size at 18 months = 200 words; at 6 years = 8,000 basic words, plus 6,000 word variations.
         Proportions of specific parts of speech change with development.
         Young children overextend words.

      TWO-WORD SENTENCES
         Two-word sentences emerge at $1\frac{1}{2}$ to 2 years of age.
         Meanings conveyed in two-word sentences:
           1. action- and object-location
           2. action-recipient
           3. agent-action-object
           4. attribution
           5. negation
           6. possession
           7. recurrence and nonexistence
           8. questions

      STAGES OF LANGUAGE DEVELOPMENT--Brown's five stages (Table 9.2)
         <u>Stage I</u>
            Two-word sentences
            Speech is telegraphic.

Stage II
- Three-word sentences--subject-verb-object
- Articles, prepositions, and inflections are used.
- Overregularization begins

Stage III
- Children can construct complete questions (wh-questions) and more precise negative statements.
- Passive voice is understood.

Stage IV and V--complicated sentence structures with subordinate clauses and conjuctions

GRAMMAR AND MEANING
- Context helps adults interpret children's speech.
- Grammar provides a context.
- Surface structure, deep structure, and metaphors

PROCESSES IN LANGUAGE DEVELOPMENT (p. 303)

INNATE MECHANISMS
- Language development progresses in a universal sequence.
- Deaf children also develop language.
- Chomsky's language acquisition device (LAD)
- Creole languages of children share certain universal features.
- There is little evidence of a sensitive period for language acquisition; if it exists, it might span ages 2 to 5 years.

LEARNING AND IMITATION
- Conditioning principles influence language development, but they are not sufficient to explain the acquisition of grammar.
- Observational learning plays an important role in language development, particularly vocabulary acquisition.

COGNITIVE DEVELOPMENT
- Many cognitive skills are acquired before language; and children understand more than they can say.
- Whorfian hypothesis proposes that language shapes our thinking.
- Vygotsky holds that children's private speech guides their thought processes and behavior.

THE CHILD'S ABILITY TO COMMUNICATE (p. 309)

WILL THE LISTENER UNDERSTAND?
- Children become increasingly skilled at adapting their speech to their audience as they get older.
- Young children's descriptions tend to be idiosyncratic.

AWARENESS OF LANGUAGE STRUCTURE AND SOCIAL USES

INDIVIDUAL DIFFERENCES AND CULTURAL INFLUENCES (p. 311)

SEX DIFFERENCES

Girls generally surpass boys in language development, especially during the preschool years.
The left hemisphere of girls develops more rapidly than in boys.

HOME ENVIRONMENT AND SOCIAL CLASS
Theories of social class differences in language development: language deficit theory and language difference theory.
Lower-class children hear relatively restricted speech; middle-class hear relatively elaborated speech.

DIALECTS
Regional and Social Group Dialects
Regional variations
Ethnic variations: Pidgin-English, Chicano, Black English
Black English
Pronunciation and grammar (e.g., use of the habitual tense) show differences from Standard English.
These differences may hinder the black child's communication within the majority society.

ISSUES IN ACTION (p. 319)

BILINGUALISM
Learning two languages does not necessarily lead to interference between the languages.
Learning two languages may promote cognitive development.
Poor school performance by bilinguals may stem from poor language models and lower economic status, among other factors.

LEARNING A "FOREIGN LANGUAGE"--immersion programs appear to be more effective than conventional ones.

SPEECH DISORDERS--faulty articulation and stuttering are the two most common disorders.
Faulty Articulation
Can occur through omission, substitution, or distortion of sounds
Two types of distortion are lisping and lalling.
Stuttering--involves interruptions in speech caused by repetitions, prolongations, and hesitations.
Three times as many boys as girls are afflicted.
Stuttering may develop through the interaction of biological and environmental factors.

ENCOURAGING LANGUAGE SKILLS IN SCHOOL
The Structured Approach--the Bereiter-Engelman program
Enrichment Techniques
Use of verbal expansions
Developing listening skills
Conversation, giving talks, and discussion
Choral speaking, singing, and dramatic play
Using Computers

Chapter 9

GUIDED REVIEW

1. The most basic sounds of a language are called _____. These sounds are combined to form _____, which are the basic units of _____ in a language.

2. Progress in language development can be measured in terms of MLUs and size of the child's _____.

3. The one-word sentences of toddlers consist mostly of _____; later, verbs, adjectives, and prepositions are used. Young children often _____ words, applying them to similar but incorrect objects or events.

4. By age _____ most children begin to use two-word sentences, which expand children's range of verbal expressions. They can communicate action- and object-_____, action-r_____, attribution, negation, and other meanings.

5. Brown has proposed that as children's MLUs increase they pass through five _____ of language development. Stage I begins with _____-word utterances that have a telegraphic quality. Stage II starts when children use three-word utterances in a _____-verb-_____ format. Their speech now includes grammatical markers, called _____, and the regular inflection rules may be applied to irregular cases--a phenomenon called _____. In stage III children become able to construct _____ and _____ statements. During stages IV and V two or more _____ can be combined with conjunctions and prepositions.

6. As their language skills develop, children can go beyond the appearance of sentences, or _____ structure, to comprehend the _____ structure. And they begin to comprehend and produce figures of speech, or _____.

7. Lenneberg (1967) holds the view that humans produce and use language largely because of _____ mechanisms. Chomsky holds a similar view and has proposed the existence of a _____ device in the brain which processes language. The LAD is used to explain the creative or _____ aspect of children's speech.

8. In many colonized societies, immigrant laborers had little opportunity to learn the dominant language and used _____ speech to communicate with people from other language backgrounds. Their children did not use this impoverished speech; instead, they formed new and more sophisticated languages called _____ languages.

9. Both imitation and reinforcement can account for some, but not all, aspects of language development. Imitation plays

Chapter 9   141

a larger role in the _____ children learn than in the grammar. Emotional reactions to words can develop through _____ processes.

10. The parallel between the development of cognition and language is clearly seen as children go from mastering concrete concepts to acquiring more _____ concepts. Although _____ is dependent on cognitive development, language may also affect _____; this notion is the basis of the _____ hypothesis.

11. Young children's communications are often incomplete and imprecise. Their descriptions and instructions are _____ in that they include information the listener does not know about. Children need to acquire knowledge of the "pragmatic" side of communication--being sensitive to the needs of the listener, becoming aware of the _____ of language, and knowing the social _____ of language.

12. There are sex differences in most aspects of language development; American _____ typically surpass _____. The superiority of girls may be due to their faster maturation, especially of the _____ of the brain, and to the finding that mothers in the U.S. _____ more to infant daughters than to sons.

13. Lower-class children typically have smaller _____ and use less complex _____ structures than middle-class children. The language _____ theory views poor children's grammar as inferior; the language _____ theory maintains that lower-class children simply learn different language rules.

14. Bernstein (1961) has shown that lower-class mothers use a _____ pattern of verbal interaction, and middle-class mothers use _____ patterns. But lower-class children are capable of producing more _____ sentences under relevant conditions.

15. A variation of a spoken language peculiar to a social group, region, or occupation is called a _____. In the U.S., social group dialects are sometimes based on minority group membership, such as the Hawaiian dialect called _____ English.

16. Black English differs from Standard English in several ways. For example some sounds, like th, are _____ differently in Black English. And some grammatical rules are different, especially those pertaining to the verb _____.

17. Children younger than 3 years of age can acquire two languages at the same time with little _____ if the languages are kept separate. Older children have a strongly established first language; they may experience

interference when learning a second language if their social environment does not provide a _____ context for the new language. Foreign language programs that use the _____ method appear to be more effective than those that use conventional methods.

18. Nearly 75% of children's speech disorders handled by speech therapists involve _____, such as lalling and _____, in which the child _____ sounds. A child who says "bo" for "both" misarticulates by _____ sounds.

19. Stuttering occurs most often among young (boys/girls). Stutterers tend to come from f_____ where there is a history of stuttering and where there are strong pressures for social competition and con_____, and to _____ competently at an early age.

20. One approach to enhancing language development that emphasizes drill and repetition is called the _____ approach. A second approach uses a broad variety of _____ techniques, such as puppetry, _____ speaking, and _____ play.

TERMS AND DEFINITIONS QUIZ

SET 1 (Match each term in the set with its definition below.):

INFLECTIONS, MEAN LENGTH OF UTTERANCE (MLU), MORPHEMES, OVEREXTEND, OVERREGULARIZATION, PHONEMES, SURFACE STRUCTURE, TELEGRAPHIC, WH-QUESTIONS

1. _____ The quality of young children's speech that is characterized by short choppy expressions containing only the words essential for communication.

2. _____ The basic vowel or consonant sounds that are distinguishable from one another in a language.

3. _____ Grammatical markers, such as s for plural and ed for past tense, which are added to words to modify their meanings.

4. _____ The average number of morphemes per utterance.

5. _____ To apply a given word in a generalized way for several objects that share one or more feature but have others that distinguish the objects.

6. _____ The smallest units of meaning in a language; they can be small words, such as "pin," or parts of a word, such as "pre" or "ing."

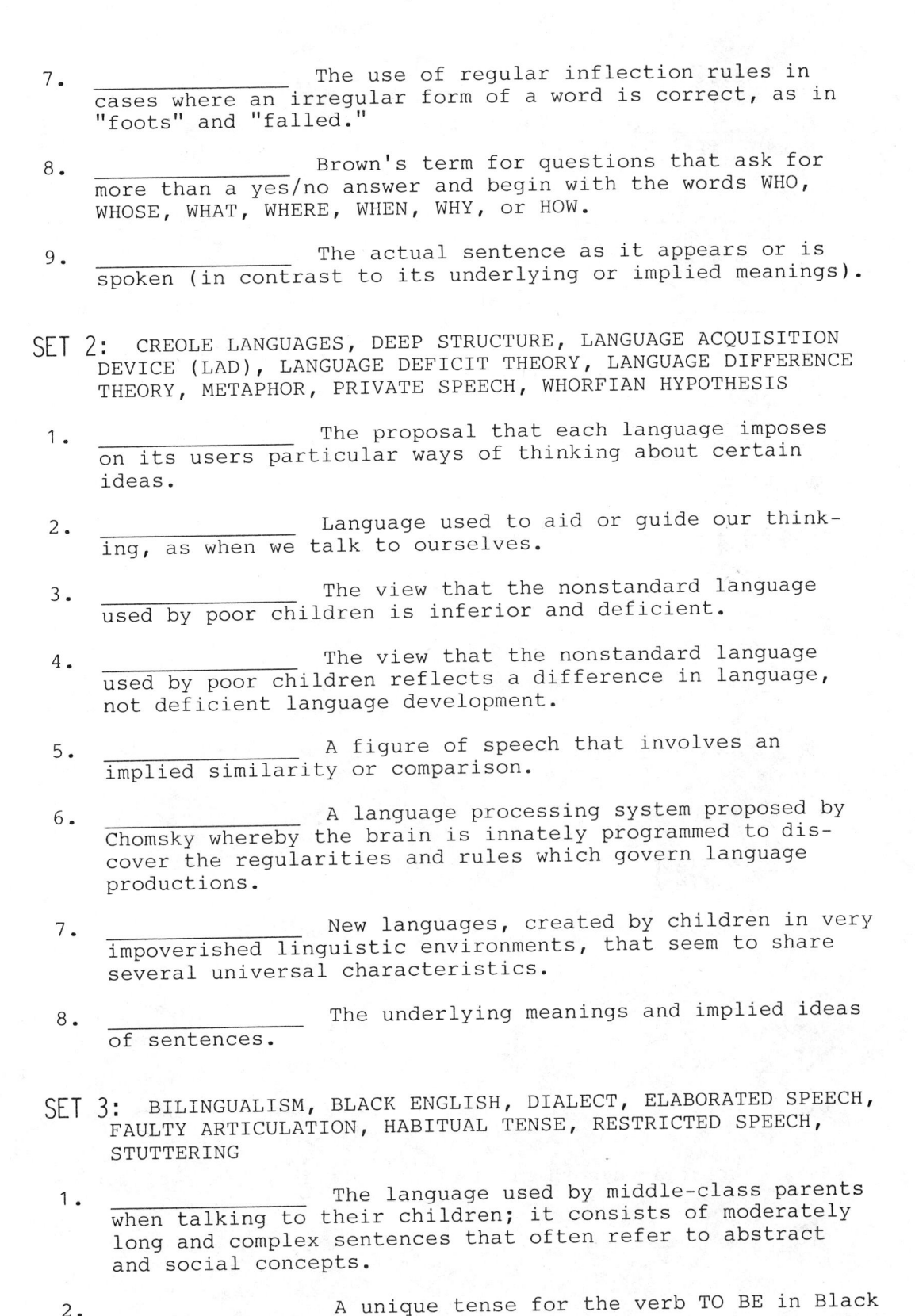

Chapter 9

7. _____ The use of regular inflection rules in cases where an irregular form of a word is correct, as in "foots" and "falled."

8. _____ Brown's term for questions that ask for more than a yes/no answer and begin with the words WHO, WHOSE, WHAT, WHERE, WHEN, WHY, or HOW.

9. _____ The actual sentence as it appears or is spoken (in contrast to its underlying or implied meanings).

SET 2: CREOLE LANGUAGES, DEEP STRUCTURE, LANGUAGE ACQUISITION DEVICE (LAD), LANGUAGE DEFICIT THEORY, LANGUAGE DIFFERENCE THEORY, METAPHOR, PRIVATE SPEECH, WHORFIAN HYPOTHESIS

1. _____ The proposal that each language imposes on its users particular ways of thinking about certain ideas.

2. _____ Language used to aid or guide our thinking, as when we talk to ourselves.

3. _____ The view that the nonstandard language used by poor children is inferior and deficient.

4. _____ The view that the nonstandard language used by poor children reflects a difference in language, not deficient language development.

5. _____ A figure of speech that involves an implied similarity or comparison.

6. _____ A language processing system proposed by Chomsky whereby the brain is innately programmed to discover the regularities and rules which govern language productions.

7. _____ New languages, created by children in very impoverished linguistic environments, that seem to share several universal characteristics.

8. _____ The underlying meanings and implied ideas of sentences.

SET 3: BILINGUALISM, BLACK ENGLISH, DIALECT, ELABORATED SPEECH, FAULTY ARTICULATION, HABITUAL TENSE, RESTRICTED SPEECH, STUTTERING

1. _____ The language used by middle-class parents when talking to their children; it consists of moderately long and complex sentences that often refer to abstract and social concepts.

2. _____ A unique tense for the verb TO BE in Black

English.

3. _____ Interruptions in speech that are produced by repetitions, prolongations, and hesitations (or "blockages") of sounds, syllables, or words.

4. _____ Speech disorders in which the child fails to sound out words properly by omitting, substituting, or distorting sounds.

5. _____ The ability to use two languages fluently.

6. _____ Any form or variety of a spoken language that is peculiar to a social group, region, or occupation.

7. _____ The language used by many lower-class parents when talking to their children; it consists of short, grammatically simple sentences which refer mostly to concrete objects and events.

8. _____ A dialect spoken by black people, generally in lower-class ghettos.

MATCHING QUIZ

1. ___ LAD
2. ___ telegraphic speech
3. ___ Black English
4. ___ social class differences
5. ___ vocabulary
6. ___ inflections
7. ___ stuttering
8. ___ overregularization
9. ___ Whorfian hypothesis
10. ___ morphemes

a. measure of language development
b. inappropriate use of a regular rule
c. smallest units of meaning
d. Noam Chomsky
e. language affects conceptual thinking
f. first occurs in Brown's stage I
g. habitual tense
h. more common in boys than girls
i. restricted versus elaborated speech
j. grammatical markers

SELF TEST

1. Each letter in the word "dog" represents a
   a. morpheme.
   b. phoneme.
   c. inflection.
   d. distortion.

2. Which of the following sounds are among NEITHER the earliest nor the latest sounds that children acquire in the English language?
   a. f and r
   b. v and j
   c. p and m
   d. h and w

3. A child's utterance, "Tommy's bike falled down," contains _____ morphemes.
   a. 4
   b. 6
   c. 8
   d. 20

4. At 18 months of age, children understand about 500 words and use one-half of these in speaking.
   a. True
   b. False

5. Which utterance best illustrates the child's awareness of the nonexistence of events or objects.
   a. "Sleep bed."
   b. "Mommy hat."
   c. "High doggy."
   d. "Done candy."

6. Which statement about stage II in language development is TRUE?
   a. Speech is no longer telegraphic.
   b. The subject-verb-object format does not yet appear in children's sentences.
   c. Children begin to use inflections in their speech.
   d. Children can only form plurals for words they know well.

7. Which of the following is an example of an inflection?
   a. the suffix ed for past tense
   b. the suffix s for plural
   c. the prefix ex to mean "former"
   d. all of the above

8. Questions beginning with "why" and "when" begin to appear in children's speech after questions with "what."
   a. True
   b. False

9. Sentences in the active voice are mastered earlier than

those in the passive voice.
a. True
b. False

10. The underlying meaning of a sentence, including implied ideas, is called
    a. surface structure.
    b. deep structure.
    c. private speech.
    d. elaborated speech.

11. Language development in children born deaf
    a. ceases if their parents don't use sign language.
    b. does not include cooing and babbling.
    c. shows similar progress to that of hearing children if they get special training.
    d. does not include one-word and two-word sentences at 1 year of age.

12. According to Chomsky (1972), the LAD works because it is biased toward the development of specific languages of the world.
    a. True
    b. False

13. Leonard (1975) demonstrated that modeling procedures are
    a. ineffective in helping children learn grammar.
    b. effective in teaching grammar, but not vocabulary.
    c. effective in teaching children subject-verb sentences.
    d. effective in teaching children to produce active sentences, but not passive sentences.

14. Children are most likely to imitate speech that is far below their own language level.
    a. True
    b. False

15. Research has shown that young children acquire ideas about _____ before they have the language to express these ideas.
    a. space
    b. time
    c. causality
    d. all of the above

16. Private speech is used to
    a. hide adult themes from children.
    b. direct special information toward a listener who does not comprehend instructions.
    c. communicate a falsehood.
    d. aid or guide one's thinking.

17. Which of the following statements about the child's ability to communicate is TRUE?
    a. Young children typically give instructions that take the listener's knowledge into account.

b. Young children often give idiosyncratic descriptions and instructions.
c. Second-graders are almost as proficient as eighth-graders in adapting their language to their audience.
d. None of the above are true.

18. When young children realize that a listener does not understand their descriptions or instructions, they
    a. simply repeat what they said in a louder voice.
    b. give an improved or clearer statement.
    c. act puzzled by the inability of the listener to understand.
    d. ignore the listener's difficulty and act as though there is no problem

19. Even 6-year-olds realize that a person who makes a statement that contains factual inconsistencies is lying.
    a. True
    b. False

20. Children from a lower socioeconomic class generally construct sentences that are less grammatical than middle-class children do.
    a. True
    b. False

21. Robinson (1965) studied the production of elaborated sentences by asking lower-class and middle-class boys to write a formal letter and an informal letter. This study found that
    a. social class differences were greatest for the informal letters.
    b. social class differences were absent for the formal letters.
    c. lower-class children generally do not use their full linguistic power.
    d. lower-class children simply have deficient linguistic abilities.

22. Which of the following aspects of the home were found by Elardo et al. (1977) to have a positive correlation with later language development?
    a. emotional distance of the mother
    b. toys that provide muscle activity and eye-hand coordination
    c. absence of the father in caretaking
    d. all of the above

23. Speakers of Black English often omit consonant sounds at the ends of words, saying _jus'_ instead of _just_, for instance.
    a. True
    b. False

24. An example of the habitual tense in Black English is
    a. "He OK?"

b. "She's workin'"
c. "She be cookin'"
d. "He's always readin'"

25. According to McLaughlin (1984), a child younger than about _____ years of age can learn two languages simultaneously with minimal interference if the languages are kept separate.
    a. 1
    b. 3
    c. 5
    d. 9

26. Immersion programs for teaching second languages in school
    a. are used only after elementary school.
    b. are carried out in classes that meet for a few hours a week.
    c. stress role learning methods.
    d. conduct the entire school experience on certain days of the week in the second language.

27. Difficulty in making "W" sounds is called lalling.
    a. True
    b. False

28. A child who says "ka" for "cat" shows the speech disorder called
    a. omission.
    b. distortion.
    c. substitution.
    d. stuttering.

29. Stuttering disorders afflict about 1% of school children.
    a. True
    b. False

30. Which of the following approaches would be the LEAST helpful in getting a shy child to speak?
    a. choral speaking
    b. singing
    c. puppetry
    d. show and tell

IMPORTANT DETAILS TO KNOW

1. What are three of the earliest and three of the latest phonemes to be acquired by children? See Figure 9.1. (p. 292)

2. From Highlight 9.3 define: emotional and verbal responsivity, maternal involvement, variety in stimulation, and appropriate play materials. (p. 315)

3. What are Pidgin-English and Chicano? (p. 317)

Chapter 9

4. In what ways does Black English differ in pronunciation from Standard English? (p. 317)

5. When does stuttering tend to begin, and what percentage of children develop this speech problem? (p. 322)

TEST YOUR RECALL

1. Name two different measures of language development. (p. 293)

2. List four basic meanings that children can communicate at the two-word stage. (p. 295)

3. Outline the major accomplishments at each of Roger Brown's stages of language development. See Table 9.2. (p. 297)

4. Give three examples of overregularization. (p. 298)

5. Describe how the language development of deaf children parallels that of hearing ones. (p. 299)

6. Show the difference between surface and deep structure with a sample sentence. (p. 302)

7. Cite facts which support Lenneberg's view that there are innate mechanisms for language development. (pp. 303-304)

8. What is the difference between pidgin speech and a creole language? (p. 304)

9. Explain how operant conditioning and imitation appear to be limited as explanations of language development. (pp. 305-306)

10. How do children use private speech? (pp. 308-309)

11. Characterize the way young children tend to give verbal instructions. (p. 310)

12. Summarize sex differences in language development. (p. 312)

13. Contrast restricted versus elaborated speech patterns. According to Bernstein (1961), how do these patterns relate to social class differences in language development? (p. 313)

14. List four aspects of the home environment that are strongly correlated with later language development. See Highlight 9.3. (p. 315)

15. State the principal ways that Black English differs from Standard English. (pp. 317-318)

Chapter 9

16. State the conditions cited by McLaughlin (1984) that produce interference in learning two languages. (p. 320)

17. What is the difference between lisping and lalling? (p. 321)

18. Discuss the possible role of biology and environment as causes of stuttering. (p. 322)

19. Describe the "structured approach" for enhancing language skills in school. (p. 323)

20. Make a list of specific "enrichment techniques" for promoting language development. (pp. 323-324)

ANSWER SECTION

GUIDED REVIEW:

1. phonemes; morphemes; meaning
2. vocabulary
3. nouns; overextend
4. 2; location; recipient
5. stages; two; subject; object; inflections; overregularization; questions; negative; clauses
6. surface; deep; metaphors
7. innate (inherited); language acquisition; productive
8. pidgin; creole
9. words (vocabularies); conditioning
10. abstract; language; thinking (cognition); Whorfian
11. idiosyncratic; structure; uses
12. girls; boys; left hemisphere; talk
13. vocabularies; sentence; deficit; difference
14. restricted; elaborated; elaborate
15. dialect; Pidgin
16. pronounced; to be
17. interference; supportive; immersion
18. misarticulations; lisping; distorts; omitting
19. boys; families; conformity; speak
20. structured; enrichment; choral; dramatic

TERMS AND DEFINITIONS QUIZ:

SET 1:
1. telegraphic
2. phonemes
3. inflections
4. mean length of utterance (MLU)
5. overextend
6. morphemes
7. overregularization
8. wh-questions
9. surface structure

SET 2:
1. Whorfian hypothesis

Chapter 9

2. private speech
3. language deficit theory
4. language difference theory
5. metaphor
6. language acquisition device (LAD)
7. creole languages
8. deep structure

SET 3:
1. elaborated speech
2. habitual tense
3. stuttering
4. faulty articulation
5. bilingualism
6. dialect
7. restricted speech
8. Black English

MATCHING QUIZ:

1. d (p. 304)
2. f (p. 297)
3. g (p. 318)
4. i (p. 313)
5. a (p. 293)
6. j (p. 297)
7. h (p. 322)
8. b (p. 298)
9. e (p. 308)
10. c (p. 293)

SELF TEST:

1. b (p. 292)
2. a (p. 292)
3. b (p. 293)
4. b (p. 293)
5. d (p. 296)
6. c (p. 297)
7. d (p. 297)
8. a (p. 300)
9. a (p. 300)
10. b (p. 302)
11. c (p. 304)
12. b (p. 304)
13. c (p. 307)
14. b (p. 307)
15. d (p. 308)
16. d (p. 308)
17. b (p. 310)
18. b (p. 311)
19. b (p. 311)
20. a (p. 312)
21. c (p. 314)
22. b (p. 315)
23. a (p. 317)
24. c (p. 318)
25. b (p. 320)
26. d (p. 320)
27. b (p. 321)
28. a (p. 321)
29. a (p. 322)
30. d (p. 321)

CHAPTER 10

Social Relations in the Family

SUMMARY IN OUTLINE

    PROLOGUE   (p. 331)

        Socialization is a reciprocal process that begins in infancy; it begins in the family, then expands into larger social networks.

    PARENT/CHILD RELATIONSHIPS   (p. 332)

        DIMENSIONS OF PARENTING--love-hostility and autonomy-control
            Four Styles of Parenting: (1) authoritative parents, (2) authoritarian parents, (3) permissive parents, and (4) indifferent/uninvolved parents--see Figure 10.1
            Do Parenting Styles Change?
                Parenting styles can be affected by parental feelings of stress, temperament of the child, unique factors in the family system, and the age of the child.

        METHODS OF DISCIPLINE PARENTS USE
            Power assertion, love-withdrawal, and induction
            Parents who rely on induction are more likely to have children who are better able to exercise self-control.
            Parents use different techniques for different situations.

    FAMILY STRUCTURE   (p. 338)

        FAMILY SIZE, BIRTH ORDER, AND SPACING
            In larger families parents often have fewer opportunities to interact and they may be more likely to use power assertion.
            Parents interact more with firstborns than laterborns.

Firstborns are slightly higher in competitiveness, educational aspiration, and self-esteem than laterborns.

SIBLING RELATONS
Older siblings serve as teachers, models, and caretakers for younger siblings.
Children distressed by separation from parents will turn to siblings for comfort and support.
Sibling rivalry is greatest when siblings are spaced 1 to 2 years apart; parents can help to minimize rivalry.

NONTRADITIONAL FAMILIES   (p. 341)

MOTHERS WHO WORK OUTSIDE THE HOME
Over 55% of mothers are employed; most, full-time.
Greater positive impact on daughters than sons
Some working mothers may feel guilty about working and become overprotective.
Maternal employment does not generally lead to negative psychological adjustment or delinquent behavior.

FATHERLESS FAMILIES
Children in fatherless families often have poor cognitive skills, but this results more from socioeconomic factors than from father absence.
Father absence in young boys is related to either "feminine" interests OR heightened "masculine" interests.
Few differences are found if the father leaves after age 5.
No sex-role differences for girls associated with father absence.

DIVORCE: ALTERED FAMILY RELATIONSHIPS--a third of all children experience the disruption of divorce.
  Only One Parent Now
    In the first year after a divorce children experience diminished parenting.
    Father contacts are usually severely reduced.
    Noncustodial parent contact is psychologically important to children's adjustment.
  When Father Gets Custody
    Children tend to adjust better when in the custody of the same-sex parent.
    Most kids say they want their parents to get back together.
    Joint custody is one way to balance children's contact with each parent.
  Stepparents--remarriage often benefits children.

THE EMOTIONAL STRESS OF DIVORCE
  Children need to process feelings of rejection, anger, and blame.
  Adapting to divorce can take several years.
  Achieving realistic hope regarding future relationships is an important accomplishment.
  Five principles for adapting to divorce: (1) Tell the

children in advance. (2) Encourage open communication.
(3) Gear explanations to the child's level of understanding. (4) Use support systems. (5) Encourage children's
contact with both parents.

SOCIALIZATION IN THE FAMILY   (p. 349)

   PROSOCIAL BEHAVIOR--positive social behaviors
      Children are more likely to help when they have something
       to gain and when the help is likely to be reciprocated.
      Helping and Sharing--increases with age
         A child's mood influences his or her prosocial
            behavior.
      Cooperation--children from more complex and urbanized
       societies tend to be less cooperative than those from
       rural societies.
      Prosocial Family Relations

   ANTISOCIAL BEHAVIOR: AGGRESSION
      When are Children Aggressive?--frustration and competition
      Types of Aggression
         Hostile aggression and instrumental aggression
         Young children show more aggression than older children
            overall, particularly boys, and much of this is
            instrumental aggression.
      Antisocial Family Relations
         Some families develop a coercive pattern of interaction.
         Childhood aggressive patterns can last into adulthood.

   PROCESSES IN SOCIAL DEVELOPMENT
      Innate Behavioral Tendencies
         Threat displays and appeasement postures
         Young children use submissive gestures when losing a
            fight.
         Reaction to an infant's "babyish" physical features
         Children's temperaments seem to be inborn.
      Operant Learning Processes
         Children's donations increased by praising their giving.
         Rewards have a stronger effect on antisocial than on
            prosocial behaviors.
      Observational Learning--models have a powerful influence
      Cognition
         Children are more willing to share if they understand
            proportions.
         Perspective taking influences social behavior.
         The cognitive process called attribution influences
            social behavior.

ISSUES IN ACTION   (p. 360)

   PROS AND CONS OF PUNISHMENT--current thought accepts the use
    of punishment in moderation.
      Does Punishment Work?
         Punishment suppresses behavior; immediate punishment
            is most effective.
         Children who expect punishment are less likely to

misbehave.
Social punishment, time-out, and response-cost
Extinction; rewarding alternative responses
<u>Side Effects of Punishment</u>--aggression and avoidance reactions
<u>Other Methods of Reducing Misbehavior</u>
Extinction, omission training, and induction techniques

MINIMIZING AGGRESSION IN CHILDREN

SEXUAL OFFENSES AGAINST CHILDREN
Types of offenses: forcible rape, nonforcible rape, sodomy, incest, and indecent liberties
Average age of victim is 11 years. Typically, offenders are male and victims are female.
Most offenders are people the victims already know.
Victims' families share some common characteristics and child-care practices.

GUIDED REVIEW

1. Schaefer (1959) identified two major dimensions of parenting styles: love-_____ and autonomy-_____. In Maccoby and Martin's (1983) classification system, _____ parenting involves a combination of love and control; _____ parenting involves hostility and autonomy.

2. Children who are reared by _____ parents tend to lack social competence, be standoffish, and have low self-esteem. Children of _____ parents tend to be impulsive and lacking in the ability to take responsibility.

3. To teach children self-control, parents use methods of _____, which include power assertion, love withdrawal, and _____. The disciplinary technique that is most likely to help children form internalized moral standards is _____.

4. The Responsive Parent Training Program stresses concrete methods derived from _____ principles. Other parent training programs emphasize _____ processes, and involve parents and children in discussion and reasoning sessions. In Parent Effectiveness Training the use of rewards and punishers is (encouraged/rejected).

5. Family structure can influence social development. Parents in large families tend to be less warmly involved with each child and use _____ discipline techniques. Firstborn children hold a special place of honor in the family, and they tend to show slightly higher competitiveness, _____ aspiration, and self-_____ than laterborns.

Chapter 10

6. Friction between children in a family, called _____, is usually stronger when siblings are spaced closer than _____ years apart and are the (opposite/same) sex.

7. Two-thirds of adopted children were born to _____ mothers. Today most children are placed quickly, and there are more interracial and _____ parent adoptions.

8. A majority of mothers of children under 18 years of age work outside the home. Daughters of employed mothers tend to view women more (positively/negatively) than daughters of nonworking mothers. The reaction of sons seems to depend on their socioeconomic class: _____ boys evaluate their fathers more negatively when their mothers work.

9. The number of children growing up in fatherless families has been increasing rapidly. Boys whose fathers leave after _____ years of age show little difference in masculinity compared to boys in two-parent families. If boys are younger when the father leaves, they tend to develop either somewhat _____ interests or heightened _____ interests and aggression. Father absence seems to have no long-term sex-role effects on _____.

10. Divorce disrupts the families of about one-_____ of all children by their middle teens. During the first year after the separation, the parenting of the custodial parent is usually _____. Children of divorce generally have very _____ contact with their father thereafter.

11. Helping and caring behaviors among people are called _____ behaviors. They are influenced by rewards, _____ development, and even people's moods. For instance when children were asked to think _____ thoughts, their donations were smaller than those asked to think _____ thoughts. Studies also show that hypocritical models tend to _____ children's donations.

12. There are cultural differences in competition and cooperation. Children from _____ or communal cultures show more cooperation than those from industrialized societies when not everyone can win.

13. The most thoroughly studied antisocial behavior is _____. Frustration and _____ are environmental conditions that promote aggression. Two types of aggression have been distinguished. When an act is committed with intent to injure another, it is termed _____ aggression. But if the act is intended as a means to a goal it is called _____ aggression. Hartup (1974) found that girls exhibit less aggression than boys and that younger children show more _____

aggression than older children.

14. Parents in virtually all cultures try to control children's aggression, but children in _____-family cultures seem to show more aggression than those from _____ families.

15. Social behavior is influenced by biological and learning processes. Two types of behaviors that seem to be under some innate control are _____ postures and people's positive reactions to the "_____" appearance of infants.

16. The role of operant conditioning in the development of social behavior is well documented, especially for anti-social conduct. Walters and Brown (1963) showed that children who were rewarded for hitting a Bobo doll were later more _____ in a competitive situation; their learning _____ from the doll to other children.

17. Bandura's experiments of filmed models demonstrated how _____ could be acquired through _____ learning. Other studies have shown that children tend to imitate the _____ behaviors of cold models.

18. Cognitive development influences social development. As children get older positive social behaviors increase, probably because they become better able to take the other person's _____ and to _____ whether help is needed.

19. Punishment does not eliminate the tendency to perform a "bad" behavior, but it can effectively _____ the act. To be most effective, punishment should occur _____ after the act. If punishment must be delayed the child should be told what behavior is being punished and _____.

20. There are many types of punishment. Gestures and criticism are examples of _____ punishment. When a child is told "stay in your room," the technique is called _____; but if the child has to pay a fine, the punishment is termed _____.

21. Punishment alone does not encourage positive behavior, so it is important to provide reinforcement for _____ responses. Punishment may have the side effects of producing _____ and _____ reactions.

22. Inappropriate behaviors can be reduced by methods other than punishment, including omission training, _____, and _____.

23. The majority of sexual offenses against children are classified as _____. Other offenses include

rape, sodomy, and _____. The average child victim is about _____ years of age, and many come from unstable or _____ families where neglect is common. The offender, usually known to the child, is almost always of the _____ gender, and the vast majority of victims are of the _____ gender.

TERMS AND DEFINITIONS QUIZ

SET 1 (Match each term in the set with its definition below.):

AUTHORITARIAN, AUTHORITATIVE, BIRTH ORDER, DISCIPLINE, INDIFFERENT/UNINVOLVED, INDUCTION, LOVE WITHDRAWAL, PERMISSIVE, POWER ASSERTION, SIBLING RIVALRY, SOCIALIZATION

1. _____ The parenting style in which the parent provides direction and strict limits, uses punishment techniques often, and fails to show interest in the child's needs and point of view.

2. _____ The parenting style in which the parent provides little guidance, uses inconsistent discipline, and is rejecting of and unresponsive to the child's needs and point of view.

3. _____ Methods used to instill self-control so that the individual can maintain acceptable and productive behavior independently and without supervision.

4. _____ Disciplinary techniques that involve threats or the use of punishment.

5. _____ The lifelong process of acquiring cultural and social skills, roles, expectations, and values.

6. _____ Punitive discipline techniques that involve, threaten, or suggest some form of parent/child separation and, therefore, loss or reduction in adult attention, support, and protection.

7. _____ Disciplinary techniques that involve reasoning and explaining why certain behaviors should and should not be performed.

8. _____ The parenting style in which parents provide clear limits and direction, but are also accepting of and responsive to the needs and persuasive arguments of the child.

9. _____ A child's birth rank position relative to his or her siblings.

10. _____ Competition between children in a family that may involve high levels of jealously, bickering,

teasing, and negative feelings.

11. _____ The parenting style in which the parent is accepting and loving, but exercises little control over the child's behavior.

SET 2: AGGRESSION, ANTISOCIAL BEHAVIOR, ATTRIBUTION, COERCIVE PATTERN, COMPETITION, DIMINISHED PARENTING, FRUSTRATION, HOSTILE AGGRESSION, INSTRUMENTAL AGGRESSION, JOINT CUSTODY, PROSOCIAL BEHAVIOR

1. _____ A type of social interaction that escalates into increasingly hostile exchanges by both parties.

2. _____ Social behaviors which promote or maintain supportive, caring, and friendly relationships between people.

3. _____ Social behaviors that promote or maintain inconsiderate, nonsupportive, and antagonistic relationships between people.

4. _____ Behavior that may cause physical or psychological injury to another person, including such acts as hitting, kicking, issuing insults, and yelling threats.

5. _____ The condition of being prevented from reaching a goal.

6. _____ A reduction in the quantity and quality of parenting a child receives from the custodial parent in the year or so following a divorce.

7. _____ The condition where two or more persons are striving for the same goal.

8. _____ The process by which we judge or explain the actions, motives, feelings, or intentions of others.

9. _____ Child custody arrangement in which the child lives with each parent half of the time.

10. _____ Behavior intended to injure another person as a goal in itself.

11. _____ Behavior involving injury to another person for the purpose of acquiring a goal.

SET 3: ALTERNATIVE RESPONSES, EXTINCTION, FORCIBLE RAPE, INCEST, INDECENT LIBERTIES, NONFORCIBLE RAPE, OMISSION TRAINING, RESPONSE COST, SOCIAL PUNISHMENT, SODOMY, TIME-OUT

1. _____ A method of suppressing behavior by rewarding the person for NOT performing undesirable behavior.

2. _____ The process whereby a behavioral tendency is weakened or eliminated by withholding the stimuli (e.g., reinforcer or US) that maintained it.

3. _____ Sexual intercouse between persons of close kinship.

4. _____ A wide variety of illegal sexual acts, including genital exposure, sexual manipulation, physical advances, and the use of obscene language.

5. _____ A method of suppressing behavior by providing opportunities to perform other, more desirable, behaviors instead.

6. _____ A method of suppressing behavior by taking away reinforcers.

7. _____ Sexual offense whereby threats, force, or drugs are used in order to achieve intercourse.

8. _____ Sexual offense involving intercouse between an adult of legal age and a minor who does not resist.

9. _____ An unpleasant social consequence (e.g., a frown or reprimand) for one's behavior.

10. _____ A method of suppressing behavior by removing the person from opportunities to gain rewards.

11. _____ Legally defined as oral or anal intercourse.

MATCHING QUIZ

1. ___ love withdrawal   a. wrongdoer pays a fine
2. ___ permissive parenting   b. style based on competent influence
3. ___ power assertion   c. leads to impulsiveness in children
4. ___ cooperation   d. boys benefit more than girls

5. ___ sibling rivalry   e. diminished parenting

6. ___ father custody   f. closely spaced and same sex

7. ___ response-cost   g. more common among rural than urban children

8. ___ authoritative parenting h. antisocial family relations

9. ___ divorce   i. more common in very large families

10. ___ coercive pattern   j. giving someone the "silent treatment"

SELF TEST

1. Which statement about parent/child relations is TRUE?
   a. In Europe, fathers spend less time with their children than mothers do.
   b. In the United States, fathers spend less time playing with their children than mothers do.
   c. The amount of time parents spend with their children differs from one culture to another.
   d. All of the above are true.

2. The authoritative parenting style involves Schaefer's _____ dimension.
   a. love and control
   b. hostility and control
   c. love and autonomy
   d. hostility and autonomy

3. Children who lack social competence, are standoffish, and have low self-esteem are likely to have parents who generally use the _____ style of parenting.
   a. authoritarian
   b. authoritative
   c. permissive
   d. indifferent/uninvolved

4. The indifferent/uninvolved parenting style involves Schaefer's _____ dimensions.
   a. love and control
   b. hostility and control
   c. love and autonomy
   d. hostility and autonomy

5. Children whose parents often use the power assertion method of discipline show a strong ability to resist temptation.
   a. True
   b. False

6. Which parent training program takes differences in developmental levels of the child into account?
   a. Responsive Parent Training Program
   b. Parent Effectiveness Training (P.E.T.)
   c. both of the above
   d. none of the above

7. Children think that parents should be permissive in their childrearing methods.
   a. True
   b. False

8. Firstborn and laterborn children are about equally likely to become leaders and successful in later professions.
   a. True
   b. False

9. Dunn and Kendrick (1982) found that children whose mothers talked to them about the new sibling's _____ were much friendlier toward the baby 14 months later.
   a. wishes
   b. likes
   c. interest in the elder child
   d. all of the above

10. Most infants who become adopted are
    a. born to parents who are married.
    b. orphaned.
    c. placed by 3 months of age.
    d. placed after 12 months of age.

11. Fathers of preschoolers often perform more household chores if their wives are employed than if their wives are full-time homemakers.
    a. True
    b. False

12. The percentage of American children who live with only one parent has increased since 1960.
    a. True
    b. False

13. Studies comparing children in families with and without resident fathers have found that father-absent
    a. girls become overly dependent.
    b. boys become feminine in their behavior regardless of how their mothers treat them.
    c. children have stronger cognitive skills.
    d. and father-present girls are similar in their femininity and aggressiveness.

14. A study of contact with noncustodial parents after the divorce found that about _____ % of the children had not seen their fathers in the past 5 years.
    a. 10
    b. 25

c. 35
d. 50

15. Research on the effect of moods on children's prosocial behavior has shown that, compared to children in a control group, those who were instructed to think about _____ donated more money to other children.
    a. sad events
    b. happy events
    c. being in school
    d. all of the above

16. According to the text, aggressive behavior includes acts that
    a. are accidental.
    b. cause physical injury.
    c. cause psychological injury.
    d. both b and c.

17. Compared with extended family cultures, in nuclear families husbands and wives have less intimacy in their relationship.
    a. True
    b. False

18. If Angie pushed Kevin down because he teased her, Angie's act would be an example of _____ aggression.
    a. competitive
    b. frustrative
    c. hostile
    d. instrumental

19. Hartup's (1974) research found that aggression becomes less instrumental and physical as children get older.
    a. True
    b. False

20. In a coercive pattern of interaction, the encounter
    a. ends at the start because the coerced individual submits immediately.
    b. involves induction methods which prevent hostility.
    c. escalates into a hostile exchange.
    d. both a and b.

21. In Fullard and Reiling's (1976) study of people's preferences for infant and adult faces, second- to sixth-graders preferred _____ faces and older subjects preferred _____ faces.
    a. infant; infant
    b. adult; adult
    c. infant; adult
    d. adult; infant

22. Children with relatively "easy" temperaments tend to be more aggressive than "difficult" children are.

a. True
b. False

23. As children get older, they become
    a. more selfish and less willing to share possessions.
    b. less likely to cooperate with others.
    c. more likely to act aggressively when they cannot use a toy they want.
    d. none of the above.

24. Research on cognitive factors in antisocial behavior has found that
    a. children's perspective-taking skills are not related to their antisocial actions.
    b. perspective-taking skills cannot be trained.
    c. aggressive children seem to "take things personally."
    d. children cannot make attributions until they reach 12 years of age.

25. Skinner's (1938) research on the effects of punishment on the operant behavior of rats showed that punishment
    a. eliminated the behavior.
    b. suppressed the behavior temporarily.
    c. strengthened the behavior temporarily.
    d. had no effect at all.

26. Deducting a dime from a child's allowance for each serious misdeed is an example of a type of punishment called
    a. response cost.
    b. time out.
    c. omission training.
    d. extinction.

27. Because punishment can produce frustration, it may cause the child to be aggressive.
    a. True
    b. False

28. Sexual intercourse with someone of close kinship is called
    a. sodomy.
    b. nonforcible rape.
    c. indecent liberties.
    d. incest.

29. The ratio of reported heterosexual-to-homosexual incidents of sexual offenses against children is 3 to 1.
    a. True
    b. False

30. In most reported cases of sexual offenses against children, the
    a. child does not know the offender.
    b. offender uses physical force against the child.
    c. child's biological father lives with the child.
    d. victim is a girl.

Chapter 10

IMPORTANT DETAILS TO KNOW

1. Make a table of the various dimensions of parenting, describing what the children tend to be like who experience each parenting style. (p. 333)

2. What proportion of adopted children are from unwed mothers? See Highlight 10.2. (p. 342)

3. What were the findings in Hartup's (1974) study concerning the children who showed the most hostile aggression? (p. 352)

4. At about what age do girls show a dramatic shift toward preferring to look at pictures of babies than of adults? (p. 355)

5. How many children are the objects of sexual offenses each year? What proportion of the offenders are male and what proportion of the victims are female? (p. 364)

TEST YOUR RECALL

1. What are Schaefer's (1959) two major dimensions of parenting styles? (p. 332)

2. Outline Maccoby and Martin's (1983) four parenting styles in terms of parent and child characteristics. (p. 333)

3. What might be the effects of the parental overuse of power assertion and love withdrawal on children? (pp. 334-335)

4. Describe the Responsive Parent Training Program. See Highlight 10.1. (p. 336)

5. Discuss the advantages and limitations of the induction method for disciplining children. (pp. 335-337)

6. In what ways and for what reasons do parents typically treat firstborns differently from laterborns? (p. 339)

7. How does spacing influence children's socialization in the family? (p. 340)

8. Describe the typical roles of older siblings--both boys and girls--toward their younger siblings. (pp. 340-341)

9. Discuss how parents could minimize sibling rivalry upon the birth of another baby. (p. 341)

10. How and when should adoptive parents tell their child about being adopted. See Highlight 10.2. (p. 342)

11. How do daughters and sons feel about their working mothers?

(p. 343)

12. To what extent do children in fatherless families face special risks in sex-role socialization? (p. 344)

13. How is the custodial parent often affected within the first year after a divorce. (p. 345)

14. Is maternal custody always the best arrangement for children? Explain. (p. 346)

15. List five principles that can help parents and children cope more effectively with divorce. (pp. 347-348)

16. How does mood affect children's willingness to make donations? (p. 350)

17. What cultural differences have been found in children's cooperative behavior? (pp. 350-351)

18. What cultural variations in children's aggression were found through the Six Cultures Project? See Highlight 10.3. (p. 353)

19. Give one example each of hostile and instrumental aggression. (p. 352)

20. Summarize in one sentence each the three lines of evidence supporting the view that human social development is partly influenced by innate factors. (pp. 354-356)

21. Describe the Bandura et al. studies (1961, 1963b) on children's imitation of aggressive models. (p. 357)

22. What were the principal findings of the studies by Dodge and Frame (1982) on children's attribution and aggression? (p. 359)

23. List the pros and cons of punishment. (pp. 361-362)

24. What alternatives to punishment could parents use? (p. 363)

25. Cite several ways of minimizing aggression in children. (p. 363)

26. Characterize the average child victim of sexual abuse. (pp. 364-365)

27. How do family characteristics and child-care practices relate to child sexual abuse? (p. 365)

Chapter 10

ANSWER SECTION

GUIDED REVIEW:

1. hostility; control; authoritative; indifferent/uninvolved
2. authoritarian; permissive
3. discipline; induction; induction
4. basic learning; cognitive; rejected
5. power-assertive; educational; esteem
6. sibling rivalry; 3; same
7. unwed; single
8. positively; lower-class
9. 5; feminine; masculine; girls
10. third; diminished; little
11. prosocial; cognitive; sad; happy; reduce
12. rural (semiagricultural)
13. aggression; competition; hostile; instrumental; instrumental
14. extended; nuclear
15. submissive; babyish
16. aggressive; generalized
17. aggression; observational; aggressive
18. perspective; assess
19. suppress; immediately; why
20. social; time-out; response-cost
21. alternative; aggression; avoidance
22. extinction; induction
23. indecent liberties; incest; 11; broken (divorced); male; female

TERMS AND DEFINITIONS QUIZ:

SET 1:
1. authoritarian
2. indifferent/uninvolved
3. discipline
4. power assertion
5. socialization
6. love withdrawal
7. induction
8. authoritative
9. birth order
10. sibling rivalry
11. permissive

SET 2:
1. coercive pattern
2. prosocial behavior
3. antisocial behavior
4. aggression
5. frustration
6. diminished parenting
7. competition
8. attribution
9. joint custody
10. hostile aggression
11. instrumental aggression

Chapter 10

SET 3:
1. omission training
2. extinction
3. incest
4. indecent liberties
5. alternative responses
6. response cost
7. forcible rape
8. nonforcible rape
9. social punishment
10. time-out
11. sodomy

MATCHING QUIZ:

1. j (p. 335)
2. c (p. 333)
3. i (p. 338)
4. g (p. 350)
5. f (p. 341)
6. d (p. 346)
7. a (p. 361)
8. b (p. 333)
9. e (p. 345)
10. h (p. 353)

SELF TEST:

1. d (p. 332)
2. a (p. 333)
3. a (p. 333)
4. d (p. 333)
5. b (p. 334)
6. d (p. 336)
7. b (p. 337)
8. a (p. 340)
9. d (p. 341)
10. c (p. 342)
11. a (p. 343)
12. a (pp. 343-344)
13. d (p. 344)
14. c (pp. 345-346)
15. b (p. 350)
16. d (p. 351)
17. b (p. 353)
18. c (p. 352)
19. a (p. 352)
20. c (p. 353)
21. d (p. 355)
22. b (p. 356)
23. d (p. 358)
24. c (p. 359)
25. b (p. 360)
26. a (p. 361)
27. a (p. 362)
28. d (p. 364)
29. b (p. 365)
30. d (p. 365)

CHAPTER 11

Socialization and Society: Peers, School, and Television

SUMMARY IN OUTLINE

<u>PEER RELATIONSHIPS</u> (p. 372)

    THE DEVELOPMENT OF PEER INTERACTION--by age 4, children spend more time with peers than with adults.

    CHILDREN PLAYING TOGETHER
        Parten's four types of play: solitary play, parallel play, associative play, and cooperative play.
        Peer negotiations aid the development of communication and social skills.

    HOW PEERS SOCIALIZE EACH OTHER
        <u>Conditioning by Peers</u>--children often use social reinforcers.
        <u>Modeling and Imitation</u>

    DEVELOPING FRIENDSHIPS
        Toddlers show elementary forms of friendship.
        School-age friendships become increasingly cooperative, intimate, and durable.
        Factors that influence the development of friendships include self-disclosure, age, race, and gender.

<u>PEER GROUPS AND SOCIALIZATION</u> (p. 379)

    A peer group has durable social relationships, shared values and goals, plus social roles and status among individuals.

    THE FORMATION OF GROUPS
        Group structure often becomes formalized by age 11.

Sherif et al. study of boys' groups

GROUP STRUCTURE: POPULARITY AND LEADERSHIP
Sociometric techniques--sociogram
Popular children are usually healthy, vigorous, mature, and attractive.
Unpopular children display negative characteristics--see Table 11.2.
Children's and teachers' social judgments of others are influenced by a person's physical attractiveness.
Popular children also tend to (1) be socially outgoing, (2) have friendly dispositions, and (3) be intellectually and/or athletically capable.

CONFORMITY
Conformity is strongest during late childhood and early adolescence.
Conformity is greatest in situations where ambiguity or uncertainty are high.
Middle-status children are the most likely to conform.
Children who are anxious, dependent, and lacking in self-confidence tend to be more conforming.

PREJUDICE AND CONFLICT
Sherif's research with boys--common goals helped reduce intergroup conflict.

PEER RELATIONS IN OTHER CULTURES
Peer groups in the Soviet Union--classroom "links"
Peer relations show similarities across cultures.

SCHOOLS AND SOCIAL DEVELOPMENT (p. 386)

PRESCHOOLS
Day-care centers tend to provide a homelike environment.
Nursery schools emphasize developing the child's social and cognitive skills.
Intellectual and social outcomes of preschool experience

ELEMENTARY SCHOOL
Four functions: (1) teaching academic skills, (2) promoting society's goals and values, (3) encouraging health and fitness, and (4) improving social skills.
Traditional classrooms--action zone
Open classroom model and structured classroom model
Computer Assisted Instruction (CAI)

THE TEACHER

SOCIAL CLASS AND RACE RELATIONS
Most teachers are middle-class and 90% are white.
Lower-class children may come into conflict with teachers and other school authorities.
Although the effects of school desegregation have not been encouraging, cooperative learning programs can improve interracial relations.

Chapter 11   173

TELEVISION (p. 394)

    HOW MUCH TV DO CHILDREN WATCH?
        Typical child, after age 3, watches 20 to 30 hours of TV per week.
        Viewing patterns vary with age, sex, social class, and race.

    HOW TV ATTRACTS ATTENTION--formal features
        High action and pace
        Visual and sound effects

    TV VIOLENCE AND AGGRESSION
        Correlational studies established that child aggression is related to viewing TV violence.
        Experimental studies have found that watching TV violence causes aggression in children, and vice versa.

    PROSOCIAL AND COGNITIVE CONTENT OF TV--some programs are effective in promoting children's prosocial and cognitive skills.

    SOCIAL ATTITUDES AND TV
        TV presents several types of social distortions by under-representing and stereotyping age, gender, and ethnic groups.

ISSUES IN ACTION (p. 400)

    PROMOTING SOCIALIZATION IN THE SCHOOL--children's popularity can be enhanced by training in social skills.
        The Role of the Teacher
           "Detached" versus "active" teachers
           Teachers can (1) evaluate and reward specific behaviors, (2) appropriately structure the activities, (3) select low-competition activities, and (4) use modeling and coaching techniques.
        Enlisting the Aid of Peers

    RELEASING HOSTILITY: CATHARSIS
        Very little support exists for the catharsis position.
        Overwhelming evidence that the observation or expression of hostility promotes future aggression in children.

GUIDED REVIEW

1. Social interaction with age-mates, or _____, increases with age. Waldrop and Halverson (1975) found that sociable behaviors of individuals are fairly (stable/unstable) across age; and that boys were more likely to play in _____, rather than with one other child.

2. Parten (1932-33) identified four types of play: solitary

play, _____ play, associative play, and _____ play. The type of play that begins to decline earliest is _____ play. Because _____ play has goals and rules, it helps children to solve social conflicts.

3. Peers reward each other chiefly with _____ reinforcers. Children who give many rewards receive _____ rewards. A victim of aggression can reduce future attacks by _____ strongly.

4. Hartup and Coates (1967) demonstrated that children's sharing could be increased through _____. Other studies have shown that observational learning can _____ shyness and childhood fears.

5. Toddlers who have regular contact with agemates form _____, or at least preferences for certain children over others. Most friendships during the preschool years form and end quickly, and center around _____ activities. Preschoolers show a distinct preference for _____-sex friends.

6. A peer _____ is not just a bunch of kids. It is durable and includes status and _____ relationships. Peer groups in early childhood have less influence and are relatively unstructured and un_____ compared with those in later childhood.

7. Social relationships in groups can be measured by _____ techniques. When children are asked to name their favorite companions, it is possible to construct a _____ of their social preferences. Group leadership and _____ can be determined in this way.

8. The popularity of children correlates with ratings of their physical _____. Children are more likely to attribute negative social behaviors to _____ peers, whereas attractive peers are judged to have _____ behaviors. Also, the social desirability of children's first _____ is related to their popularity.

9. Children who are leaders tend to be popular. But successful leadership also depends on the child's _____ in relevant task skills.

10. The Costanzo and Shaw (1966) study of peer influence on the individual's judgments found that _____ is greatest during late childhood, and that (boys/girls) were more likely to conform. Other work has found that conformity to outside pressure is increased in situations that are _____, when pressure is applied to peer group members of _____ status, and where the pressured children have little c_____ in themselves.

Chapter 11   175

11. Sherif's work with older boys demonstrated that intergroup conflict and prejudice could be increased through _____ games. Later on, conflict was reduced by having the two groups work toward a common _____ that required _____.

12. In Soviet classrooms peer groups, called _____, seem to foster responsibility among group members.

13. American preschools that are intended to create a homelike environment for youngsters of working mothers are called _____, while _____ have traditionally catered to nonworking mothers. Both types attempt to develop children's social skills; typically, nursery schools put more emphasis on the development of _____ skills.

14. Preschool programs designed to help disadvantaged children keep up with middle-class children are called _____. Children who attend these programs are less likely to be "left-back" in school later, to become delinquent, and to be _____ after leaving high school.

15. In traditional classrooms, teachers generally use lectures and drills. Because of the seating arrangement, student-teacher interactions are often restricted to the "_____." One new classroom approach which emphasizes individual learning in a portable and fluid working space is called the _____ model. Another individualized approach, called the _____ model, stresses the acquisition of _____ academic skills using reinforcement, feedback, and highly structured learning materials. Children from structured classrooms show higher math and _____ scores and greater task _____; those from open classrooms show higher nonverbal _____ scores and are more likely to c_____ with other children. Some schools are trying _____-Assisted Instruction.

16. Lower-class students often encounter conflict when confronted with the _____ values of teachers and schools. At home their parents are likely to ignore academic goals or striving, and their own low motivation and self-_____ hamper success. So far there is little evidence that desegregation has reduced _____ or raised black _____; but some studies suggest that black students' scores on tests of _____ may have increased.

17. The typical child watches TV _____ hours each week. Generally, viewing time _____ during childhood, _____ in adolescence, and tends to be higher among _____-class children.

18. Children's attention to TV depends on the _____ features of the visual and sound production. Young chil-

dren often don't understand the shows they watch, missing the central _____ and mistaking real and nonreal events. Nevertheless, TV is an effective _____ medium.

19. Studies of televised aggression clearly show there is a strong relationship between the amount of _____ children watch and their aggressive tendencies. This relationship is _____--watching violence makes children more aggressive, and being aggressive leads them to watch more aggression. Children at 8 or 9 years of age may be especially _____ to the influence of TV.

20. Several television programs have been designed to enhance children's development. For example, "Mr. Rogers' Neighborhood" has been shown to promote _____ behaviors in young children. And "Sesame Street" has been effective in raising children's _____ skills. Children who watched "Sesame Street" the most enjoyed school (more/less).

21. TV presents a _____ view of social reality. Greenberg (1982) reported that only about 15% of the characters on TV were children, _____, and old people combined. Only about _____% of all TV characters are women. Sex role behaviors and ethnic minorities are often depicted in _____ or traditional ways.

22. Poorly socialized and *is* _____ children are more likely to have problems later on. Teachers can model, evaluate, and _____ prosocial behaviors, and they can _____ or select activities which engage children in positive social behaviors. Teachers in other cultures, such as in the Soviet Union, make effective use of _____ to promote socialization.

23. The "safe" release of emotional energy, called _____, was thought to be a "healthy" process that would prevent intensely violent acts. However research with children has found that the observation and expression of hostility promotes _____. Playing with aggression-related _____ or watching aggressive models can increase children's aggression. The expression of hostility sometimes seems to reduce aggression, but this may be because it _____ people from their frustration and anger. Puppetry and _____-play can be used effectively to show children how to solve social conflicts peacefully.

TERMS AND DEFINITIONS QUIZ

SET 1 (Match each term in the set with its definition below.):

ASSOCIATIVE PLAY, CLIQUES, COOPERATIVE PLAY, FRIENDSHIP, PARALLEL PLAY, PEER GROUP, PEERS, SELF-DISCLOSURE, SOCIOMETRIC TECHNIQUES, SOLITARY PLAY

1. _____ Research procedures used to measure social relationships, such as popularity and leadership, in group structures.

2. _____ Playing alone and independently of others.

3. _____ Sharing feelings, concerns, and other personal information.

4. _____ A group of age-mates with an established, durable set of social relationships, including individual roles and status, and shared values and goals.

5. _____ Play where there is some sharing and interaction, but little coordinated activity, reciprocity, or mutual regard among participants.

6. _____ Play involving several people engaged in a single task that has shared rules and goals.

7. _____ Small, intimate groups of peers.

8. _____ Age-mates.

9. _____ A strong emotional bond that involves frequent social interactions and mutual emotional support, understanding, and acceptance.

10. _____ Playing beside another person, and perhaps engaging in similar activities, but without interacting.

SET 2: CATHARSIS, COMPUTER-ASSISTED INSTRUCTION (CAI), DAY-CARE CENTERS, FORMAL FEATURES, LINKS, NURSERY SCHOOLS, OPEN CLASSROOM MODEL, SOCIOGRAM, STRUCTURED CLASSROOM MODEL

1. _____ The visual and sound characteristics that the child experiences while viewing TV.

2. _____ In psychoanalytic theory, the "safe" release of pent-up hostile energy, by, for example, engaging in mild acts of aggression, watching aggressive sports or shows, or expressing one's feelings verbally.

3. _____ An individualized classroom approach where students have much freedom in choosing learning activities and schedules.

4. _____ An individualized classroom approach emphasizing the mastery of common learning objectives through the use of structured materials that are logically ordered toward increasing complexity.

5. _____ Custodial settings for the daytime care of children whose parents work or are otherwise unavailable.

6. _____ A diagram depicting social preferences among members of a group.

7. _____ Preschools that prepare children for school with academic and social activities; usually the children attend for only 10 to 20 hours a week.

8. _____ Teaching in which lessons are presented by a computer, which coaches the student much as a human tutor would do.

9. _____ Groups of children in Soviet classrooms who share mutual responsibility for controlling each member's behavior in striving toward group goals.

MATCHING QUIZ

1. ___ middle-status children
2. ___ sociogram
3. ___ peer ratings
4. ___ physical attractiveness
5. ___ catharsis
6. ___ cooperative play
7. ___ structured classroom model

a. leads to higher reading and math skills
b. basis for "release therapy"
c. involves shared goals and rules
d. reveals social preferences within a group
e. correlated with popularity
f. are the most likely to conform
g. strong predictor of later emotional problems

SELF TEST

1. Children's social interactions with peers do NOT generally include sharing toys until _____ of age.
   a. 1 year
   b. 2 years
   c. 3 years
   d. 4 years

2. Waldrop and Halverson (1975) found that children who were outgoing and helpful at 2½ years of age tended to remain sociable at 7.
   a. True
   b. False

3. During a session of playing, children's parallel play seems to bridge the gap in going from _____ to _____ play.
   a. associative; cooperative
   b. cooperative; solitary
   c. solitary; associative
   d. cooperative; associative

4. Parten's (1932-33) study of social participation found that the most frequently occurring type of play at 2 years of age is
   a. associative.
   b. cooperative.
   c. parallel.
   d. solitary.

5. The study by Hartup and Coates (1967) of the influence of modeling on prosocial behavior found that the
   a. children would imitate a prosocial act only if the model was reinforced for the act.
   b. children's willingness to share was reduced by watching a model donate trinkets to another child.
   c. children did not imitate simply because of the consequences of the model experienced.
   d. none of the above.

6. Toddlers who attend day care often establish durable friendships with specific peers.
   a. True
   b. False

7. Young children's preferences for playing with same-sex children
   a. becomes increasingly strong during grade school.
   b. is shown by both boys and girls.
   c. is not affected by social experiences.
   d. both a and b

8. In Sherif's research, the boys at the summer camp were assigned to two groups, and
   a. efforts were made by the researchers to prevent animosity from developing between the groups.

Chapter 11

b. no efforts were made to promote cohesiveness within each group.
c. these groups were very similar in athletic ability and intelligence.
d. these groups quickly joined together into a single group with one leadership hierarchy.

9. Sociograms taken on a group of children can reveal different patterns of relationships if the sociograms are based on different questions, such as "Which three classmates do you like the most?" and "Which three classmates would you like to have on your basketball team?"
   a. True
   b. False

10. Which of the following characteristics is most likely to enhance a child's acceptance by a typical group of peers?
    a. being mentally retarded
    b. being physically attractive
    c. having an unusual first name
    d. having greater than average intelligence

11. Which one of the following names is likely to have the greatest social disadvantage to an American child's popularity?
    a. Nancy
    b. Anne
    c. Diana
    d. Inez

12. Conformity to one's peer group is greatest at about 9 years of age.
    a. True
    b. False

13. Ambiguity and uncertainty _____ the child's tendency to conform to the views of others.
    a. decrease greatly
    b. decrease slightly
    c. increase
    d. do not affect

14. In Russian classrooms, the success of the link in controlling each member's behavior has no effect on the rewards the link members receive from the teacher.
    a. True
    b. False

15. Children who have attended preschool are _____ than children who have not.
    a. more independent
    b. less polite
    c. more aggressive
    d. all of the above

16. Adams and Biddle (1970) found that the students who have

the most interaction with their teachers in traditional classrooms are those who sit _____ of the room.
a. in the back
b. toward the sides
c. in the front-central region
d. in the "structured zone"

17. Compared with traditional classroom methods, the _____ place greater emphasis on requiring active student participation in learning.
a. open classroom model
b. structured classroom model
c. both a and b
d. none of the above

18. School children from the lower socioeconomic classes are likely to
a. have teachers who are also from the lower classes.
b. find many rewards and encouragement for school achievement at home.
c. have difficulty working toward far-off goals.
d. all of the above.

19. Overall, evidence from studies following school desegregation indicates that
a. self-esteem of minority children increases greatly.
b. cooperative learning programs seem to improve interracial relations among classmates.
c. school achievement of blacks declines.
d. none of the above.

20. Which of the following statements about childhood TV viewing is TRUE?
a. The typical 6-year-old watches less than 15 hours of TV a week.
b. Boys and girls spend about the same amount of time watching TV.
c. TV viewing time decreases after 3 years of age.
d. None of the above is true.

21. The factors that make up the formal features of TV include _____, such as rapid variation in scenes and characters.
a. pace
b. visual aspects
c. sound aspects
d. action

22. The typical viewer probably sees about 300 killings a year on TV.
a. True
b. False

23. Longitudinal studies of Finnish and American children found that the relationship between children's aggression and watching TV violence is bidirectional.

a. True
b. False

24. Watching programs, such as "Mr. Rogers' Neighborhood," that are designed to benefit children's development appears to enhance children's
    a. understanding others' feelings.
    b. cooperation.
    c. sharing.
    d. all of the above.

25. Blacks seem to be the only ethnic group whose depiction on TV has improved over the years.
    a. True
    b. False

26. Children who are unpopular and poorly socialized are more likely to drop out of school than other children are.
    a. True
    b. False

27. Oden and Asher (1977) demonstrated that _____ can be an effective technique for enhancing the social relationships of isolated children.
    a. parallel play
    b. associative play
    c. sociometrics
    d. coaching

28. Classmates rarely reinforce unruly behavior by other students.
    a. True
    b. False

29. Proponents of catharsis as a "constructive" and "safe" way to release hostility have suggested that children should _____ when angry.
    a. hit a punching bag
    b. stamp their feet
    c. draw violent pictures
    d. all of the above

30. Which of the following statements about catharsis is FALSE?
    a. Children who play with toy guns are more likely to fight with other children.
    b. Expressing or observing hostility releases hostility and reduces further aggression.
    c. Aggression toward a substitute object may simply distract the child from the originally frustrating situation.
    d. None of the above is false.

IMPORTANT DETAILS TO KNOW

1. What social behaviors with age-mates do children show at age 2 years? (pp. 372-373)

2. What are the characteristics of Parten's four types of play? Which types predominate in 2-year-olds? (pp. 373-374)

3. What are peer groups like in the early grade school years and at age 11 years? (p. 379)

4. List the academic skills and classroom behaviors that were found to be stronger in children from structured classrooms and from open classrooms. (pp. 390-391)

5. How much time does the average child spend watching TV? (p. 395)

6. Describe the age trends in TV viewing among boys and girls during childhood and adolescence. (p. 395)

7. What percentage of TV characters are women? And what percentage are children, adolescents, and old people? (pp. 398-399)

TEST YOUR RECALL

1. Outline the development of peer interactions from 2 to 7 years of age. (pp. 372-373)

2. List Parten's four types of play. (pp. 373-374)

3. Why are peer negotiations important to children's social development? (p. 375)

4. Describe the findings of the Hartup and Coates (1967) study on modeling and imitation of sharing behavior. (p. 376)

5. How do children start and maintain friendships? (p. 377)

6. What factors are related to a child's choice of friends? (p. 378)

7. List several research topics that might be studied by using sociometric techniques on children. (pp. 380-381)

8. Describe the characteristics of popular children. (pp. 380-382)

9. How is physical attractiveness advantageous to children's social development? (p. 381)

10. What characteristics are associated with children who are

selected as leaders? (p. 382)

11. Describe the developmental course of peer conformity that was found by Costanzo and Shaw (1966). (p. 382)

12. How is status in a peer group related to children's willingness to conform? (p. 383)

13. Describe how Sherif and his associates were able to reduce group prejudice between the "Bull Dogs" and "Red Devils." (p. 385)

14. Contrast the usual functions of day-care centers and nursery schools. (p. 387)

15. Offer some suggestions on what to look for when selecting a preschool. (p. 388)

16. What are the possible benefits from well-run Head Start programs? See Highlight 11.1. (p. 388)

17. What major differences have been found in the learning outcomes of the open and structured classroom models? (pp. 390-391)

18. What are some of the common characteristics of "good" and/or "effective" teachers. (p. 391)

19. Why do lower-class children often "run a collision course" with schools? (p. 392)

20. List the tentative conclusions reached by those who have studied the effects of school desegregation. (p. 393)

21. Describe the Singers' approach to helping children become wise about TV's messages. See Highlight 11.2. (p. 397)

22. What conclusions have come from experiments on the effects of children viewing TV violence? (pp. 397-398)

23. Discuss the kinds of social distortions children are likely to see on television. (pp. 398-399)

24. List several ways that teachers can promote socialization in the schools. (pp. 400-402)

25. What is catharsis? (p. 402)

ANSWER SECTION

GUIDED REVIEW:

1. peers; stable; groups
2. parallel; cooperative; solitary; cooperative
3. social; more; retaliating
4. observational learning; reduce
5. friendships; play; same
6. group; role; unstable
7. sociometric; sociogram; popularity
8. attractiveness; unattractive; positive; names
9. competence
10. conformity; girls; ambiguous (uncertain); middle; confidence
11. competitive; goal; cooperation
12. links
13. day-care centers; nursery schools; cognitive (intellectual)
14. Head Start; unemployed
15. action zone; open classroom; structured classroom; basic; reading; persistence; intelligence; cooperate; Computer
16. middle-class; esteem; prejudice; self-esteem; academic achievement
17. 20 to 30; increases; declines; lower
18. formal; theme; educational
19. violence; bidirectional; susceptible
20. prosocial; cognitive; more
21. distorted; adolescents; 25; stereotyped
22. isolated; reward; structure; peers
23. catharsis; aggression; toys; distracts; doll

TERMS AND DEFINITIONS QUIZ:

SET 1:
1. sociometric techniques
2. solitary play
3. self-disclosure
4. peer group
5. associative play
6. cooperative play
7. cliques
8. peers
9. friendships
10. parallel play

SET 2:
1. formal features
2. catharsis
3. open classroom
4. structured classroom
5. day-care centers
6. sociogram
7. nursery schools
8. Computer Assisted Instruction (CAI)
9. links

MATCHING QUIZ:

    1. f (p. 383)   5. b (p. 403)
    2. d (p. 380)   6. c (p. 374)
    3. g (p. 400)   7. a (p. 390)
    4. e (p. 381)

SELF TEST:

    1. a (p. 372)   16. c (p. 389)
    2. a (p. 372)   17. c (pp. 389-390)
    3. c (p. 374)   18. c (p. 392)
    4. c (p. 374)   19. b (p. 393)
    5. c (p. 376)   20. b (p. 395)
    6. b (p. 377)   21. a (p. 395)
    7. d (p. 378)   22. b (p. 396)
    8. c (p. 379)   23. a (pp. 397-398)
    9. a (p. 380)   24. d (pp. 398-399)
  10. b (pp. 380-382)   25. a (p. 399)
  11. d (p. 381)   26. a (p. 400)
  12. b (p. 382)   27. d (p. 401)
  13. c (p. 383)   28. b (p. 402)
  14. b (p. 385)   29. d (p. 403)
  15. d (p. 388-389)   30. b (pp. 403-404)

CHAPTER 12

The Self: Building a Personal Identity

SUMMARY IN OUTLINE

    PROLOGUE (p. 409)

        Personal identity, self, self-concept
        Self-concept begins to develop in infancy.

    THE DEVELOPING SELF (p. 410)

        GROWTH TOWARD AUTONOMY, INITIATIVE, AND INDUSTRY
            Autonomy: The Road to Independence
                Encouragement to explore challenging situations is important.
                Toddlers make rapid gains in self-control.
            Initiative and Industry
                Competence and confidence aided through self-initiated activities.
                Between ages 6 and 11 most children want to complete projects and to build a sense of industry, and to avoid developing a sense of inferiority.
                Children make many social comparisons.
                Youngsters also learn about themselves through self-observation and social feedback.

        THE SELF-CONCEPT--consists of self-esteem and self-image
            The Child's Age and Abilities
                Self-concept becomes increasingly complex and abstract with age.
                Abilities and self-concepts influence each other reciprocally.
            The Child's Family and Social Contacts
                Child-rearing styles are related to measures of self-

esteem.

MOTIVATING ASPECTS OF ONE'S SELF
Self-image consists of perceived self and ideal self.
Two motivating aspects of one's self: (1) the discrepancy between one's perceived and ideal self, and (2) protection of one's self-concept, such as through the use of defense mechanisms.

ACHIEVEMENT MOTIVATION
Fear of failure is associated with goals set too high or too low.
Children who perform below their potential are called underachievers.
Achievement orientation varies across tasks and appears to be lower among girls than boys.

SOCIAL COGNITION (p. 418)

EMPATHY
Empathy is a social-cognitive process with cognitive and emotional components.
Children try to comfort others by age 18 months.
Older children are more likely than younger ones to include facial or personal clues in judging how others might feel.

KNOWING ABOUT FRIENDSHIP
Children's expectations of friendship change with age.
Selman's 5 stages of friendship development:
Stage 0: Momentary Playmateship (3-7 years)
Stage 1: One-way Assistance (4-9 years)
Stage 2: Fair-weather Cooperation (6-12 years)
Stage 3: Mutually Shared Relationships (9-15 years)
Stage 4: occurs in the adolescent years

UNDERSTANDING SOCIAL ROLES AND MOTIVES
Children's conceptions of authority change with age.
Pretend play and attribution processes help children understand social roles and motives.

SEX ROLES AND GENDER IDENTITY (p. 421)

GENDER: A KEY ASPECT OF SELF
<u>The Role of Sex Roles</u>
Two-year-olds have some understanding of conventional sex role behavior.
Boys generally feel more ambitious, in control of things, and confident in their problem solving skills than girls do.
Girls generally feel more sensitive, generous, and helpless.
<u>Forming a Gender Identity</u>
Androgynous gender identity
Gender identity is dependent on cognitive growth.
Gender constancy is not fully understood by young

children.

BIOLOGY AND GENDER IDENTITY
   XY chromosome pair produces H-Y antigen which causes prenatal development of the testes.
   Androgen levels help regulate sexual development after 6 weeks of gestation.

THE FAMILY AND GENDER IDENTITY
   Parents have gender-related expectations for and perceptions of their newborns.
   Parents; behavior toward sons and daughters is often guided by traditional sex roles.

SOCIETY AND GENDER IDENTITY
   Preferences for sex-appropriate activities emerge by 2 or 3 years of age.
   Stories about sex-unconventional behavior are seen as "stupid" by many preschoolers.
   Peers reward each other for conventional sex role behavior
   TV and books teach children about sex roles.
   Sex roles vary across cultures.

<u>MORAL DEVELOPMENT</u> (p. 428)

Internalization of moral standards allows children to develop inner controls for regulating their own behavior.

   MORAL REASONING
      <u>Jean Piaget's Contributions</u>--three stages:
         Moral realism (ages 4-7)--belief in immanent justice.
         Intermediate stage.
         Moral relativism (after age 10)--justice is an abstract concept.
      <u>Lawrence Kohlberg's Theory</u>
         Three levels (and six stages)--see Tables 12.2 and 12.3
         Level I: Preconventional (stages 1 and 2)
         Level II: Conventional (stages 3 and 4)
         Level III: Postconventional (stages 5 and 6)
      <u>An Evaluation</u>
         Contrary to Piaget's theory, young children do consider a wrongdoer's intentions.
         Cross-cultural evidence supports Kohlberg's sequence of stages.
         Rates of moral development vary across cultures.
         There is evidence that some children skip stages or regress.
         Not all cultures value postconventicnal thinking.

   MORAL CONDUCT AND SELF-REGULATION
      Classic study by Hartshorne and May (1928)
      <u>Delay of gratification</u>--ability to delay increases with a variety of social and cognitive conditions
      <u>Resistance to Temptation and Cheating</u>--moral conduct is affected by the perceived risk of detection.

Chapter 12

ISSUES IN ACTION (p. 439)

SEX-ROLE LIBERATION

SEX-ROLES AND SEXUAL INFORMATION
Most children learn about sex from their peers.
A minority of schools offer courses in sex education.

ENHANCING THE CHILD'S SELF
Moral Standards
Achievement Orientation and Competence--how teachers can bolster children's self-concepts.

GUIDED REVIEW

1. Every child has a unique personality or _____. According to _____, healthy ego development in toddlerhood is highlighted by the sense of _____. Then children strive to develop a sense of _____, followed by a sense of _____. These advances in personality development are accompanied by increases in the _____ comparisons children make. If the outcome of these comparisons is negative, school-age children may develop a sense of _____.

2. Children's self-concepts have two important components: self-_____ and self-_____. Negative self-concepts are related to high levels of a _____, poor school adjustment, and poor _____ performance. Positive self-concepts are associated with the opposite attributes. The self-concept becomes more detailed and complex as children get older partly because of _____ development.

3. Coopersmith (1967) discovered that boys with (high/low) self-esteem are more likely than boys with _____ self-esteem to have parents who enforce rules in a con_____ manner, and use rewards, discussion, and re_____ to promote socialization. When punishment is used, high self-esteem boys tend to perceive it as _____.

4. The self-concept is thought to have motivating properties. For example, when the discrepancy between one's perceived self and _____ self is too low, development may be _____; but too much discrepancy can lead to _____. Children use _____ to protect their self-concept.

5. The process by which we perceive, know, and reason about the social relations and thoughts of others is called _____. Empathy has two components, _____ and _____. The ability to empathize increases with age and depends on the child's feelings of responsi-

bility and _____ to intervene. Other social-cognitive skills also improve, including children's understanding of friendship, _____ roles, and the motives of others.

6. Notions of conventional sex role behaviors are learned very early. Societal sex roles usually become a part of one's _____ self. The degree to which sex roles are adopted is called one's _____ identity. People who have adopted characteristics of the roles of both sexes into their identities are described as _____.

7. Biological factors influence gender identity. Females who are exposed to high levels of prenatal _____ may develop male organs at birth, and show more _____ behaviors later on. If males are exposed to _____ during gestation, they tend to become less athletic and aggressive than other boys.

8. Family experiences influence gender identity. At birth, parents' expectations lead them to _____ their newborn's attributes as fitting conventional sex roles. As development proceeds, parents continue to see _____ as strong and _____ as weak. They also assign tasks, buy toys, decorate the child's _____, and reward behaviors according to conventional sex roles.

9. Peers and teachers reward children for behavior that is sex-_____. TV and children's _____ also present information about sex roles.

10. The process of accepting other people's standards of conduct as one's own is called _____, and it allows children to _____ their behavior more effectively and independently as they grow older.

11. When children make judgments about why certain behaviors are "good" or "bad," they are engaged in _____. According to Piaget, the way children reason about moral issues parallels _____ development. The first stage of moral reasoning coincides with the _____ stage of cognition and passes sequentially through _____ stages. The child first reasons at the level of _____. Here rules are seen as absolute and unchangeable; and the child believes that wrongdoers will be punished eventually--a notion called _____. At the intermediate stage, children come to understand that _____ are made and changed by people. At the highest stage the child becomes a moral _____ and believes we should take a wrongdoer's in_____ and motives into account.

12. Kolhberg's theory includes _____ stages of moral development divided into three levels: Level I is labeled _____ and is characterized by egocentric think-

ing. Level II is called _____, and involves a high degree of _____ to social rules. At the postconventional level children can deal with _____ concepts and reason according to self-_____ ethical _____.

13. Children progress through these levels at different rates. Generally _____-class youngsters function at higher levels than those from the _____-class. This is partly because of class differences in participating in society's con_____ processes.

14. Contrary to Piaget's theory, it appears that very young children can take a wrongdoer's _____ into account, but they seem to weigh consequences more heavily. Research on Kohlberg's theory has found that individuals in many rural and impoverished societies progress through the stages at a _____ rate than people from cities and technological societies. In technological societies, Stage _____ reasoning predominates, Stage _____ reasoning is rare, and Stage _____ judgments virtually never occur. Other research has found that children's moral thinking can _____ stages and regress to earlier ones.

15. Harshorne and May (1928) found that the overall relationship between moral opinions and moral behavior is fairly (consistent/inconsistent) among children.

16. Self-regulation is shown by the child's resistance to _____ and delay of _____. The ability to delay increases with the child's _____ and social _____. Modeling can affect children's delay more easily when the models (lengthen/shorten) their own delay behavior. In addition, delay can be _____ by asking children to think about "happy" events. Children who cheat on exams tend to have _____ IQs and friends who cheat.

17. Resistance to temptation is affected by learning processes. Models who are _____ for misconduct are less likely to be imitated than those who are _____. Peers also influence the ability to resist temptation. One study of Halloweeen trick-or-treaters found that children are less likely to steal when (alone/in a group) and their identities are (protected/known).

18. Sexual misinformation obtained from peers can be harmless, but it can also lead to problems. Parents who want to inform their children about sex are advised to take the child's _____ level into account. Today a (majority/minority) of schools offer courses in sex education. Most parents _____ such courses.

19. The self-concepts of underachieving children can be enhanced by teaching them to set _____ goals, to

accept personal responsibility for their behavior, and to seek _____ about their performance.

TERMS AND DEFINITIONS QUIZ

SET 1 (Match each term in the set with its definition below.):

ACHIEVEMENT ORIENTATION, DEFENSE MECHANISMS, IDEAL SELF, PERCEIVED SELF, SELF, SELF-CONCEPT, SELF-CONTROL, SELF-ESTEEM, SELF-IMAGE, SOCIAL COGNITION

1. _____ Sometimes called the "real" self; it is the picture we have of our own characteristics.

2. _____ The mental picture an individual has of his or her self and the self the person would like to be; it includes the perceived self and the ideal self.

3. _____ The individual's evaluation of personal worthiness or value based on self-image and knowledge of society's values.

4. _____ Our picture of the person or self we would like to be.

5. _____ Protective strategies and methods used by the individual to prevent information from threatening or damaging the self-concept.

6. _____ A person's sense of personal awareness and unique combination of dispositions, beliefs, values, and interests.

7. _____ The ability to govern one's own behavior and desires, such as in complying with requests and waiting when something desired must be delayed.

8. _____ The organized internal or personal idea we have about our own characteristics; it includes the self-image and self-esteem.

9. _____ An internalized motivation to complete successfully tasks which the person considers to be worth doing.

10. _____ The process of perception, knowing, and reasoning about the social relations, ideas, and feelings of people, including oneself.

Chapter 12

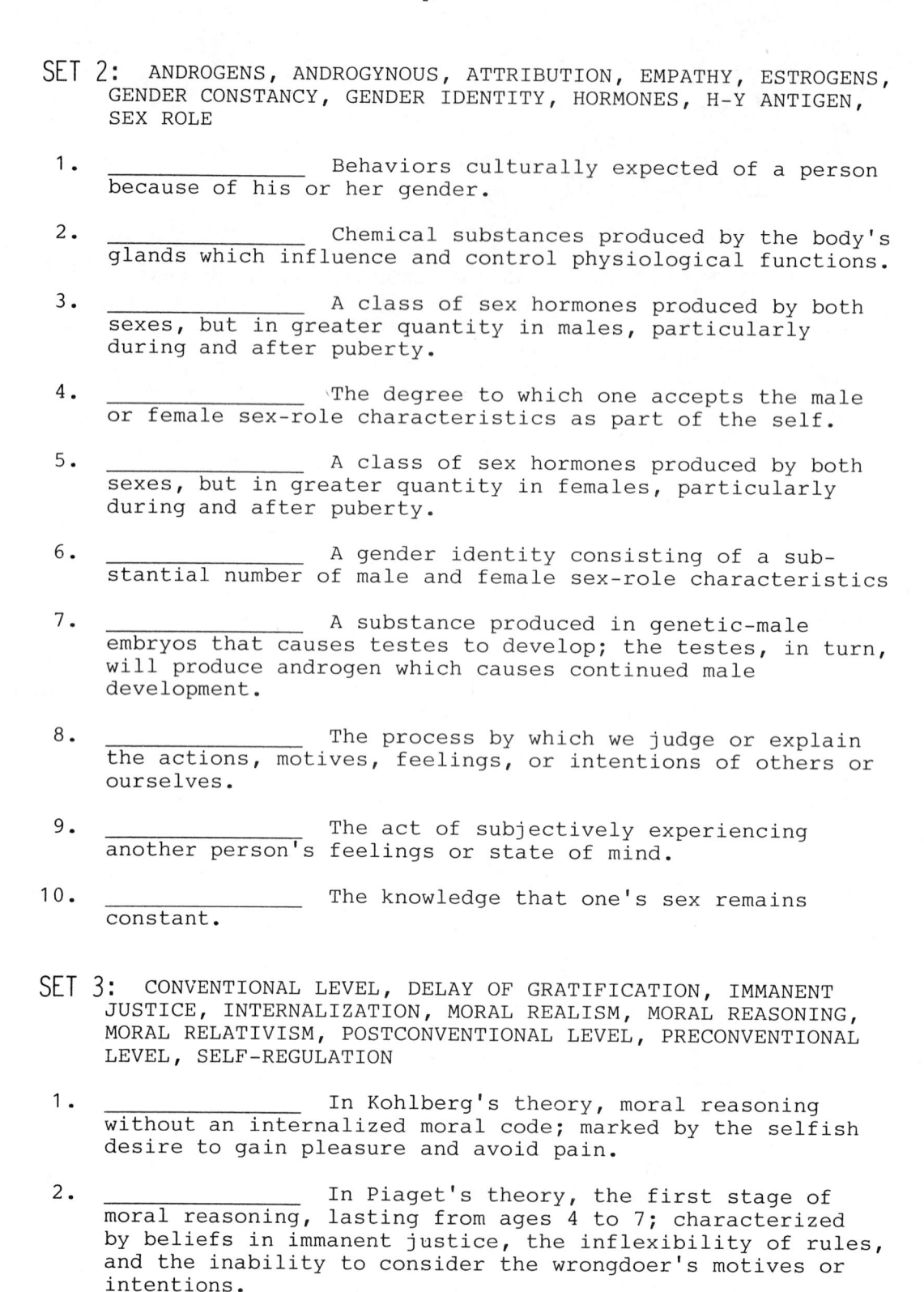

SET 2: ANDROGENS, ANDROGYNOUS, ATTRIBUTION, EMPATHY, ESTROGENS, GENDER CONSTANCY, GENDER IDENTITY, HORMONES, H-Y ANTIGEN, SEX ROLE

1. _____ Behaviors culturally expected of a person because of his or her gender.

2. _____ Chemical substances produced by the body's glands which influence and control physiological functions.

3. _____ A class of sex hormones produced by both sexes, but in greater quantity in males, particularly during and after puberty.

4. _____ The degree to which one accepts the male or female sex-role characteristics as part of the self.

5. _____ A class of sex hormones produced by both sexes, but in greater quantity in females, particularly during and after puberty.

6. _____ A gender identity consisting of a substantial number of male and female sex-role characteristics

7. _____ A substance produced in genetic-male embryos that causes testes to develop; the testes, in turn, will produce androgen which causes continued male development.

8. _____ The process by which we judge or explain the actions, motives, feelings, or intentions of others or ourselves.

9. _____ The act of subjectively experiencing another person's feelings or state of mind.

10. _____ The knowledge that one's sex remains constant.

SET 3: CONVENTIONAL LEVEL, DELAY OF GRATIFICATION, IMMANENT JUSTICE, INTERNALIZATION, MORAL REALISM, MORAL REASONING, MORAL RELATIVISM, POSTCONVENTIONAL LEVEL, PRECONVENTIONAL LEVEL, SELF-REGULATION

1. _____ In Kohlberg's theory, moral reasoning without an internalized moral code; marked by the selfish desire to gain pleasure and avoid pain.

2. _____ In Piaget's theory, the first stage of moral reasoning, lasting from ages 4 to 7; characterized by beliefs in immanent justice, the inflexibility of rules, and the inability to consider the wrongdoer's motives or intentions.

3. _____ The most advanced stage of moral reasoning

in Piaget's theory, beginning about age 10; characterized by flexible reasoning and judgments that consider the wrongdoer's intentions and motives.

4. _____ In Kohlberg's theory, moral reasoning based on an internalized moral code that stresses conformity to socially approved rules and conventions.

5. _____ Thinking about and judging issues or situations in terms of whether they are "good" or "bad."

6. _____ A measure of how long a person will wait to obtain rewards.

7. _____ The process of taking other people's standards and rules and transforming them into guidelines for one's own conduct.

8. _____ The belief that all wrongdoers are eventually punished.

9. _____ In Kohlberg's theory, moral reasoning based on an internalized moral code that involves rules that are abstract, unselfish, and universal.

10. _____ The operation of inner controls which permit people to exercise internalized standards without being controlled by other people or environmental restraints.

MATCHING QUIZ

1. ___ defense mechanisms
2. ___ authoritative parenting
3. ___ underachievers
4. ___ internalization
5. ___ postconventional level
6. ___ H-Y antigen
7. ___ one-way assistance
8. ___ androgynous

a. high self-esteem in children
b. a stage in understanding friendship
c. belief in immanent justice
d. important to sexual differentiation
e. may have high fear of failure
f. means of gaining knowledge about the self
g. motivational aspect of the self
h. leads to self-regulation

9. ___ social comparisons   i. self-chosen ethical principles

10. ___ moral realism   j. a form of gender identity

SELF TEST

1. A toddler who resists performing a prohibited act demonstrates
   a. self-control.
   b. initiative.
   c. industry.
   d. inferiority.

2. A preschooler shows her developing sense of initiative when she asks questions.
   a. True
   b. False

3. Children learn about their abilities relative to those of their peers by
   a. making social comparisons.
   b. self-observation.
   c. social feedback.
   d. all of the above.

4. Children whose behavior is ridiculed or scorned by a teacher often receive similar treatment from their classmates.
   a. True
   b. False

5. A girl who says "I'm the smartest kid in my class" reveals part of her
   a. sense of initiative.
   b. sense of autonomy.
   c. self-esteem.
   d. perceived-esteem.

6. Which statement about self-esteem is TRUE?
   a. Children's self-esteem is not related to their adjustment in life.
   b. Children who have high self-esteem tend to be highly anxious.
   c. People who seek help for psychological problems often have low self-esteem.
   d. Self-esteem is not affected by the goals children set for themselves.

7. Children's self-images are related to their personality development, but not their cognitive development.
   a. True
   b. False

8. Children's self-esteem is related to
   a. their success or failure in school.
   b. the parenting style they experience.
   c. the acceptance they receive from peers.
   d. all of the above.

9. The self-concept includes
   a. self-esteem.
   b. the perceived self.
   c. the ideal self.
   d. all of the above.

10. When Howard tries to protect his self-concept by deciding that "football is dumb" after he doesn't make the football team, he is using a(n)
    a. moral convention.
    b. defense mechanism.
    c. androgyny.
    d. preconventional concept.

11. Which statement about achievement motivation is FALSE?
    a. Children who fear failure often set high goals for themselves.
    b. Children who fear failure often set low goals for themselves.
    c. The strength of children's achievement motivation depends on the self-concept they have developed.
    d. Almost all highly competent schoolchildren know that they have strong ability and set high achievement standards for themselves.

12. The process of perception, knowing, and reasoning about the relationships, ideas, and feelings of people, including oneself, is called
    a. the perceived-self.
    b. the self-concept.
    c. social cognition.
    d. conventional attributions.

13. According to Selman (1981), children at the _____ stage of knowledge about friendship expect friends to colloborate on common interests, rather than satisfying their own self-interests.
    a. momentary playmateship (stage 0)
    b. one-way assistance (stage 1)
    c. fair-weather cooperation (stage 2)
    d. mutually shared relationships (stage 3)

14. Children at 3 years of age have very little awareness of sex roles.
    a. True
    b. False

15. Androgyny is the same thing as bisexuality.
    a. True
    b. False

16. Atypical prenatal exposure to large quantities of
    a. hormones is the chief cause of androgyny.
    b. estrogen makes boys more "masculine."
    c. hormones has no effect if it occurs between the sixth and twelfth week of gestation.
    d. androgen produces a large clitoris in female embryos.

17. Compared to parents of newborn boys, parents of girls perceive their babies as less
    a. attentive.
    b. coordinated.
    c. strong.
    d. all of the above.

18. Parents play less roughly and vigorously with their daughters than with their sons.
    a. True
    b. False

19. Margaret Mead's (1935) study showed that all New Guinea societies had sex roles that were the opposite of American sex roles.
    a. True
    b. False

20. According to Piaget, which of the following children's behaviors would a moral realist judge most harshly?
    a. Tommy drops a glass because someone bumped into him.
    b. Lisa opens the kitchen door which inadvertently smashes ten cups her mother placed on the floor.
    c. Jimmy throws a ball that hits and breaks a glass on the dining room table.
    d. Janet accidently drops and breaks three dishes while helping to clean the kitchen.

21. According to Kohlberg, a child whose moral reasoning is at the _____ level is concerned with conforming to socially approved rules.
    a. intermediate
    b. preconventional
    c. conventional
    d. postconventional

22. According to Kohlberg, a person whose moral reasoning is at the _____ level applies abstract, unselfish, and universal rules of conduct.
    a. preconventional
    b. conventional
    c. intermediate
    d. postconventional

23. Contrary to Piaget's theory of moral development, 5-year-olds can and do use a wrongdoer's intentions in making moral judgments.
    a. True
    b. False

24. Which statement about Kohlberg's theory of moral development is FALSE? Research has found that
    a. moral reasoning can skip stages.
    b. moral reasoning can regress.
    c. 75% of American adults typically use postconventional reasoning to judge conduct.
    d. people in many impoverished and rural communities progress through the stages more slowly than people from cities and technological societies.

25. People who use higher stages of reasoning to judge moral issues are far more likely to behave morally than those who use lower stages.
    a. True
    b. False

26. Research on delay of gratification has shown that
    a. children from the lower classes show less ability to delay gratification than those from more affluent backgrounds.
    b. observational learning affects the ability to delay.
    c. cognitive factors affect the ability to delay.
    d. all of the above.

27. Children who observe a model fail to resist temptation are not likely to imitate that conduct if the model _____ for the misdeed.
    a. is rewarded
    b. experiences no consequences
    c. is punished
    d. none of the above

28. To encourage children to develop androgynous gender identities, efforts should be started very early in their lives.
    a. True
    b. False

29. Which statement about sex roles is TRUE?
    a. Boys cannot be as sensitive and gentle as girls.
    b. Pointing out real examples of androgynous behavior probably doesn't help produce sex role liberation.
    c. Using pronouns, such as "he" and "she," in sexist stories affects children's ideas about sex roles.
    d. none of the above

30. The self-concepts of low-achieving children may be enhanced if the teacher
    a. avoids public comparisons of high- and low-achieving students.
    b. seeks opportunities to praise low-achievers.
    c. has them serve as tutors for younger children.
    d. all of the above.

IMPORTANT DETAILS TO KNOW

1. Characterize children's descriptions of their self-images in early childhood, later childhood, and in adolescence. (pp. 413-414)

2. Describe the child's gender constancy at age 2 to 3, and before and after age 7. (pp. 422-423)

3. How does an embryo develop the male or female anatomy? (p. 423)

4. What were the appropriate sex roles in the Arapesh, Mundugumor and Tchambuli societies? (p. 427)

5. To what extent do individuals use preconventional, conventional, and postconventional reasoning between 7 and 16 years of age. See Figure 12.5. (p. 433)

TEST YOUR RECALL

1. Give two examples of striving for autonomy in 2-year-olds. (pp. 410-411)

2. Describe the procedure and results of the research by Ruble et al. (1976) on social comparisons among children. (p. 412)

3. Name the two major components of the self-concept. (p. 413)

4. Describe how children's self-esteem is related to their effective functioning. (p. 413)

5. How does the child's self-concept typically change with development? (pp. 413-414)

6. Discuss the relationships between parenting style and levels of self-esteem in children. (pp. 414-415)

7. Explain how the difference between one's ideal self and perceived self can influence motivation. (p. 415)

8. Cite the principal ways children reveal a fear of failure. (p. 416)

9. Discuss how the ability to empathize affects children's social behavior. (pp. 418-419)

10. Describe Robert Selman's first four stages of friendship development. (pp. 419-420)

11. How do children's conceptions of authority change with development? (p. 420)

Chapter 12　　201

12. Trace the development of children's understanding of gender constancy. (pp. 422-423)

13. What is the role of H-Y antigen in sexual differentiation? (p. 423)

14. To what extent can sex hormones influence sex-appropriate behavior in boys and girls? See Highlight 12.1. (p. 424)

15. Characterize the ways that parents tend to treat boys and girls differently. (pp. 425-426)

16. Cite several sources of societal influence on children's gender identity. (pp. 426-427)

17. Briefly describe cross-cultural differences in acceptable sex-role behavior. (p. 427)

18. Summarize Piaget's stages of moral development. (p. 429)

19. List Kohlberg's three levels of moral development. (p. 430)

20. Evaluate Kohlberg's theory of moral development. (pp. 432-434)

21. Cite the findings of the Hartshorne and May (1928) study on moral behavior. (p. 434)

22. Discuss the factors that are related to children's delay of gratification. (pp. 435-436)

23. Describe the method and results of the study by Diener et al. (1976) on cheating among trick-or-treaters. (p. 438)

24. Summarize Bernstein's (1976a, b) advice on how to tell children about sex. See Highlight 12.3. (p. 441)

25. How can teachers bolster the self-concepts of children? (pp. 443-444)

ANSWER SECTION

GUIDED REVIEW:

1. self; Erikson; autonomy; initiative; industry; social; inferiority
2. esteem; image; anxiety; academic; cognitive
3. high; low; consistent; reasoning; justified
4. ideal; stagnated; failure; defense mechanisms
5. social cognition; cognitive; emotional; competence; social
6. ideal; gender; androgynous
7. androgen; masculine; high levels of estrogen

8. perceive; boys; girls; room
9. conventional; books
10. internalization; regulate
11. moral reasoning; cognitive; preoperational; three; moral realism; immanent justice; rules; relativist; intentions
12. six; preconventional; conventional; conformity; abstract; chosen; principles
13. middle; lower; contractual
14. intentions; slower; 4; 5; 6; skip
15. inconsistent
16. temptation; gratification; age; class; shorten; increased; low
17. punished; rewarded; alone; known
18. cognitive; minority; favor
19. moderate (reasonable); feedback

TERMS AND DEFINITIONS QUIZ:

SET 1:
1. perceived self
2. self-image
3. self-esteem
4. ideal self
5. defense mechanisms
6. self
7. self-control
8. self-concept
9. achievement orientation
10. social cognition

SET 2:
1. sex role
2. hormones
3. androgens
4. gender identity
5. estrogens
6. androgynous
7. H-Y antigen
8. attribution
9. empathy
10. gender constancy

SET 3:
1. preconventional level
2. moral realism
3. moral relativism
4. conventional level
5. moral reasoning
6. delay of gratification
7. internalization
8. immanent justice
9. postconventional level
10. self-regulation

MATCHING QUIZ:

1. g (p. 416)
2. a (p. 414)
3. e (p. 416)
4. h (p. 428)
5. i (p. 430)

6. d (p. 423)
7. b (p. 419)
8. j (p. 422)
9. f (p. 412)
10. c (p. 429)

SELF TEST:

1. a (p. 411)
2. a (p. 411)
3. d (p. 412)
4. a (p. 412)
5. c (p. 413)
6. c (p. 413)
7. b (p. 413)
8. d (pp. 414-415)
9. d (p. 415)
10. b (p. 416)
11. d (p. 416)
12. c (p. 418)
13. d (p. 420)
14. b (pp. 421-422)
15. b (p. 422)

16. d (p. 424)
17. d (p. 425)
18. a (p. 425)
19. b (p. 427)
20. b (p. 429)
21. c (p. 430)
22. d (p. 430)
23. a (p. 432)
24. c (p. 433)
25. b (p. 434)
26. d (p. 436)
27. c (p. 436)
28. a (p. 440)
29. c (p. 440)
30. d (pp. 443-444)

CHAPTER 13

Emotions and Psychological Problems of Childhood

SUMMARY IN OUTLINE

CHILDREN'S EMOTIONAL DEVELOPMENT (p. 450)

WHAT IS AN EMOTION?--consists of subjective feelings, thoughts, behaviors, and physiological changes

EMOTIONS OF CHILDHOOD
Basic emotions of newborns include disgust, distress, interest, joy, and startle.
Other basic emotions are affection, anger, fear, and sadness.
<u>Complex Emotions</u>
Toddlers can express mixed emotions, but don't understand them very well.
Shame and guilt develop in the early childhood years and involve social-cognitive processes that coordinate two or more basic emotions.
<u>Knowing When to Express What You Feel</u>
Display rules vary across cultures.
Children learn to use display rules to exaggerate and dampen their true emotions.

KNOWING AND MANAGING EMOTIONS--preschool children can accurately identify expressions of happiness, sadness, and anger.
<u>Coping with Emotions</u>
<u>Understanding What Triggers Emotions</u>
<u>Understanding the Effects Emotions Have</u>--by 6 years of age, children know that emotions can affect one's cognitive abilities.

EMOTION AND PERSONALITY--long-lasting emotional states (moods) that characterize one's behavior are considered part of the personality.

CHILDHOOD NEUROSES (p. 455)

Psychological impairment that involves maladaptive ways of coping with stress and emotions
Three characteristics of neurotic children: (1) anxieties, fears, and perceived stress; (2) unhappiness; and, (3) impaired social relationships and schoolwork.

FEARS, PHOBIAS, AND ANXIETY PROBLEMS
Usual versus Serious Fears
Defensive reactions to danger are adaptive and occur early in life.
Intense, frequent, or extensive fears generally require treatment.
Fears in Childhood
Girls usually show more fears than boys.
Social class differences in children's fears have been found.
How Fears Change with Age
Fears become less concrete and more abstract with age.
Anxieties relating to school and social relations become more pronounced in late childhood.
Treatment for early school phobia is likely to be less complex than for late school phobia.
Death phobia can arise from misconceptions about the meaning of death.
What Causes Children's Fears?
Individual differences in temperaments
Conditioning, observational learning, and cognition

CHILDHOOD DEPRESSION
Depression becomes neurotic when it is severe, frequent, and long lasting.
Much less frequent in early childhood than in adolescence.

PSYCHOPHYSIOLOGICAL DISORDERS (p. 463)

Physical symptoms or illnesses that are produced or intensified by emotional stress

ASTHMA
Results from physical allergies, respiratory infections, and psychological factors.
About 3% of children have asthma.
Personality traits do not seem to cause asthma.
Medical treatment and family therapy can reduce attacks.

ULCERS
Stress is a psychological factor in ulcers and colitis.
Although the effectiveness of psychotherapy has not been established, biofeedback may be useful; medical care is needed.

EATING DISORDERS
Anorexia nervosa results in death in 10-15% of the cases.
More frequent in females than males.
Occurs more often in late childhood and adolescence.
Treatment involves medical care, operant procedures, and counseling.

CHILDHOOD PSYCHOSES (p. 468)

AUTISM AND CHILDHOOD SCHIZOPHRENIA
Nine characteristics of psychotic children--see Table 13.2
Two major characteristics, impaired socialization and disturbed speech patterns, are associated more with autism than schizophrenia.
Autism is apparent in the first few years; schizophrenia begins later.

CAUSAL FACTORS IN CHILDHOOD PSYCHOSIS
The Child's Experience
Caring for a psychotic child may lead some parents to develop "refrigerator" traits.
Experiential factors are not the primary cause of childhood psychosis.
Maturational Factors
The role of biochemical imbalances is uncertain.
Brain damage seems to be a causal factor in autism.
There is evidence for a genetic predisposition in autism and childhood schizophrenia.

IMPACT OF PSYCHOTIC CHILDREN ON THEIR FAMILIES
Enormous strain on the family
Contact with similarly afflicted families can be helpful.

TREATMENT AND PROGNOSIS
Prognosis best if the child (1) can talk before age 5, (2) has no severe symptoms in early childhood, and (3) is not committed to an institution.
Treatment is aimed at reducing or eliminating maladaptive behavior, often through operant conditioning.

ISSUES IN ACTION (p. 474)

THE DEATH OF SOMEONE CLOSE
Children should not be shielded from the concept of death; it should be explained directly and truthfully.
Children can participate in the mourning process.
Dying children should know as much as they can comprehend about their own illness.

OVERCOMING CHILDREN'S FEARS
Some "don'ts" on handling fears
Methods for handling fears: (1) explanations, (2) teaching relevant skills, (3) observational learning, (4) desensitization or counterconditioning, and (5) reinforcement.

Probably the most effective approach uses a combination of methods.

DIAGNOSTIC LABELS--although they provide an economical means of communication among professionals, they can stimatize children and impede improvement.

SEEKING PROFESSIONAL HELP

GUIDED REVIEW

1. The large number of complex emotions children develop seem to stem from a set of _____ emotions that infants express, such as disgust, interest, and joy. Toddlers become increasingly adept at expressing _____ emotions, such as happiness and fear simultaneously.

2. By way of social-cognitive processes, children come to coordinate two or more _____ emotions to produce new, more advanced, emotions. One of these advanced emotions--the feeling of loss of love or esteem of others--is called _____. Another involves the sense of having fallen short of one's own internal standards; this emotion is called _____, and it seems to emerge after _____ years of age.

3. Children learn to use _____ to exaggerate or dampen what they actually feel. By late _____, emotional expression is rarely free of these cultural or personal controls.

4. Sometimes temper tantrums can be _____ by eliminating the conditions that produce them. Parents who give in when tantrums occur may _____ tantrum behavior. It is sometimes helpful to use _____ after the tantrum has subsided.

5. Psychological disorders involving maladaptive ways of handling stress or emotions are called _____. Maladaptive behaviors, such as escape or _____, are maintained because they reduce the immediate feeling of _____. Intense and irrational fears are called _____; vague feelings of apprehension are called _____.

6. During childhood (girls/boys) usually show more fears. The fact that the objects of children's fears become less concrete and more _____ as they grow older is related to changes in _____ development. Fears in late childhood often center around _____ relations.

7. School phobias can surface in early or late childhood. Those that occur early may be related to problems of

_____ from the parents. When they occur late, they are often preceded by poor school _____ and parent/child relationships.

8. Before age 5, children often think death is _____, that is, the person can come back. Children's conception of death becomes fairly complete after _____ years of age. Some children develop a death _____ because of their misunderstandings about death.

9. Fears are learned, but some children may be vulnerable to developing fears because of their inborn _____.

10. Although all people "feel depressed" on occasion, depression becomes a neurotic disorder when it is _____, frequent, and _____. Neurotic depression probably occurs _____ often in early childhood than in adolescence.

11. Physical problems that are produced or intensified by emotional stress are termed _____ disorders. Asthma appears to result from a combination of respiratory infection, physical _____, and a variety of _____ factors. Asthma is more common among (males/females) and among (adults/children). Most asthmatic children show great improvement before adulthood. Research has found little relationship between asthma and the _____ of the parent or child. Asthmatic children show as much maladjustment as their _____ and cardiac patients who are free of asthma. In many cases asthmatic children are relieved of their symptoms when not in the presence of their _____.

12. Other psychophysiological problems include ulcers and _____, obesity, and _____ nervosa. Ulcers and colitis can arise from psychological stress. They are usually treated medically, and _____ techniques seem promising. Anorexia nervosa involves a drastic reduction in food intake, and usually afflicts (male/female) adolescents. Even when slim, anorexics _____ their body size. Treatment usually requires _____ care, and _____ conditioning methods have been successful in helping patients regain weight temporarily.

13. Autism is distinguished from childhood _____ on the basis of its earlier onset, and autistics are more likely to show impaired _____ and disturbed _____ patterns. Fortunately childhood psychoses are rare, afflicting about _____ children out of 10,000.

14. Many children grow up under extremely dire conditions, yet are competent and well-adjusted individuals. They are described as _____ children because they bounce back from life's adversities.

15. Bettelheim (1967) proposed that childhood psychoses result from cold and unresponsive _____. But _____-injured children have parents with traits similar to those of parents of psychotics. The primary cause of childhood psychoses appears to be _____, rather than experiential.

16. A primary causal factor in childhood psychoses now appears to be _____ damage, which severely affects cognitive functioning. Twin research suggests that _____ factors also play a role. The results of research on _____ imbalances are still inconclusive.

17. Traditional psychotherapies have produced (little/much) success in treating childhood psychoses. Operant conditioning methods have improved the prognosis, but it is still not good. The goals of current treatment are to suppress self-_____ and self-_____, and to facilitate the learning of basic language, social, and self-_____ skills.

18. When someone close dies, children are often told falsehoods and are restricted from the _____ process. The concept of death can be explained to children truthfully if the explanation matches the child's level of _____ development.

19. Many techniques are available to help eliminate children's fears. Parents can provide expl_____ of the feared situation, training in _____ skills, examples of fearless behavior, and _____ for fearless behaviors. Another approach involving progress through a hierarchy of stimuli resembling the feared source is called counterconditioning or _____.

20. A child with a serious problem needs help and there are a number of community resources that can help in finding a therapist. These include ph_____, school psychologists or counselors, the cl_____, and community _____ centers.

TERMS AND DEFINITIONS QUIZ

SET 1 (Match each term in the set with its definition below.):

ANXIETY, BIOFEEDBACK, DEATH PHOBIA, DEPRESSION, DISPLAY RULES, NEUROSIS, PHOBIAS, PSYCHOPHYSIOLOGICAL DISORDERS, SCHOOL PHOBIA

1. _____ A technique whereby a person's physiological processes, such as blood pressure, are monitored by the person so he or she can gain voluntary control over these processes through operant conditioning.

2. _____ Feeling of tension and apprehension that has a relatively vague or unidentified source.

3. _____ Broadly defined as psychological impairments that involve maladaptive ways of coping with anxiety, fear, or stress.

4. _____ An intense and irrational fear related to school.

5. _____ The feeling of sadness; a neurotic disorder when it is severe, frequent, and long-lasting.

6. _____ Cultural or personal rules regarding the expression of emotions.

7. _____ Physical symptoms or illnesses, such as ulcers, that are produced or intensified by emotional stress.

8. _____ An intense and irrational fear of death, an abstract concept that is not well understood by the young child.

9. _____ Intense, irrational fears that are associated with specific events or situations.

SET 2: ANOREXIA NERVOSA, ANXIETY, AUTISM, CHILDHOOD SCHIZOPHRENIA, COLITIS, DESENSITIZATION OR COUNTER-CONDITIONING, PSYCHOSIS, ULCERS

1. _____ A childhood psychosis that typically arises after infancy and seems to represent a departure from adequate functioning.

2. _____ A respiratory disorder that involves coughing, wheezing, and gasping for air; generally a psychophysiological problem.

3. _____ A childhood psychosis distinguished from schizophrenia by its very early onset, impaired socialization, and disturbed speech patterns.

4. _____ Extreme loss of appetite resulting in dramatic weight loss; thought to be a psychophysiological disorder.

5. _____ A conditioning procedure used for reducing or eliminating fears.

6. _____ Lesions or open sores often found in the stomach and upper intestine; generally a psychophysiological problem.

7. _____ Inflammation of the lower intestine;

generally a psychophysiological problem.

8. _____ A severe psychological impairment, characterized by frequent loss of contact with reality.

MATCHING QUIZ

1. ___ guilt
2. ___ display rule
3. ___ anorexia nervosa
4. ___ autism
5. ___ depression
6. ___ desensitization
7. ___ school-related fears
8. ___ biofeedback
9. ___ asthma

a. used in hiding true emotions
b. less common in early than late childhood
c. a complex emotion
d. procedure to reduce fears
e. more common among upper-class children
f. may begin as a physical allergy
g. typically begins in infancy
h. usually more common among females than males
i. potential aid in treating ulcers

SELF TEST

1. Which of the following is a basic emotion that children express from infancy onward?
   a. interest
   b. shame
   c. guilt
   d. none of the above

2. Children learn to use display rules to _____ the emotion they feel.
   a. exaggerate
   b. dampen
   c. substitute another emotion for
   d. all of the above

3. The study by Hyson (1983) of toddlers' and preschoolers' ability to control their emotions found that toddlers were too dumbfounded to react during the pediatrician's examination, but the preschoolers reacted immediately with protests.

a. True
b. False

4. The category of psychological problems that relates to anxieties, fears, and stresses children perceive in their lives is called
   a. psychosis.
   b. schizophrenia.
   c. neurosis.
   d. autism.

5. Marvin is afraid to go outside, saying "I don't know what, but something awful will happen." He has a(n)
   a. psychosis.
   b. phobia.
   c. nervosa.
   d. anxiety.

6. Grade-school-aged children often retain their fears for at least a year.
   a. True
   b. False

7. Which of the following is a 5-year-old LEAST likely to fear?
   a. animals
   b. unfamiliar people
   c. ghosts
   d. threat of bodily harm

8. The authors of your text recommend that parents display a negative attitude about their child beginning school so the child can rebel against them.
   a. True
   b. False

9. The development of children's fears seem to be influenced in part by inborn behavioral tendencies called
   a. psychoses.
   b. temperaments.
   c. phobias.
   d. anxieties.

10. When a school phobic boy was allowed to stay home because he was crying and pleading very strongly, his fear was
    a. classically conditioned.
    b. punished.
    c. reduced.
    d. rewarded.

11. Children seem to develop the greatest number of new fears during early childhood.
    a. True
    b. False

12. Parents who are afraid of heights may transmit their fear

to their child by
a. counterconditioning.
b. desensitization.
c. observational learning.
d. display rules.

13. Depression becomes a neurotic disorder when it is
a. severe.
b. long-lasting.
c. frequent.
d. all of the above.

14. Asthma and ulcers are classified as _____ disorders.
a. neurotic
b. psychophysiological
c. psychotic
d. depressive

15. About _____ % of the child population suffers from asthma.
a. 15
b. 10
c. 6
d. 3

16. The experiment (Long et al., 1958) in which dust was sprayed into the hospital rooms of asthmatic children found that the dust caused serious respiratory difficulty in two-thirds of the children.
a. True
b. False

17. Which statement about childhood asthma is TRUE?
a. Asthma is caused by parents being overprotective.
b. Asthmatics and childhood cardiac cases show similar degrees of maladjustment.
c. Asthmatics are far more maladjusted than their siblings are.
d. None of the above is true.

18. Children and adolescents constitute about one-fourth of hospitalized colitis cases.
a. True
b. False

19. Anorexia nervosa usually
a. begins in late childhood or adolescence.
b. occurs in individuals who have never dieted.
c. is cured easily.
d. all of the above.

20. Psychoses are characterized by frequent loss of contact with reality.
a. True
b. False

21. Which of the following speech disturbances do many

psychotic children show?
a. being mute
b. saying meaningless phrases
c. echolalia
d. all of the above

22. The incidence rate for childhood psychoses is about _____ per 10,000 children.
a. 3
b. 10
c. 50
d. 300

23. Resilient children tend to
a. be high achievers.
b. have good social skills.
c. have high self-esteem.
d. all of the above.

24. The chief cause of childhood psychoses is the child's experience with a "refrigerator" mother.
a. True
b. False

25. Although the treatment for psychotic children has improved in recent years, the goals of treatment are modest for most of these children.
a. True
b. False

26. Which statement about childhood psychoses is FALSE?
a. A major goal of treatment is to improve self-help skills.
b. Parents who are trained in operant conditioning methods can help maintain and improve the behaviors the child learns in treatment.
c. Psychoses are more common among boys than girls.
d. Children who are psychotic nevertheless learn quickly.

27. The authors of your text advise that, when someone a child knows dies, the child should be allowed to participate in in the mourning process.
a. True
b. False

28. What should parents NOT do when they notice that their child is afraid?
a. ignore the fear
b. coerce or scold the child
c. ridicule the fear or the child
d. all of the above

29. The technique of reducing fears by pairing the feared object with pleasant or neutral events is called
a. operant conditioning.
b. desensitization.

c. teaching relevant skills.
d. observational learning.

30. Which of the following methods is effective in helping reduce a child's fear?
    a. teaching the child relevant skills
    b. observational learning
    c. rewarding behavior that is less fearful
    d. all of the above

IMPORTANT DETAILS TO KNOW

1. What do boys and girls from different social classes fear? (pp. 457-458)

2. What are the most common fears of toddlers and older children? (p. 458)

3. How do children's beliefs about the concept of death change between ages 4 and 8? (p. 460)

4. What are the relationships regarding the development of asthma and the person's age and gender? (p. 464)

5. What percentage of the children in the Long et al. (1958) study had respiratory difficulty when subjected to dust from their homes? (p. 464)

6. In the Neuhaus (1958) study, how did the asthmatic children compare with siblings, cardiac patients, and normals? (p. 465)

7. What is the incidence rate of childhood psychosis, and what percentage of psychotic children are boys? (p. 469)

TEST YOUR RECALL

1. Describe the developmental changes in children's expression and understanding of complex emotions. (p. 451)

2. How do children use display rules? (p. 452)

3. What did Hyson's (1983) study reveal about developmental changes in children's coping with negative emotions? (p. 453)

4. To what extent do children at different ages understand how an emotion can affect themselves? (p. 454)

5. How do anxieties and phobias differ? (p. 454)

6. How is social class related to the types of fears children

Chapter 13

develop? (pp. 457-458)

7. Characterize how fears change with age. (p. 458)

8. Contrast early versus late school phobia. (p. 459)

9. Give an example of how a phobia might result from a child's misunderstanding of the concept of death. (p. 460)

10. List some causes of children's fears. (pp. 460-462)

11. Characterize a person with a neurotic depression. (pp. 462-463)

12. Name three types of psychophysiological disorders. (p. 464)

13. Asthma appears to result from a combination of what three factors? (p. 464)

14. What were the results of a study by Neuhaus (1958) on asthmatic children and their siblings? (p. 465)

15. Discuss the types of treatment that have been used in treating anorexia nervosa. (p. 467)

16. How is autism different from childhood schizophrenia? (p. 468)

17. What is Bettelheim's view on the role of mothers in the development of childhood psychosis? What is the current view of psychologists on this issue? (p. 470)

18. List four intuitive reasons for assuming a biological basis for childhood psychosis. (p. 470)

19. Describe the impact of psychotic children on their families. (p. 472)

20. Under what conditions do psychotic children have the best prognosis? (p. 472)

21. How have operant conditioning methods been used in the treatment of psychotic children? (p. 472)

22. What advice would you give parents on explaining the death of someone close to a child? (p. 475)

23. Indicate what parents should avoid doing in order to help children overcome fears. (pp. 476-477)

24. What effective methods can be used in reducing childhood fears? (pp. 477-478)

25. How are diagnostic labels used and sometimes abused in the treatment of childhood disorders? (pp. 478-479)

26. List several sources of help for obtaining information in locating a therapist. (p. 479)

ANSWER SECTION

GUIDED REVIEW:

1. basic; mixed
2. basic; shame; guilt; 3
3. display rules; childhood
4. avoided; reinforce; reasoning
5. neuroses; avoidance; fear; phobias; anxieties
6. girls; abstract; cognitive; social
7. separation; attendance
8. reversible; 8; phobia
9. temperaments
10. severe; long-lasting; less
11. psychophysiological; allergies; psychological; males; children; personalities; siblings; parents
12. colitis; anorexia; biofeedback; female; overestimate; medical; operant
13. schizophrenia; socialization; speech; 3 or 4
14. resilient
15. mothers; brain; maturational (biological)
16. brain; genetic; biochemical
17. little; stimulation; mutilation; help
18. mourning; cognitive
19. explanations; relevant; reward (reinforcement); desensitization
20. physicians; clergy; mental health

TERMS AND DEFINITIONS QUIZ:

SET 1:
1. biofeedback
2. anxiety
3. neuroses
4. school phobia
5. depression
6. display rules
7. psychophysiological disorders
8. death phobia
9. phobias

SET 2:
1. Childhood schizophrenia
2. asthma
3. autism
4. anorexia nervosa
5. desensitization or counterconditioning
6. ulcers
7. colitis
8. psychosis

Chapter 13

MATCHING QUIZ:

1. c (p. 451)
2. a (p. 452)
3. h (p. 466)
4. g (p. 468)
5. b (p. 463)
6. d (p. 477)
7. e (p. 458)
8. i (p. 466)
9. f (p. 464)

SELF TEST:

1. a (p. 450)
2. d (p. 452)
3. b (p. 453)
4. c (p. 455)
5. d (p. 456)
6. a (p. 457)
7. b (p. 458)
8. b (p. 459)
9. b (p. 461)
10. d (p. 462)
11. a (p. 461)
12. c (p. 462)
13. d (p. 462)
14. b (p. 464)
15. d (p. 464)
16. b (p. 464)
17. b (p. 465)
18. b (p. 465)
19. a (p. 466)
20. a (p. 468)
21. d (p. 468)
22. a (p. 469)
23. d (p. 471)
24. b (p. 470)
25. a (p. 472)
26. d (p. 473)
27. a (p. 476)
28. d (pp. 476-477)
29. b (p. 477)
30. d (pp. 477-478)

CHAPTER 14

Adolescent Physical, Cognitive, and Sexual Development

SUMMARY IN OUTLINE

PROLOGUE   (p. 487)

   Adolescence was not considered separate from adulthood in the 1800s.
   Adolescence in Western societies begins at puberty (age 12-13) and lasts until about age 20.

PHYSICAL DEVELOPMENT   (p. 488)

   Many physical changes occur with puberty.
   Androgen and estrogen production increase.

   THE GROWTH SPURT
      Physical Growth--rapid gains in height and weight; sex differences
      Motor Development
         Sex differences in strength and endurance
         Males continue to show improvement in motor skills; females typically show less improvement.

   FEMALE SEXUAL MATURATION
      Growth spurt begins before breast buds and pubic hair develop.
      Many changes in the reproductive system
      First menstruation is called menarche; girls often have neutral or negative reactions to it.

   MALE SEXUAL MATURATION
      Sexual maturity starts about 1 year before the growth spurt.

Ejaculations at 14 or 15 years; fertile a year or more later.

EARLY VERSUS LATE MATURERS
Compared with late maturers, early maturing boys are larger and stronger, have better athletic skills, tend be leaders, and are more socially active and mature.
Compared with late maturers, early maturing girls tend to be shorter and stockier, and may be "out of step" in early adolescence.

ADOLESCENT COGNITION   (p. 495)

FORMAL OPERATIONAL THOUGHT--highest stage in Piaget's theory.
<u>Using Abstract Concepts</u>--adolescent thinking is less dependent on concrete perception.
<u>Contemplating Hypothetical and Future Events</u>
<u>Considering All Possible Combinations</u>
- Pendulum problem
- Logical and systematic problem solving

<u>Coordinating Related Variables</u>
- Balance scale problem
- Reason systematically about the interactions of 2 or more variables.
- Can reason about proportions and logical propositions.

ATTAINING FORMAL OPERATIONAL THOUGHT
Most adolescents fail to show full development of formal operations; most adults show incomplete attainment.
Formal operational thought improves in adolescence.
High positive correlation between IQ and formal thinking.

ADOLESCENT SOCIAL COGNITION--hampered by adolescent egocentrism (imaginary audience and personal fable)

THE ROLE OF THE SCHOOL
Nearly all teens start high school; 70-75% graduate.
Academic achievement declined after 1960, but this decline seems to have stopped.
Most teens have positive attitudes about school, but want more emphasis on academic achievement, vocational training, and social/psychological objectives.

ADOLESCENT SEXUALITY   (p. 502)

CULTURAL INFLUENCES ON SEXUALITY
Western societies hold a double standard for the sexes.
Differences of Hopi, Ashanti, and Vedda regarding sexual relations

SEXUAL ATTITUDES
The Sorensen (1973) study
<u>Parent and Adolescent Sexual Attitudes</u>
Most teens respect their parents, but most also feel that their attitudes about sex differ from their parents'.

Chapter 14

    Sexual attitudes are typically more conservative for parents than teens.
    Today most parents approve of college age children having sexual relations when in love.
    Adolescents receive little sex information from their parents.
  <u>Adolescent Views on Sex and Personal Relationships</u>
    Fewer boys than girls feel a need for love in sexual relations.
    Sexual attitudes of teens vary with age and education.

SEXUAL BEHAVIOR--historical trends show rapid changes in the 1920s and after the mid-1960s.
  <u>Heterosexual Contacts</u>
    Petting has grown more intense as the incidence of intercourse has increased.
    Boys and girls typically feel differently about their first intercourse.
    Sorensen found two types of nonvirgins, serial monogamists and sexual adventurers.
  <u>Homosexual Contacts</u>
    Sex play is fairly common in preadolescent boys.
    Most early homosexual encounters are experimental; most of these teens develop heterosexual orientations.
    Homosexuality is no longer viewed as an illness.
    The causes of homosexuality are not known.

<u>ISSUES IN ACTION</u> (p. 513)

  SEXUALLY TRANSMITTED DISEASE: "VENEREAL" DISEASE
    VD has become epidemic since 1960, particularly among 15- to 30-year-olds.
    Incidence is much higher for males than females.
    Gonorrhea, genital herpes, syphilis, and AIDS

  UNWED PREGNANCY AND MOTHERHOOD
    Alarming increase in the number of unwed pregnancies.
    About 10% of unmarried girls at ages 15 to 19 become pregnant.
    Most sexually active teens in the U.S. don't regularly use reliable contraceptives.
    In other Western countries the teenage pregnancy rate is less than half the rate in the U.S.
    Over 90% of unwed teenage mothers keep their babies.
    Teens who marry to avoid having an out-of-wedlock child tend to have marital difficulty.

GUIDED REVIEW

1. Adolescence begins with _____ and ends around age 20. Adolescent body growth is regulated, in part, by the _____ gland, which stimulates other glands to produce two classes of sex hormones, _____ and _____.

2. The growth spurt begins about age _____ in girls; boys start their spurt about _____ years later. During this time there are rapid gains in height and weight, and changes in body proportions. Motor abilities increase in _____, speed, and coordination.

3. Puberty begins with a rapid enlargement of testes in boys and _____ in girls. The growth of _____ hair and of the breasts or penis occur in early adolescence; later, the _____ deepens and body hair comes in. These are called _____ sex characteristics. At 12.8 years of age, the average American girl experiences _____. Boys are capable of producing e_____ by about age 15.

4. For the past century people have been _____ at earlier ages. Earlier maturity of girls is shown by their younger age at _____. These changes are thought to be due to improved health conditions. This trend seems to have reached a biological lower-_____ in the United States.

5. Early-maturing males are more likely to be admired for their _____ skills and to be active in _____ and social affairs. They appear to be much more socially mature and have more positive self-_____ than late-maturing boys. For females, few consistent differences are found between early- and late-maturers, perhaps because of the lesser importance placed on _____ prowess.

6. According to _____'s theory of cognitive development, adolescents attain _____ thought. Their thinking now includes several distinctive abilities: they can effectively use _____ concepts, deal with _____ and future situations, systematically break down a complex problem and test all possible _____ of its components, and they can coordinate related _____.

7. Research has found that a (minority/majority) of adolescents and adults attain full formal operations. Martorano (1977) found that formal reasoning improves throughout adolescence, with the largest gain occuring between _____th and _____th grades.

8. According to Elkind (1967), adolescent social cognition is still hampered by _____. This includes the feel-

ing of being "on stage," or having an _____ audience, and the idea that others do not have similar feelings, which is called the personal _____

9. When asked to describe themselves and others, children focus on _____ qualities, like appearance, whereas adolescents stress psychological qualities.

10. Schools are charged with fostering cognitive growth, yet in American schools academic achievement has _____, particularly in the area of _____ academic skills, such as writing.

11. Overall, student attitudes are (positive/negative) toward the schools. They feel that less stress should be given to _____ and more emphasis should be given to academic, _____, and social/psychological areas.

12. There are wide cultural variations in the way adolescent sexuality is treated. In the United States a _____ is applied, one for males and one for females.

13. Adolescents today view sexual morality as a (public/personal) matter. Sexual acts are more likely to be approved if _____ is involved and disapproved if _____ is involved. Yankelovich (1974) found that with increasing age and _____, young people become more approving of unconventional sexual behaviors.

14. This century's shift toward sexual permissiveness was first evident in the _____s, and then again the the 1960s, about the time the "_____" was introduced.

15. Victorian courting was often arranged by parents and watched over by a _____. By the 1920s couples dated without adults around, and the practice of _____ became common. Today the incidence of _____ has increased.

16. The largest group of sexually active teens and those with a preference for going steady are called _____. Some of these youths live together, a practice called _____. Only a small percentage of youth--the sexual adventurers--adopt a _____ pattern of sexual behavior, and those who do, report more _____ with parents and society.

17. The chief adolescent outlet for sex often is _____. The trend toward masturbating at younger ages is particularly strong among (boys/girls). Sorensen (1973) found that teens of both sexes use _____ during masturbation.

18. Homosexual sex _____ is fairly common during childhood, but it _____ as adolescence nears. The vast majority of first homosexual contacts are with

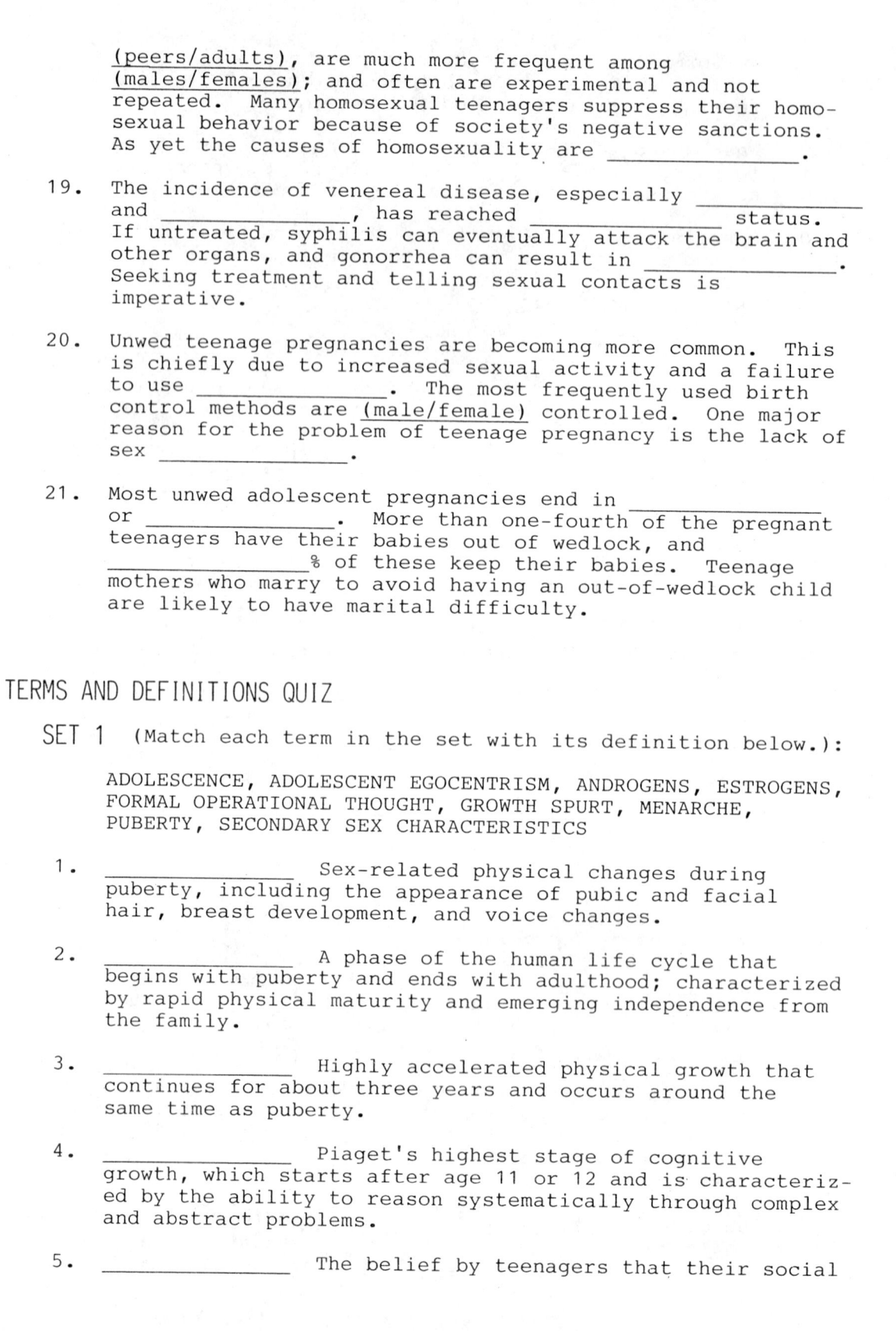

(peers/adults), are much more frequent among (males/females); and often are experimental and not repeated. Many homosexual teenagers suppress their homosexual behavior because of society's negative sanctions. As yet the causes of homosexuality are _____.

19. The incidence of venereal disease, especially _____ and _____, has reached _____ status. If untreated, syphilis can eventually attack the brain and other organs, and gonorrhea can result in _____. Seeking treatment and telling sexual contacts is imperative.

20. Unwed teenage pregnancies are becoming more common. This is chiefly due to increased sexual activity and a failure to use _____. The most frequently used birth control methods are (male/female) controlled. One major reason for the problem of teenage pregnancy is the lack of sex _____.

21. Most unwed adolescent pregnancies end in _____ or _____. More than one-fourth of the pregnant teenagers have their babies out of wedlock, and _____% of these keep their babies. Teenage mothers who marry to avoid having an out-of-wedlock child are likely to have marital difficulty.

TERMS AND DEFINITIONS QUIZ

SET 1 (Match each term in the set with its definition below.):

ADOLESCENCE, ADOLESCENT EGOCENTRISM, ANDROGENS, ESTROGENS, FORMAL OPERATIONAL THOUGHT, GROWTH SPURT, MENARCHE, PUBERTY, SECONDARY SEX CHARACTERISTICS

1. _____ Sex-related physical changes during puberty, including the appearance of pubic and facial hair, breast development, and voice changes.

2. _____ A phase of the human life cycle that begins with puberty and ends with adulthood; characterized by rapid physical maturity and emerging independence from the family.

3. _____ Highly accelerated physical growth that continues for about three years and occurs around the same time as puberty.

4. _____ Piaget's highest stage of cognitive growth, which starts after age 11 or 12 and is characterized by the ability to reason systematically through complex and abstract problems.

5. _____ The belief by teenagers that their social

universe is directed toward them.

6. _____ A class of sex hormones produced by both sexes, but in greater quantity in males, particularly during and after puberty.

7. _____ A class of sex hormones produced by both sexes, but in greater quantity in females, particularly during and after puberty.

8. _____ The period of rapid sexual maturation in humans that begins with the enlargement of ovaries and testes.

9. _____ A girl's first menstruation.

SET 2: DOUBLE STANDARD, GENITAL HERPES, GONORRHEA, IMAGINARY AUDIENCE, PERSONAL FABLE, SERIAL MONOGAMISTS, SEXUAL ADVENTURERS, SYPHILIS, VENEREAL DISEASE

1. _____ Elkind's term for the constant scrutiny adolescents often feel they are under; part of adolescent egocentrism.

2. _____ Elkind's term for the belief by teenagers that they are so unique or special that others cannot understand their needs or feelings.

3. _____ Different expectations for the conduct of boys and girls, especially regarding the morality of sexual behavior.

4. _____ Unmarried adolescents who have a series of affectionate and sexual relationships with one person at a time.

5. _____ Adolescents who are highly promiscuous in their sexual conduct.

6. _____ Any of several diseases transmitted by sexual activity.

7. _____ A contagious venereal disease that results in an internal infection of the genitals; infected males may notice a burning sensation when urinating and a mucous seepage from the penis, but the disease is less easily detected in females.

8. _____ A viral disease that is sexually transmitted; symptoms include small fluid-filled blisters that recur periodically.

9. _____ A contagious venereal disease caused by bacteria; it produces a complex series of symptoms beginning with open sores and, if untreated, attacks such organs

as the eyes, heart, and brain.

MATCHING QUIZ

1. ___ formal operational thought   a. secondary sex characteristic

2. ___ personal fable   b. more athletic and popular

3. ___ serial monogamist   c. gender-related rules about sexual conduct

4. ___ venereal disease   d. parents are not a major source

5. ___ pubic hair   e. a minority of adults show full attainment

6. ___ early maturing male   f. most frequent between ages 15-30 years

7. ___ double standard   g. an aspect of teenage egocentrism

8. ___ sex information   h. preference for going steady

SELF TEST

1. Adolescence in the United States
   a. begins 2 years before the growth spurt starts.
   b. began at 13 years of age in the early 1800s.
   c. lasts from about 13 to 20 years of age.
   d. begins after the reproductive system has fully matured.

2. The pituitary gland
   a. regulates body growth but not sexual maturation.
   b. produces most of the body's estrogen.
   c. produces most of the body's androgen.
   d. is part of the endocrine system which influences maturation.

3. Which statement about adolescent physical development is TRUE?
   a. Adrenal androgens regulate the appearance of body hair in boys and girls.
   b. Girls produce adrenal estrogens, not androgens, which affect their secondary sex characteristics.
   c. Boys do not produce androgen until they are 13 years old.
   d. Girls do not produce estrogen until they are 11 years old.

Chapter 14

4. Boys grow at a faster rate than girls during the growth spurt.
    a. True
    b. False

5. Boys show LESS development in _____ during adolescence than girls do.
    a. muscle strength
    b. arm dexterity
    c. speed and agility
    d. none of the above

6. The average age at which girls in the United States reach menarche is _____ years.
    a. 11.6
    b. 13.5
    c. 14.2
    d. none of the above

7. Boys are capable of producing ejaculations by about _____ years of age.
    a. 8
    b. 10
    c. 12
    d. 14

8. Early maturing boys tend to have relatively negative self-concepts, compared to late maturing boys.
    a. True
    b. False

9. Compared to late maturers, early maturing girls are more likely to
    a. be less socially mature.
    b. have less social status at age 15.
    c. have a short and stocky build.
    d. feel out of step in high school.

10. Which of the following is NOT a major characteristic of formal operational thought?
    a. using abstract concepts
    b. irreversible logic
    c. contemplating hypothetical events
    d. considering all possible combinations

11. According to Piaget, prior to reaching the formal operational stage of cognitive development, children generally cannot coordinate several related variables to solve a problem.
    a. True
    b. False

12. By the end of adolescence, most teenagers show full attainment of formal operational thought.
    a. True
    b. False

13. Specific training in relevant cognitive skills _____ adolescents' performance on formal-operational tasks.
    a. does not affect
    b. improves
    c. interferes with female, but not male,
    d. interferes with male, but not female,

14. According to Elkind (1967), adolescent egocentrism includes two aspects which are called
    a. the double standard.
    b. formal and informal reasoning.
    c. imaginary audience and personal fable.
    d. pendulum and balance.

15. Adolescents are more likely than children to focus on aspects of one's overt qualities (such as appearance) when describing themselves or other people.
    a. True
    b. False

16. Research on the role of schools on development in adolescence has shown that
    a. only about 55% of all adolescents graduate high school.
    b. most adolescents believe that school is unnecessary, and they would drop out if they could.
    c. the large decline in academic achievement in the 1960s and 1970s seems to have stopped.
    d. teenagers would like greater emphasis placed on sports in high school.

17. Most adolescents feel that their attitudes about sex are different from those of their parents.
    a. True
    b. False

18. In Sorensen's (1973) survey, about _____% of the teenagers reported that their parents had discussed birth control with them.
    a. 8
    b. 18
    c. 36
    d. 56

19. Yankelovich's (1974) survey found that the more education teenagers and young adults have the
    a. more accepting they are of casual premarital sex.
    b. more accepting they are of homosexual relations.
    c. less tolerant they are of unconventional sexual behavior.
    d. both a and b

20. The percentage of females who have remained virgins has declined to about _____% since the early 1900s.
    a. 15
    b. 30
    c. 45

d. 60

21. Today, the percentage of teenage females who have had sexual experience is the same as for males.
    a. True
    b. False

22. Unmarried adolescents who have a sexually active relationship with one person at a time are called sexual adventurers.
    a. True
    b. False

23. The sexual adventurers in Sorensen's (1973) study reported that they
    a. were sexually faithful to their partners.
    b. preferred to "go steady."
    c. sought another steady relationship after breaking up with a partner.
    d. none of the above.

24. By 20 years of age, about _____% of males and _____% of females masturbate.
    a. 85; 60
    b. 50; 50
    c. 60; 35
    d. 35; 10

25. Homosexual sex play prior to puberty declines later and generally does not lead to a homosexual orientation in adulthood.
    a. True
    b. False

26. The American Psychiatric Association _____ homosexuality to be an illness.
    a. no longer considers
    b. still considers
    c. once again considers
    d. never did consider

27. The incidence of gonorrhea among 15- to 19-year-olds has increased by _____% since 1960.
    a. 50
    b. 100
    c. 300
    d. 1,000

28. Which of the following sexually transmitted diseases attacks the liver, heart, and brain if not treated?
    a. gonorrhea
    b. genital herpes
    c. syphilis
    d. none of the above

29. The basic reason for the high incidence of teenage

pregnancy in the United States is that sexually active adolescents do not regularly use reliable birth control methods.
a. True
b. False

30. About _____% of unwed pregnant adolescents get married before their baby is born.
a. 90
b. 62
c. 30
d. 12

IMPORTANT DETAILS TO KNOW

1. When does adolescence begin and end? (p. 487)

2. What gland is especially important in regulating sexual maturation? What hormone is related to the development of facial hair and acne? (p. 488)

3. Describe androgen and estrogen production in males and females during pubertal development. See Figure 14.1 (p. 481)

4. Compare boys' and girls' blood pressure and the size of their hearts and lungs. (p. 490)

5. In the sexual maturation of boys, when do they usually (1) begin a period of penis enlargement, (2) become capable of ejaculation, and (3) become fertile? (p. 492)

6. In what areas of the world does menarche currently occur relatively early and late? See Highlight 14.1. (p. 493)

7. According to Piaget, why do children at the concrete operational level think "Lily is darkest" in the problem on coordinating propositions? (p. 498)

8. Relatively complete development of formal operational thought has been found to occur in what percentage of adults and university graduate students? (p. 498)

9. What percentage of Americans graduate high school? (p. 501)

10. Compare the cultural views on adolescent sexuality among the Hopi and Ashanti. (p. 503)

11. What are the effects of syphilis and gonorrhea if left untreated? (p. 513)

12. What proportion of unwed 15- to 19-year-olds becomes pregnant? Why is this so? (p. 514)

13. Out of the total number of unwed pregnant teens, what percentage have their babies out of wedlock. (p. 515)

TEST YOUR RECALL

1. Describe how body growth and sexual maturation are regulated. (p. 488)

2. Outline the changes in physical growth for boys and girls. (p. 490)

3. Trace the changes in motor development for both sexes. (pp. 490-491)

4. List the sequential changes in female sexual maturation. (pp. 491-492)

5. Specify the developmental sequence of male sexual maturation. (p. 492)

6. Discuss the trend toward earlier adolescent maturation. See Highlight 14.1. (p. 493)

7. Compare the differences in socialization and personalities of early and late maturing males. (pp. 493-494)

8. Explain the advantages and disadvantages of being an early maturing female. (p. 494)

9. List the four major abilities that characterize formal operational thought. (p. 495)

10. Give an example that illustrates how a teen at the stage of formal operations would solve a problem by "considering all possible combinations." (p. 496)

11. Describe the method and results of Martorano's (1977) study on the development of formal operations. (p. 498)

12. Explain Elkind's view of adolescent "egocentrism." (p. 499)

13. Give an example of how adolescent egocentrism might be reduced. (p. 500)

14. How do teens generally feel about their high schools? (p. 501)

15. Cite examples of cross-cultural differences in adolescent sexuality. (p. 503)

16. Discuss how parent and teen attitudes on sexuality are both similar and different. (p. 504)

234   Chapter 14

17. How do teens generally feel about sexual behavior and the quality of the personal relationships involved? (p. 505)

18. Describe the broad historical changes in sexual permissiveness that occurred in 20th century America. (pp. 505-506)

19. Discuss the relationships "serial monogamists" tend to have. (p. 508)

20. State some trends in the data on teenage masturbation. See Highlight 14.2. (p. 509)

21. Describe the personal qualities of those teens Sorensen called "sexual adventurers." (pp. 509-510)

22. Discuss the usual consequences of homosexual sex play among preadolescents. (p. 510)

23. List the various ways that homosexual teens cope with their sexuality. (p. 511)

24. What are the possible consequences of untreated syphilis and gonorrhea? (p. 513)

25. Why do sexually active teens fail to use contraception? (p. 515)

26. Discuss the problems faced by teenage mothers who marry to avoid having an out-of-wedlock child. (p. 515)

ANSWER SECTION

GUIDED REVIEW:

1. puberty; pituitary; androgens; estrogens
2. 10 or 11; 2; strength
3. ovaries; pubic; voice; secondary; menarche; ejaculations
4. maturing; menarche; limit
5. athletic; school; concepts; athletic
6. Piaget; formal operational; abstract; hypothetical; combinations; variables (factors)
7. minority; 8; 10
8. egocentrism; imaginary; fable
9. overt
10. declined; basic
11. positive; athletics; vocational
12. double standard
13. personal; love; hurt; education
14. 1920s; Pill
15. chaperone; petting; intercourse
16. serial monogomists; cohabitation; promiscuous; conflict
17. masturbation; girls; fantasy

Chapter 14

18. play; declines; peers; males; uncertain
19. gonorrhea; genital herpes; epidemic; sterility
20. contraceptives; male; education
21. miscarriage; abortion; 90

TERMS AND DEFINITIONS QUIZ:

SET 1:
1. secondary sex characteristics
2. adolescence
3. growth spurt
4. formal operational stage
5. adolescent egocentrism
6. androgens
7. estrogens
8. puberty
9. menarche

SET 2:
1. imaginary audience
2. personal fable
3. double standard
4. serial monogamists
5. sexual adventurers
6. venereal disease
7. gonorrhea
8. genital herpes
9. syphilis

MATCHING QUIZ:

1. e (p. 498)
2. g (p. 499)
3. h (p. 508)
4. f (p. 513)
5. a (p. 488)
6. b (p. 494)
7. c (p. 502)
8. d (p. 504)

SELF TEST:

1. c (p. 487)
2. d (p. 488)
3. a (p. 488)
4. a (p. 490)
5. d (p. 490)
6. d (p. 493)
7. d (p. 492)
8. b (p. 494)
9. c (p. 494)
10. b (p. 495)
11. a (p. 497)
12. b (p. 498)
13. b (p. 498)
14. c (p. 499)
15. b (p. 500)
16. c (p. 501)
17. a (p. 504)
18. b (p. 504)
19. d (p. 505)
20. b (p. 505)
21. b (p. 505)
22. b (pp. 508-509)
23. d (p. 509)
24. a (p. 509)
25. a (p. 510)
26. a (p. 510)
27. c (p. 513)
28. c (p. 513)
29. a (p. 514)
30. d (p. 515)

CHAPTER 15

Adolescent Social, Emotional, and Personality Development

SUMMARY IN OUTLINE

ADOLESCENT SOCIAL RELATIONSHIPS (p. 522)

THE FAMILY--most adolescents get along well with parents and siblings.
Parent/Adolescent Conflicts
Conflicts exist in some families, but they are neither inevitable nor the rule.
Boys and girls feel they know their mothers better than their fathers.
Values of parents and their teens are quite similar.
Teens think parents should set and enforce rules of conduct.
Sibling Relations
Strong sibling rivalries are not common in adolescence.
Same-sex siblings feel closer than opposite-sex siblings do.
Birth order and spacing affect sibling relations.

PEER RELATIONSHIPS--most frequent teen activities are talking with peers, watching TV, and studying.
Parents, Peers, and Pressure to Conform
Younger teens report more pressure to conform than older ones.
The value teens attach to the opinions of parents or peers depends on the issue.
Friendships and Peer Groups
Friendships are more stable and intimate than in childhood.
Teens report more frequent positive feelings with friends than with their families.

Boys' friendships tend to be casual and activity centered.
Girls tend to have a small number of intimate friends.
Friends tend to be the same sex, age, and race.
Teens form cliques and crowds.
- The Youth Culture
  - Some teens are adult oriented, others are peer oriented, and many fall in between these two extremes.

THE SELF AND SOCIETY (p. 530)

DEVELOPMENT OF THE SELF--according to Erikson, adolescence is a time to establish a sense of identity.
- Achieving Identity
  - Moratorium--period of delay
  - According to Erikson, failure to achieve identity can result in a sense of role confusion or identity diffusion.
  - Identity statuses: achievement, foreclosure, moratorium, and diffusion--see Table 15.2.
  - Identity achievement increases with age.
  - Identity formation differs for college students and working age-mates.
- Adolescent Self-Concepts
  - Most teens are preoccupied with their appearance.
  - Self-esteem gradually improves throughout adolescence.
  - Self-concepts show considerable stability through the teen years.
  - Body weight and starting a new school can affect self-esteem.
  - Teens are concerned about how others view them.
- The Minority-Group Adolescent's Self-Concept
  - Cultural conflict makes it more difficult to form a coherent identity.
  - Self-esteem depends partly on the social and political context.

MORAL DEVELOPMENT AND VALUES IN ADOLESCENCE
- Moral Reasoning--Kohlberg's theory
  - Only a minority of teens and adults reason at the postconventional level.
  - Consequences and culture influence moral reasoning.
- Moral Conduct, Values, and Self-Regulation
  - Internal locus of control versus external locus of control
  - The incidence of cheating in school remains high during adolescence.
  - Moral reasoning and political/social ideology are related.

VOCATIONAL CHOICE
Ginzberg's sequential periods of vocational decision making: fantasy period, tentative period, and realistic period
Although the traditional career orientations of boys and girls are changing slowly, females still prefer the

"helping professions."
Social-class background is related to vocational choice.

PROBLEMS OF ADOLESCENCE (p. 539)

HIGH SCHOOL DROPOUTS
Dropouts face severe social and vocational problems.
Involuntary dropouts, retarded dropouts, and capable dropouts
Factors related to who drops out include race, social class, academic problems, home climate, and self-esteem.

JUVENILE DELINQUENCY
More boys than girls are arrested for every type of crime except prostitution.
Only a minority of teen offenders are apprehended.
Who Becomes Delinquent?
Rate of teen crime is increasing more rapidly for girls than boys.
Social-class differences in delinquent behavior seem to be greater for apprehended youths than for unapprehended youths.
Biological factors play a role in delinquency.
The Delinquent's Family
Five family factors associated with the development of delinquency: broken homes, quality of the parent/child relationship, disciplinary techniques, family-management skills, and personality and behavioral traits.
The Delinquent's Friends
Most delinquent acts occur in the company of friends.
Many juvenile delinquents join gangs.
The Delinquent's Personality--characteristics of
delinquents: impulsive, defiant, resentful of authority, lower self-esteem, dislikes classmates, sometimes "difficult" temperaments, low tolerance for misbehavior, greater use of punishment.

DRUG USE AND ABUSE
Tobacco
Recent trends among adults and teens; sex differences
Why teens start smoking
Alcohol
Statistics on American drinking habits
Influence of family and friends is powerful.
Alcohol is a depressant; this may reinforce drinking behavior.
Marijuana
Effects of marijuana
Incidence and reasons for use
Other Drugs
Hallucinogens: LSD, mescaline, and PCP
Three other categories: stimulants (amphetamines, cocaine), depressants (alcohol, methaquelone, barbiturates), and narcotics (morphine, codeine, heroin)

Teen use of "serious" drugs has not increased in recent years.

TEENAGE SUICIDE
The rate for teenage suicide has risen sharply.
More females attempt suicide, but more males kill themselves.
Suicidal youths often have a history of problems; usually there is a stressful precipitating event.

ISSUES IN ACTION (p. 552)

REDUCING DELINQUENCY
Prevention
Predictors include environmental factors, behavioral signs, and biological markers.
Family-management training for parents
Improving the child's reading skills
Participation in Head Start
Treating the Delinquent
Three components of a successful approach: (1) the use of operant conditioning, (2) skilled supervision, and (3) small community-based group homes.

VOCATIONAL INFORMATION--systematic exploration of personal attributes with the aid of guidance counselors and psychological tests.

GUIDED REVIEW

1. Many parents feel ambivalent about their adolescent's push toward independent self-_____, and on occasion may be overly restrictive. Teenagers may resist, and parent/adolescent _____ sometimes arise. Some psychologists believe these conflicts are intense, widespread, and result in a _____ gap. _____ feel that parent/adolescent conflict is a necessary process in the formation of the _____. But surveys have found that intense conflict is not typical.

2. Research has shown that important attitudes and values held by parents are _____ by their teenagers. This similarity probably limits generational conflict. Studies have found that British children rate (adults/peers) more positively than they rate (adults/peers) on basic personality attributes, and the values of adolescents become more like their (friends'/parents') as they approach adulthood.

3. Peer pressure to conform reaches a peak in (early/late) adolescence. When chosing between the opinions of peers or parents, teenagers place more value on peer opinions for issues involving _____ consequences, but parents' opinions are favored in long-range goals and basic _____ codes.

4. The smallest peer group is a _____. Girls usually have a small number of (casual/best) friends; boys are more likely to have many _____ or good friends. As teens get older, they report increasing in _____ with friends. Cliques are (larger/smaller) than crowds, and in early adolescence are usually made up of _____-sex members. In late adolescence (crowds/cliques) fade away as _____ become sexually integrated.

5. The major task of personality during adolescence is to form a sense of _____. Most societies help in this process by providing a _____ during which adolescents try on many roles and values as they try to attain the status of identity _____. The status where commitments have been made without entering a moratorium is called identity _____. Adolescents who neither have nor are seeking firm commitments are classified in the identity _____ status.

6. The adolescent's physical appearance is very important. Most teens would like to change how they look. Being overweight can impair one's _____; for (boys/girls) this occurs only in early adolescence.

7. A child's ideal-_____ is based primarily on the parents, but the older adolescent tends to use a com_____ of many admired people. Young adolescents are highly concerned with how _____ view them and consequently may feel more self-_____ than they did as children.

8. Establishing an identity can be especially difficult for _____ group members. Powell (1973) found that when blacks were poor and comprised a _____ percentage of the population, their self-esteem was lower than whites; but when their ethnic community was large and cohesive, as in one Southern city, their self-esteem was (equal to/higher than) that of whites.

9. Although moral reasoning advances during adolescence, only a minority operate at Kohlberg's _____ level. Research has shown that the consequences affect not only moral conduct, but moral _____, too.

10. Ginzberg (1972) proposed that vocational decision making develops through three periods which he named the _____ period, the tentative period, and the _____ period. Working 10 to 15 hours a week during the high school years can _____ development.

11. Voss et al. (1966) have described three types of dropouts: the voluntary, the _____, and the capable dropout. Probably _____ of all dropouts are capable of completing school. The dropout rate is much higher

among teens with _____-class backgrounds, and among blacks. Dropouts not only have problems at school, they are more likely to have poor _____ relationships.

12. The incidence of juvenile delinquency increased in the 1960s and 1970s, but then began to _____. In interviews on delinquent behavior _____% of un-apprehended youth claimed to have committed a delinquent act. Unapprehended delinquents are more likely to come from the _____-class; apprehended youths tend to come from the _____-class.

13. Biological factors seem to play a role in a person's becoming a delinquent. Twin studies and _____ studies have confirmed this link. The results of other research suggest that delinquents tend to have muscular physiques, and their behavior in infancy suggests that they were born with "difficult" _____.

14. Studies have also shown that delinquency is related to _____ parenting and inappropriate models. Many delinquents come from homes where parents are hostile, unsupportive, and inclined to use the _____ discipline technique. These youths often have _____ friends or are members of _____. Delinquents tend to be highly intolerant and punitive toward _____.

15. Today teenage (girls/boys) are more likely to start smoking cigarettes than are _____.

16. Drinking has become a major problem for teenagers. Most teens are introduced to alcohol by their (friends/parents). Alcohol acts as a d_____, which may serve as a _____ because of the relaxation it produces. But alcohol consumption is also reinforced by _____ and parents. Some people may have a _____ predisposition to consume alcohol.

17. Marijuana is classified as a _____. Its use among teenagers is widespread, and the age of first-use is _____. Chronic use may produce _____ damage and _____ symptoms.

18. Other drugs fall into the three major categories of stimulants, depressants, and _____. When use is chronic, stimulants can lead to _____ dependence, but depressants and narcotics can result in _____ and _____ dependence.

19. The suicide rate among American teens has steadily (decreased/increased). Girls attempt suicide more than boys do, but boys are more likely to die in their attempt possibly because they use "_____" methods. Attempts are more likely to be made by people with a long

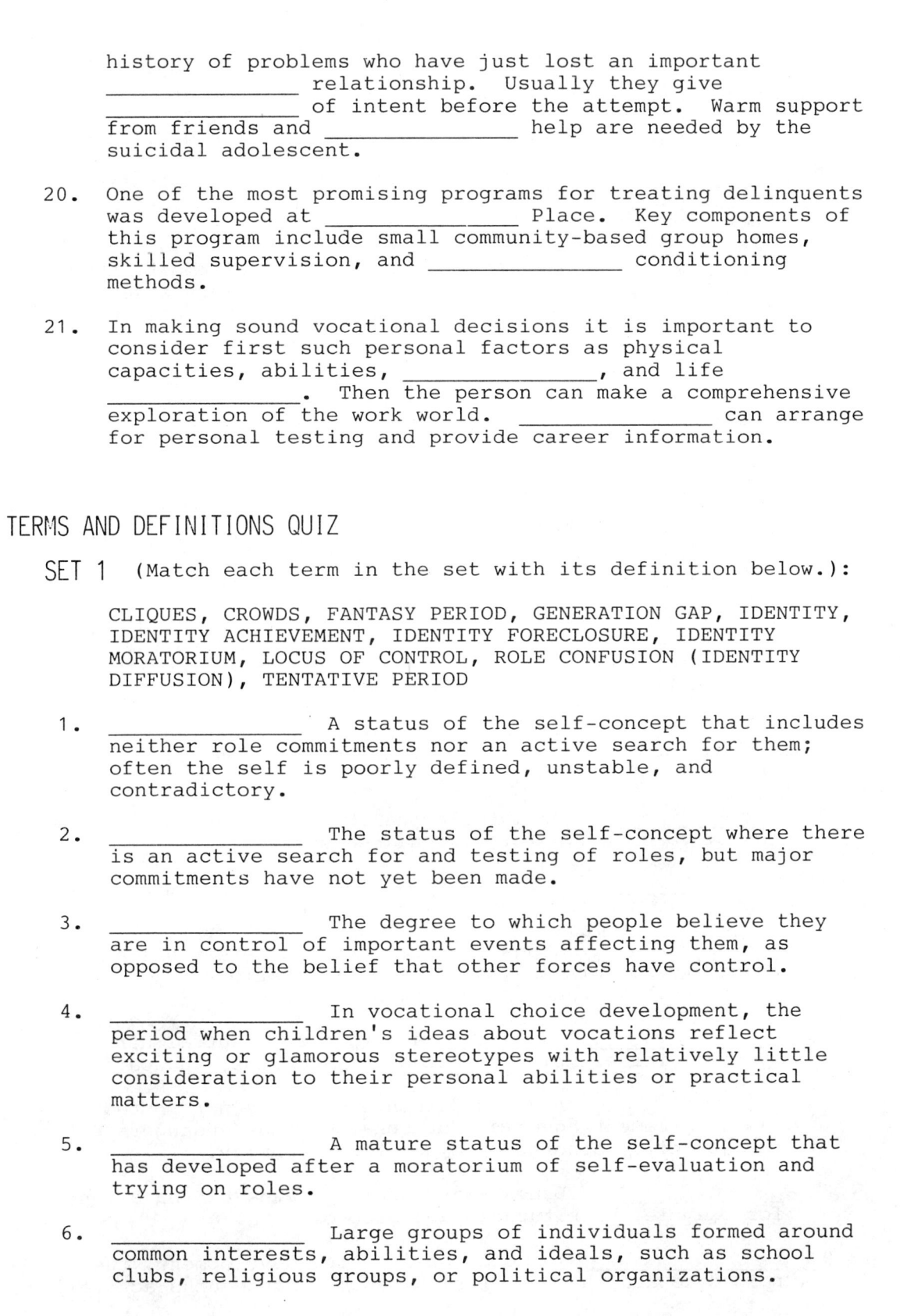

history of problems who have just lost an important _____ relationship. Usually they give _____ of intent before the attempt. Warm support from friends and _____ help are needed by the suicidal adolescent.

20. One of the most promising programs for treating delinquents was developed at _____ Place. Key components of this program include small community-based group homes, skilled supervision, and _____ conditioning methods.

21. In making sound vocational decisions it is important to consider first such personal factors as physical capacities, abilities, _____, and life _____. Then the person can make a comprehensive exploration of the work world. _____ can arrange for personal testing and provide career information.

TERMS AND DEFINITIONS QUIZ

SET 1 (Match each term in the set with its definition below.):

CLIQUES, CROWDS, FANTASY PERIOD, GENERATION GAP, IDENTITY, IDENTITY ACHIEVEMENT, IDENTITY FORECLOSURE, IDENTITY MORATORIUM, LOCUS OF CONTROL, ROLE CONFUSION (IDENTITY DIFFUSION), TENTATIVE PERIOD

1. _____ A status of the self-concept that includes neither role commitments nor an active search for them; often the self is poorly defined, unstable, and contradictory.

2. _____ The status of the self-concept where there is an active search for and testing of roles, but major commitments have not yet been made.

3. _____ The degree to which people believe they are in control of important events affecting them, as opposed to the belief that other forces have control.

4. _____ In vocational choice development, the period when children's ideas about vocations reflect exciting or glamorous stereotypes with relatively little consideration to their personal abilities or practical matters.

5. _____ A mature status of the self-concept that has developed after a moratorium of self-evaluation and trying on roles.

6. _____ Large groups of individuals formed around common interests, abilities, and ideals, such as school clubs, religious groups, or political organizations.

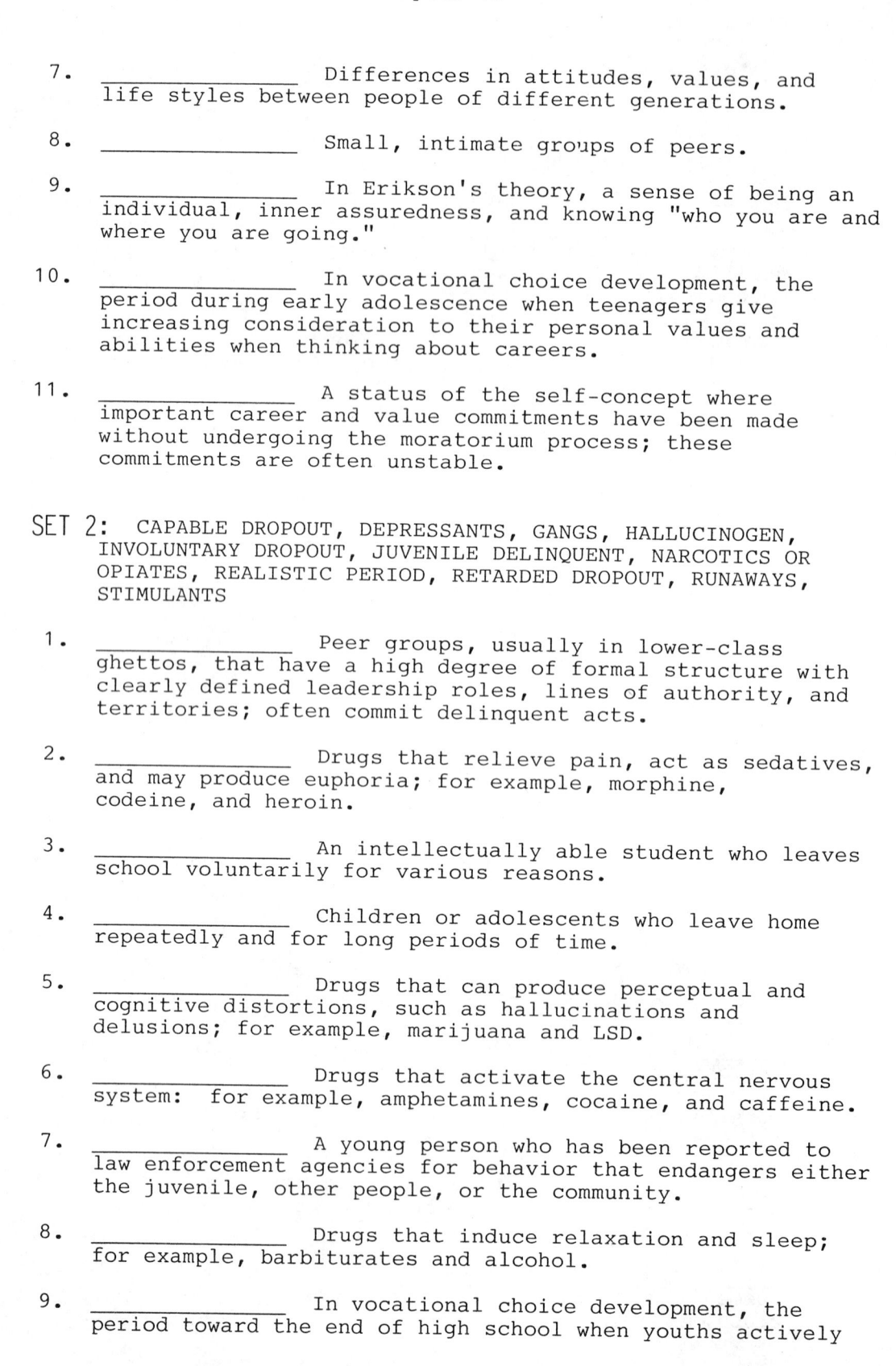

7. _____ Differences in attitudes, values, and life styles between people of different generations.

8. _____ Small, intimate groups of peers.

9. _____ In Erikson's theory, a sense of being an individual, inner assuredness, and knowing "who you are and where you are going."

10. _____ In vocational choice development, the period during early adolescence when teenagers give increasing consideration to their personal values and abilities when thinking about careers.

11. _____ A status of the self-concept where important career and value commitments have been made without undergoing the moratorium process; these commitments are often unstable.

SET 2: CAPABLE DROPOUT, DEPRESSANTS, GANGS, HALLUCINOGEN, INVOLUNTARY DROPOUT, JUVENILE DELINQUENT, NARCOTICS OR OPIATES, REALISTIC PERIOD, RETARDED DROPOUT, RUNAWAYS, STIMULANTS

1. _____ Peer groups, usually in lower-class ghettos, that have a high degree of formal structure with clearly defined leadership roles, lines of authority, and territories; often commit delinquent acts.

2. _____ Drugs that relieve pain, act as sedatives, and may produce euphoria; for example, morphine, codeine, and heroin.

3. _____ An intellectually able student who leaves school voluntarily for various reasons.

4. _____ Children or adolescents who leave home repeatedly and for long periods of time.

5. _____ Drugs that can produce perceptual and cognitive distortions, such as hallucinations and delusions; for example, marijuana and LSD.

6. _____ Drugs that activate the central nervous system: for example, amphetamines, cocaine, and caffeine.

7. _____ A young person who has been reported to law enforcement agencies for behavior that endangers either the juvenile, other people, or the community.

8. _____ Drugs that induce relaxation and sleep; for example, barbiturates and alcohol.

9. _____ In vocational choice development, the period toward the end of high school when youths actively

examine career information and their personal motives, abilities, and qualifications.

10. _____ A student who leaves school because of either a family emergency or a physical disability.

11. _____ A student who leaves school and who lacks either the ability or the skills to do academic work.

MATCHING QUIZ

1. ___ moratorium
2. ___ internal locus of control
3. ___ fantasy period
4. ___ broken homes
5. ___ long-range goals
6. ___ tobacco smoking
7. ___ alcoholism
8. ___ clique
9. ___ postconventional

a. families of juvenile delinquents
b. issue for which parental opinions are respected
c. activity often centers around talking
d. more frequent among girls than boys
e. a high level of moral reasoning
f. a period to try on and test various roles
g. childhood vocational choices
h. associated with successful school achievement
i. males outnumber females 5 to 1

SELF TEST

1. Bowerman and Kinch's (1969) study found that preferences for peers was stronger than for family by _____ grade.
   a. fourth
   b. sixth
   c. eighth
   d. tenth

2. According to Davis' sociological theory, conflict between generations intensifies as differences in their _____ increase.
   a. cultural outlook
   b. educational opportunities

c. occupational trends
   d. all of the above

3. A generation gap exists when there are sharp differences between people of different ages in their
   a. attitudes.
   b. values.
   c. life styles.
   d. all of the above.

4. For which of the following statements did Sorensen (1973) find that a majority of teenagers agreed?
   a. "I've never really gotten to know my mother."
   b. "I've never really gotten to know my father."
   c. "I have a lot of respect for my parents' ideas and opinions."
   d. "I don't feel any strong affection for my parents."

5. In which of the following family situations is a sibling LEAST likely to become timid and dependent? He or she has a(n)
   a. older sister.
   b. older brother.
   c. younger sister.
   d. younger brother.

6. Adolescents tend to be more influenced by the opinions of their parents over their peers in deciding whether to go to college.
   a. True
   b. False

7. Girls' cliques tend to have memberships that contain a broader spectrum of social classes than boys' cliques do.
   a. True
   b. False

8. Compared with adult-oriented youth, peer-oriented teenagers are more likely to
   a. be "clean cut."
   b. spend their free time partying.
   c. spend a lot of time making or building things.
   d. see themselves as dependable individuals.

9. A teenager who reports that she has "always known what career I wanted and never considered any other seriously" probably reflects the personality status of identity
   a. achievement.
   b. moratorium.
   c. foreclosure.
   d. diffusion.

10. An adolescent who reports that he hasn't settled on a career decision but is studying several alternatives probably reflects the personality status of identity
    a. achievement.

b. moratorium.
c. foreclosure.
d. diffusion.

11. College students who have achieved an ego identity tend to have relatively high levels of anxiety.
    a. True
    b. False

12. Adolescents who feel good about themselves in their early teens are likely to _____ in their later teens.
    a. have low self-esteem
    b. feel similarly about themselves
    c. show no consistent pattern of feelings
    d. both a and c

13. American society provides no moratorium for minority adolescents to establish an identity.
    a. True
    b. False

14. Postconventional moral reasoning is characterized by
    a. flexibility in one's thinking.
    b. the ability to consider several complicating factors simultaneously.
    c. take a wrongdoer's intentions into account.
    d. all of the above.

15. A teenager's career choice that takes likes and dislikes into account, and begins to involve personal interests and abilities, reflects the _____ period of vocational decision making.
    a. tentative
    b. fantasy
    c. realistic
    d. postconventional

16. Compared with teenagers from lower-class homes, middle-class youth are more likely to
    a. aspire to prestigious careers.
    b. achieve a high-level job in adulthood.
    c. have parents who set high achievement standards.
    d. all of the above.

17. High school dropouts generally report that there is very little mutual understanding and acceptance in their family relationships.
    a. True
    b. False

18. Which statement about juvenile delinquency is TRUE?
    a. A juvenile delinquent is legally defined as any youth who has committed a criminal act and is younger than 16 years of age.
    b. About 12% of all youth are likely to have arrest records by the end of adolescence.

c. Juveniles commit very few burglaries.
d. Girls are now as likely as boys to be arrested for juvenile behavior.

19. Jessor and Jessor's (1977) research on unapprehended youth found that delinquent behavior increases for boys and girls during the high school years.
a. True
b. False

20. About 40% of unapprehended teenagers report having committed delinquent acts.
a. True
b. False

21. Delinquents usually have parents who use an authoritarian style of parenting.
a. True
b. False

22. The parents of delinquent adolescents
a. tend to monitor their children's whereabouts closely.
b. use punishment very consistently.
c. often have arrest histories of their own.
d. all of the above.

23. Haviland's (1977) study comparing the punitiveness of delinquents and nondelinquents found that the
a. nondelinquents recommended much harsher punishment for someone who was caught stealing.
b. delinquents used less punishment when training a rat.
c. two groups used more punishment than reward when training a rat.
d. both a and c

24. Compared to male adolescents, females smoke cigarettes _____ and drink alcohol _____.
a. more; more
b. more; less
c. less; more
d. less; less

25. Excessive use of alcohol may result from which of the following processes?
a. reinforcement
b. modeling
c. heredity
d. all of the above

26. About 15% of a recent sample of high school seniors reported having tried marijuana before reaching high school.
a. True
b. False

27. Chronic use of depressants and narcotics produce physical

and psychological dependence.
a. True
b. False

28. Which of the following methods of committing suicide is a male LEAST likely to use?
    a. shooting
    b. taking poison
    c. hanging
    d. jumping off a bridge

29. Which of the following behavioral signs appears to be a predictor of future delinquency?
    a. impulsiveness
    b. aggressiveness
    c. academic problems
    d. all of the above

30. A follow-up of Achievement Place boys showed that they had _____ than other delinquent boys.
    a. been arrested more often
    b. been convicted of more crimes
    c. higher records of truancy
    d. higher grades

IMPORTANT DETAILS TO KNOW

1. What crimes are teenage boys and girls commonly arrested for? (p. 542)

2. In the confidential interviews by Gold and coworkers, what percentage of unapprehended youth reported having committed delinquent acts? What acts did girls report more than boys? See Figure 15.2 (p. 542)

3. Compare the number of delinquent acts claimed by lower- and middle-class highschoolers. (p. 543)

4. When did the number of new heroin addicts reach its peak? (p. 548)

5. What recent trends have been found in adult and teenage cigarette smoking? (p. 548)

6. From Table 15.5 determine the percentage of the "class of 1981" that (1) first tried marijuana in 9th grade or earlier and (2) had tried marijuana sometime before graduating. Also, compare these percentages with those for the "class of 1975." (p. 550)

7. What percentage of the "class of 1981" had tried narcotics? See Table 15.6. (p. 551)

8. The use of which drugs, other than marijuana, can result

in physical and/or psychological dependence? (p. 551)

TEST YOUR RECALL

1. How do parents often feel about their teenagers becoming independent and moving away from home? (p. 522)

2. Discuss the extent and types of conflict that occurs between teens and their parents. (p. 523)

3. Describe the relative importance that teens give to the opinions of peers and adults concerning different types of issues. (pp. 526-527)

4. Characterize the quality of adolescent friendships as distinct from those of childhood. (p. 527)

5. How are the friendships of girls different from those of boys? (p. 528)

6. Distinguish between the social relationships found in cliques and crowds. (pp. 528-529)

7. How do cliques and crowds change across the teenage years? (p. 529)

8. Characterize the "peer oriented" adolescent. (p. 529)

9. Using Erikson's theory, contrast the adolescent who gains a sense of identity with another teen who has a sense of role confusion. (p. 531)

10. Briefly list and define the four identity statuses described by Marcia (1966, 1967). See Table 15.2. (p. 532)

11. Summarize the findings of research on identity development in college students. (p. 533)

12. Discuss factors shown to be related to changes in self-esteem throughout adolescence. (p. 533)

13. How do advances in cognitive abilities influence adolescent self-concepts? (p. 534)

14. Cite the findings of the study by Powell (1973) on race and geographical differences in adolescent self-esteem. (p. 534)

15. Contrast the personal characteristics of two teens: one with an internal locus of control and one with an external locus of control. (p. 536)

16. Name and describe Ginzberg's (1972) sequential periods of

vocational decision making. (pp. 537-538)

17. How does social-class background often relate to choosing a vocation? (p. 538)

18. What characteristics are related to dropping out of school? (pp. 540-541)

19. What have studies of unapprehended youth revealed about the incidence of juvenile delinquency? (p. 542)

20. Describe the characteristics of those adolescents who are likely to become delinquent. (pp. 542-543)

21. Characterize the family conditions and relationships associated with juvenile delinquency. (pp. 544-545)

22. List the personality traits that differentiate between delinquents and nondelinquents. (p. 546)

23. Describe the method and results of Haviland's study (1977) on the punitiveness of delinquents and nondelinquents. (pp. 546-547)

24. Why do adolescents start smoking? (p. 548)

25. Discuss the influence of family and peers on teenage consumption of alcoholic beverages. (p. 549)

26. Describe the use of marijuana among American teenagers. (p. 550)

27. What factors appear to contribute to adolescent suicide? (pp. 552-553)

28. Describe the treatment program used with delinquents at Achievement Place. (p. 554)

29. List the kinds of information teenagers need to know about themselves in order to make a satisfying vocational choice. (p. 555)

ANSWER SECTION

GUIDED REVIEW:

1. regulation; conflicts; generation; Psychoanalysts; self (self-concept)
2. shared; adults; peers; parents'
3. early; immediate; moral
4. friendship; best; casual; intimacy; smaller; same; crowds; cliques
5. identity; moratorium; achievement; foreclosure; diffusion

6. self-esteem; boys
7. self; composite; others; conscious
8. minority; small; higher than
9. postconventional; reasoning (judgment)
10. fantasy; realistic; benefit
11. retarded; half; lower; family
12. decline; 80; middle; lower
13. adoption; temperaments
14. inadequate (poor); power assertive; delinquent; gangs; misbehavior
15. girls; boys
16. parents; depressant; reinforcer; peers; genetic
17. hallucinogen; decreasing; lung; withdrawal
18. narcotics (opiates); psychological; psychological; physical
19. increased; active; social; warnings; professional
20. Achievement; operant
21. interests; style; Guidance counselors

TERMS AND DEFINITIONS QUIZ:

SET 1:
1. role confusion (identity diffusion)
2. identity moratorium
3. locus of control
4. fantasy period
5. identity achievement
6. crowds
7. generation gap
8. cliques
9. identity
10. tentative period
11. identity foreclosure

SET 2:
1. gangs
2. narcotics or opiates
3. capable dropout
4. runaways
5. hallucinogen
6. stimulants
7. juvenile delinquent
8. depressants
9. realistic period
10. involuntary dropout
11. retarded dropout

MATCHING QUIZ:

1. f (p. 531)
2. h (p. 536)
3. g (p. 537)
4. a (p. 544)
5. b (p. 527)
6. d (p. 548)
7. i (p. 549)
8. c (p. 528)
9. e (p. 535)

Chapter 15

SELF TEST:

1.	d	(p. 523)	16.	d	(p. 538)
2.	d	(p. 523)	17.	a	(p. 541)
3.	d	(p. 523)	18.	b	(p. 542)
4.	c	(p. 524)	19.	a	(p. 542)
5.	b	(p. 525)	20.	b	(p. 542)
6.	a	(p. 527)	21.	b	(p. 544)
7.	b	(p. 529)	22.	c	(p. 545)
8.	b	(p. 529)	23.	c	(p. 547)
9.	c	(p. 532)	24.	b	(pp. 548-549)
10.	b	(p. 532)	25.	d	(p. 549)
11.	b	(p. 533)	26.	a	(p. 550)
12.	b	(p. 533)	27.	a	(p. 551)
13.	b	(p. 534)	28.	b	(p. 552)
14.	d	(p. 535)	29.	d	(p. 554)
15.	a	(p. 537)	30.	d	(p. 554)